SCHOOLROOM POETS

CHILDHOOD, PERFORMANCE, AND

THE PLACE OF AMERICAN POETRY,

1865–1917

Angela Sorby

University of New Hampshire Press

DURHAM, NEW HAMPSHIRE

PUBLISHED BY UNIVERSITY PRESS OF NEW ENGLAND

HANOVER AND LONDON

UNIVERSITY OF NEW HAMPSHIRE PRESS
Published by University Press of New England
One Court Street, Lebanon, NH 03766
www.upne.com

5 4 3 2 1

Library of Congress Cataloging-in-Publication Data

Sorby, Angela.
Schoolroom poets : childhood, performance, and the place of American
poetry, 1865–1917 / Angela Sorby.
   p. cm. — (Becoming modern)
Includes bibliographical references (p.) and index.
ISBN 1–58465–457–0 (alk. paper) — ISBN 1–58465–458–9 (pbk. : alk.
paper)
 1. Children's poetry, American—History and criticism. 2. American
poetry—19th century—History and criticism. 3. Children—Books and
reading—United States—History—19th century. 4. Children—Books and
reading—History—20th century. 5. Poetry—Study and teaching—United
States—History—19th century. 6. Poetry—Study and teaching—United
States—History—20th century. 7. Oral interpretation of poetry—History—
19th century. 8. Oral interpretation of poetry—History—20th century. 9.
American poetry—20th century—History and criticism. 10. Children—
United States—Intellectual life. I. Title. II. Series.
PS310.C5S67 2005
 811'.309—dc22   2004019574

CONTENTS

ACKNOWLEDGMENTS

I am grateful to the many people who have made contributions to this project, from its inception as a dissertation through the research, writing, and publication stages. Heartfelt thanks to Milton Bates, Lauren Berlant, Colleen Boggs, Bill Brown, Marshall Brown, Kate Chavigny, Phyllis Deutsch, Matthew Gartner, Jonnie Guerra, Heather Hathaway, Anita Israel, Virginia Jackson, Sandra Lee Kleppe, Diana Korzenik, Christopher Looby, Tim Machan, Maureen McLane, Cristanne Miller, Robert Mitchell, Mark Morrisson, David Nicholls, Peggy Reid, Catherine Robson, Lisa Ruddick, Sarah Sherman, Moon-Ju Shin, and Sarah Wadsworth. I am also indebted to my extended family, especially my parents, Janet and Evan Sorby.

Additionally, I wish to thank the following organizations: the Mellon Foundation, for a summer stipend; the Mrs. Giles Whiting Foundation, for a dissertation-year fellowship; the Brauer Fund, for a semester stipend; the Linfield College Faculty Fund, for a travel grant; the Longfellow Friends, for a Korzenik fellowship; Marquette University, for a summer faculty fellowship; and the Emily Dickinson International Society, for a Vivian Pollak Scholar-in-Amherst fellowship.

Research for the project was facilitated by librarians at the Center for Research Libraries, Chicago; the Newberry Library, Chicago; the Houghton Library, Harvard University; the Gutman Library, Harvard University; the Longfellow National Historic Site Archives, Cambridge (Mass.); the Jones Library, Amherst (Mass.); the Amherst College Library; the Haverhill (Mass.) Public Library; the Haverhill Whittier Club Archives; the Hampton Institute Library, Hampton (Va.); and the Lilly Library, Bloomington (Ind.).

A version of chapter 3 appeared in *American Studies* 39:1 (Spring 1998): 59–74, and a version of chapter 4 appeared in *Modern Language Quarterly* 60:2 (June 1999): 197–222. Thanks to the editors of these publications for their early support, and for permission to reprint.

Schoolroom Poets is dedicated with love to Christopher Roth, who read the whole manuscript many times, prepared the index, and made the completion of this book possible.

ABBREVIATIONS

CPW   *Complete Poetical Works of James Witcomb Riley*

ED   Emily Dickinson

FP   *Favorite Poems of Henry Wadsworth Longfellow*

H   *The Song of Hiawatha*

HWL   Henry Wadsworth Longfellow

JGW   John Greenleaf Whittier

JWR   James Witcomb Riley

PW   *Poetical Works of John Greenleaf Whittier*

Learning By Heart

On New Year's Day, 2003, a cluster of letters to the *New York Times* appeared on its editorial page. The nation was on the brink of war and the economy was sliding, but these letters were responding, with some urgency, to an op-ed piece by Carol Muske-Dukes titled "A Lost Eloquence." In that piece, Muske-Dukes recalls her mother's uncanny ability to weave poems into the daily life of her children, summoning apt quotations in response to the ordinary trials of family life:

> She is 85, a member of perhaps the last generation of Americans who learned poems and orations by rote in classes dedicated to the art of elocution. This long-ago discredited pedagogical tradition generated a commonplace eloquence among ordinary Americans who knew how to (as they put it) "quote." Poems are still memorized in some classrooms but not "put to heart" in a way that would prompt this more quotidian public expression.[1]

As Muske-Dukes remembers the poems her mother repeated, she also evokes her own childhood, when she learned poems "with my body as well as my brain." Ann Hanson wrote in response: "Maybe it's a North Dakota thing. I'm only 58, but like Carol Muske-Dukes's mother . . . I carry around with me vast stores of poetry (mostly 19th century) committed to memory and heard forever in my mother's voice." Another letter writer, Henry Emurian, mused that "the beauty of a poem, once learned, is not in the recitation of words. The poem, committed to memory, becomes a vehicle of communion for the self and the soul."[2]

This book theorizes and historicizes some common assumptions about American poetry—assumptions that underwrite the *New York Times* exchange: once upon a time, within living memory but just barely, people knew poems, repeated them, and wove them into their daily lives. Once upon a time, in other words, poetry mattered to middle-class people in a way that it no longer does. These assumptions have circulated as clichés, among the (now relatively small) group of Americans who care about poetry. The book jacket of John Hollander's *American Poetry: The Nineteenth Century* puts it another way: "In nineteenth-century America, poetry was part of everyday life, as familiar as a hymn, a love song, a patriotic exhortation . . . Parodies, dialect poems, song lyrics, and children's verse evoke the liveliness of an era when poetry was accessible to all."[3] Nineteenth- and early-twentieth-century popular poetry, then, was truly *popular*, and its popularity had something to do with repetition, with "quotidian public expression," with the body, with memory, with "the self and soul," with "access," and with a group of readers large enough to be conflated with "all." What is extraordinary about these claims is that while they are frequently repeated in passing, they have not been fully interrogated by scholars. While novel-reading has been subject to close scrutiny by James Machor, Janice Radway, Cathy Davidson, and others, postbellum poetry reading has received comparatively little attention.[4] We "know," on some level, that American poetry played a role in social, and especially educational, history, but this knowledge has not moved from the realm of memory into written history. Instead, our sense of "a lost eloquence" has generated mainly nostalgia among poets and critics such as Carol Muske-Dukes—and nostalgia, significantly, not just for poems but for forms of life that we imagine we have lost. It becomes necessary to ask, in the face of such nostalgia: What exactly has been lost? What poems constituted this archive, on which earlier generations could draw so freely? And how did these poems achieve, and maintain for several generations, their place in American memory?

To understand popular poetry—that is, to "evoke [its] liveliness," or to tap what Stephen Greenblatt calls its social energy—it is necessary to recover how it was used, both practically and ideologically, by both individual readers and the institutions that supported them.[5] I want to begin, then, with the old-fashioned term "schoolroom poet," a term that I think carries some useful historical baggage.[6] The idea of a schoolroom poet implies a specifically pedagogical function for poetry that can underwrite a version of literary history that privileges the surprisingly practical uses to which poems were put. By 1917—the point of America's entry into World War I, the end point of this study, and arguably the end point of America's long nineteenth century—the so-called "schoolroom poets" were the best-known literary figures in the nation. The first generation, the New England schoolroom poets Henry Wadsworth Longfellow, John Greenleaf Whittier, James Russell Lowell, and Oliver Wendell Holmes, were already established icons of middle-class taste, while the next generation of writers, led by the westerners James Whitcomb Riley and Eugene Field, had positioned themselves as wholesome, accessible performers of the schoolroom tradition. In addition, by 1917 the schoolroom canon had picked up many "hit singles" from poets such as Elizabeth Akers

Allen ("Rock Me to Sleep"), Sarah Josepha Hale ("It Snows," "Mary's Lamb"), Walt Whitman ("O Captain! My Captain"), Samuel Woodworth ("The Old Oaken Bucket"), Francis Miles Finch ("The Blue and the Gray"), and Joyce Kilmer ("Trees"). These American poems—along with British standbys by Shakespeare, Cowper, Hemans, Burns, and Tennyson—provided an archive of popular memory that was maintained by educational institutions: schools, primarily, but also museums, lyceums, theaters, newspapers and children's magazines, and clubs. The schoolroom canon is fairly circumscribed—the same poems appear over and over in various contexts—and taken as a whole, the list presents work that most Americans educated in the United States between 1865 and 1917 (and indeed well into the twentieth century) would recognize.

One of the challenges posed by the schoolroom canon is that it requires a rethinking of periodization: what constitutes the "historical context" of a particular work? A poem such as Longfellow's "Psalm of Life," for instance, appeared in 1839, in his Voices of the Night; in the 1840s and '50s, the poem was singled out for praise by critics such as George Gilfillan and Joel T. Headly.[7] This might be understood as its reception history. But after the Civil War, "A Psalm of Life" emerged as a standard recitation-piece in American schools (bolstered by its inclusion in *McGuffey's Sixth Eclectic Reader*), and it is through its constant repetition in the postbellum period that its most significant cultural work was accomplished, as I will discuss in chapter 1. What matters, in other words, is not when and how poets published but rather when and how readers read. I have chosen to focus on the period between 1865 and 1917 because this is when readers established the "tradition" of schoolroom poetry. However, this tradition, once established, continued until at least the mid-twentieth century, when nostalgia volumes, such as Hazel Felleman's *Best-Loved Poems of the American People,* began to appear.[8] Felleman's anthology is still in print, and available not just in specialty bookstores where one typically finds poetry but also at Wal-Mart.

How did people read this poetry, and how did it become "best-loved"? The beginnings of an answer can be found in the nineteenth-century schoolroom. If the term "schoolroom poet" is taken seriously, it can reveal what it means to read a poem as an educational experience—nor as an educational *performance*—replete with all the discipline that schooling imposes, and all the desire that it unleashes. But schoolroom poetry can never be merely private; it is always intersubjective, involving cultural transmissions or exchanges. The sociologist Maurice Halbwachs has argued that "collective memory" can be said to exist because people develop memories socially;

they require institutions, such as the family (with its photograph albums and keepsakes), the school system (with its yearbooks and canons), the local community (with its landmarks and newspapers), and the nation (with its archives, museums, and holidays) to organize their understanding of themselves and their past. All my chapters thus emerge from institutional situations that allowed for intersubjectivity, for some kind of active exchange, between the poem and its readers. Chapter 1, set in the public school system, addresses the nation-building (and national subject-building) work of Longfellow, both as an authority figure and as a poet. Chapter 2, inspired in part by the Haverhill Homestead, a restored museum-house, re-reads Whittier's "Snow-Bound" as both a museum catalog and a meditation on the (racialized) horizon of expectations that the "Colonial Revival" produced. Chapter 3, turning to the pages of *St. Nicholas Magazine,* addresses the construction of children's desires through Mary Mapes Dodge's publication of "ideal," and not-so-ideal, verses. Chapter 4 follows the stage career of the poet James Whitcomb Riley, who bridged the gap between high and low (and adults' and children's) entertainment. Chapter 5 uses a newspaper poet, Eugene Field, to explore the shifting boundaries between childhood and adulthood at the turn of the century. A final chapter considers the figure of Emily Dickinson, as she was infantilized—in the schoolroom and in *St. Nicholas*—during her first emergence as a mass cultural phenomenon (and, I will argue, as a new kind of schoolroom poet) in the 1890s. Each chapter thus examines how specific institutions—schools, museums, theaters, newspapers, and magazines—staged popular poems as social events, as memories, and as ways of constructing intimate and far-flung (or to use Benedict Anderson's term, "imagined") communities.

By way of introduction, however, I want to outline more broadly what pedagogical poetry looked (or rather, sounded) like and how it came to define, enliven, but also limit most people's understanding of poetry. It is necessary to approach schoolroom poetry with a sense of the body as a vehicle for public performance, with a sense of how institutions shape specific interpretive communities, and with an acute sense of the pleasures of repetition. Ultimately, the popular experience of poetry came to be defined as juvenile and yet (or *therefore*) powerful; internal and yet public; local and yet national; fixed and yet variable. Readers were taught to repeat poems as a measure of their social competence, making poetry a disciplinary practice that reinforced social and literary conventions. But their reading experience also allowed them to take ownership of the poems they "learned by heart," so that many readers read with a degree of interpretive freedom—a freedom derived, ironically, from the very familiarity and fixity of the schoolroom canon. The tension here—between poetry as an acculturating force and poetry as the key to self-knowledge or self-invention—was not so much resolved as negotiated by readers as they both performed and internalized verses.

FORMS OF CHILDHOOD

In 1897, in a primary-school classroom in Boston, Massachusetts, Olive Dana's class commemorated John Greenleaf Whittier's birthday with a costume pageant. Dana sent a transcript of the event to the *Journal of Education,* titling it "A Whittier Folk-Gathering," so that other teachers could replicate the event. The celebration opened with a *tableau vivant* of one of the most famous—what popular-anthology editors would call "best-loved"—poems of the American nineteenth century, Whittier's "Barefoot Boy." A child dressed as the Barefoot Boy posed in front of a Barefoot Boy picture (probably the Prang chromolithograph of Eastman Johnson's 1860 painting, although Dana does not specify). She narrates:

> First shall come the "Barefoot Boy,"—an old acquaintance of ours, and brother to every country lad in our land. We give him hearty welcome here again, and we echo the poet's words (class recites):

> > Blessings on thee, little man,
> > Barefoot boy, with cheek of tan!
> > With thy turned-up pantaloons,
> > And thy merry whistled tunes;
> > With thy red lip, redder still,
> > Kissed by strawberries on the hill;
> > With the sunshine on thy face,
> > Through the torn brim's jaunty grade.
> > From my heart I give thee joy,—
> > I was once a barefoot boy!

> Who has given us so faithful a picture of boyhood, carefree, unfettered, self-reliant; loving nature too well to be conscious overmuch of his affection, of her tuition, or of his own loyal surrender? The poet had been the lad pictured, but the portrait is for all generations of country boys.[9]

Whittier's original poem (only part of which the children quote) is a late-romantic dialogue between a corrupted adult speaker and his uncorrupted youthful self. But the way that Dana deploys the poem has an effect on its use-value, and hence, I would argue, on its meaning. First, she turns the poem from an internal monologue into a collective experience: the Barefoot Boy arrives, and is greeted by a classroom crowd as part of a "folk-gathering" that also includes characters from Whittier's "Little Red Riding Hood" and "Snow-Bound." In this way, the poem remains an internal monologue (since the children have memorized it, it is coming from "inside" of them), but it also becomes a public performance. It thus works to create a community of readers with two kinds of memory in common: the memory of a school celebration, and the memory of a text. The children have something in common externally—they are speaking in concert—but also internally, in their "hearts," having learned the poem by heart so that they can perform it. These bonds reinforce not only the children's experience as peers but also their experience as subjects, as selves, constructed and maintained by the institution of the school.

Moreover, the text they remember is not just Whittier's text; it is Whittier's text cut down to one stanza and framed by Dana. She presents a text that is not just "accessible" in the sense of being easy to read but also "accessible" in the sense that anyone can abridge it, act it out, or comment on it. Just as the Barefoot Boy is trotted out as an "old acquaintance," so too is the poem itself: like an oral text, this poem, and indeed all the popular canon, is open to revision. Whittier's original poem, published in the *Little Pilgrim* magazine in 1852, mourns the loss of the poet's own childhood, and the mourning tone is reinforced by the magazine's editorial content that stresses, as so many antebellum periodicals did, the fragility of life.[10] But in Dana's interpretive community that same boy is not lost but physically robust and present—and brought out in costume to prove it. He exists for "all generations," not as a lost romantic self but as a clear and present child, reachable and recoverable through repetition.

Although Whittier's poem hinges on the naturalness and transparency of the boy, in the "Whittier Folk-Gathering" the boy is in costume: the natural becomes theatrical, and boyhood is not a condition but a performance. Thus the childlike qualities of "The Barefoot Boy" are wholly accessible: anyone can take off his or her shoes and act the part. Dana takes ownership of "The Barefoot Boy" and invites her students to do the same, and in the process the poem's meaning is not just interpreted but changed. Instead of standing for the poet's lost self, the boy becomes a figure of possibility, representing one role (among many) that a schoolchild can play. If romantic poetry worked to project an internal self, pedagogical interpretive communities such as this one made that internal self part of a public performance.

My emphasis on the role of Olive Dana and her students in making meaning has its theoretical roots in the reception theory of Hans Robert Jauss.[11] Jauss posits the idea of a "horizon of expectations" that makes texts legible in different ways to different interpretive communities. A horizon of expectations is a complex of conscious and unconscious assumptions that governs not only how a text is read but also how it *can* be read; it does not mandate one reading, but it limits the number of readings that can be produced, based on what is imaginable and speakable at a given historical moment. In my argument (because of the historical circumstances of the later nineteenth and early twentieth centuries), institutions play a large role in establishing the horizons of expectation for popular poetry. At the same time, Jauss stresses that modern scholars bring their own expectations (also conditioned by institutions) to bear, which means that when I read "The Barefoot Boy" I am reading a different text than Dana did. It is impossible to fully recover and redeploy nineteenth-century horizons of expectation, but it is useful to partially excavate them in order to understand why certain poems were seen as beautiful and useful. At the same time, my own (institutional, scholarly, twenty-first-century) assumptions remain in play, helping to make visible latent meanings (for instance, the discourse on whiteness in Whittier's *Snow-Bound*) that emerged from nineteenth-century cultural anxieties but that readers at the time could not, or would not, have articulated.

The scene in Dana's classroom represents late-nineteenth-century horizons of expectation in several ways: it turns the poem into a pedagogical tool; it uses it as an occasion for social exchange; it stages a "natural" romantic text as a "theatrical" performance piece; and it opens the text to oral interpretation by readers. But first and most essentially, the scene in Dana's classroom is representative because it involves a performance by, and about, children. The Barefoot Boy is a child, he is being "played" by a child, children are reciting Whittier's poem, and the transcript of the event appeared in a journal aimed at early childhood education experts. This is more than a coincidence. When I began research for this project, I was expecting, like so many scholars starting out in the 1990s, to write about women poets and the feminization of American poetry. Instead, what I discovered was the *infantilization* of American poetry: poets framed as children, children seen as poets, children posited as readers, children recruited as performers, and adults wishing themselves back into childhood. If nineteenth-century novels were, as Hawthorne complained, dominated by scribbling women, then nineteenth-century poetry, especially in the later decades, was dominated by children. Longfellow, Whittier, Riley, and Field—four very different poets—were all dubbed "children's laureates," and readers of all ages read their work from (what they saw as) a child's perspective. Indeed, I will argue that commerce with real and imagined children became the primary source of social energy in American poetry between 1865 and 1917 and that this phenomenon, the infantilization of American poetry, was intimately related to its role as a medium of middle-class pedagogy and performance.

Numerous observers have casually noted the child-centeredness of American poetry without pausing to consider its significance. Looking back at the nineteenth century from the 1950s, Van Wyck Brooks commented, "Of the popular poets, Longfellow, Whittier, Holmes, something seemed destined to survive in the general mind of the nation. These authors, whom every child could understand, remained as classics indeed, but mainly for children."[12] In the early 1970s Leslie Fiedler made a similar observation in a characteristically eccentric article titled "The Children's Hour; or, The Return of the Vanishing Longfellow: Some Reflections on the Future of Poetry." Fiedler, as a mid-twentieth-century critic, takes for granted that his readers know, and agree, that the nineteenth century was indeed the original "children's hour" of American poetry, and he ends his essay on a nostalgic note:

> In my fifty-third year, however, I feel free at last to evoke in public the kinds of poems which I have never ceased to love, but which I've long felt obliged to recite in the catacombs, as it were; pretending, when my own kids were young enough, that it was for their sake only I kept alive the old chestnuts; and then, as they grew older, that it was for the sake of remembering together the time when they were young—as if there were ever a time when, at the levels touched by song, we were any of us anything else.[13]

What remains unexamined in Fiedler's essay, as well as in our more recent critical discourse, is the mixture of sentiment and nostalgia, combined with the infantilization of poems, poets, and readers, that informs his conclusion. He assumes that the "old chestnuts" represented by Longfellow create social space that can be occupied only by children: the poet and the reader become as children, fortified by the presence of actual child auditors.

Donald Hall records a similarly vague impression in his introduction to *The Oxford Book of Children's Verse in America*. As he reflects on his editorial process, he notes somewhat ruefully that selecting "children's" poems was difficult because almost all nineteenth-century American poems seemed to qualify for inclusion:

> There are strange currents in American nineteenth-century lit-
> erature, especially I think a current of childishness. Not in Whit-
> man, perhaps, except when he turned to rhyme in "O Captain,
> My Captain,"—but surely in Dickinson (not at her best); surely
> in Whittier, Holmes, Lowell, Poe, and Longfellow. This child-
> ishness infects the poets, not the novelists . . . In the popular cul-
> ture of the nineteenth century, to be a poet was to be childlike.[14]

None of the poets that Hall names began as children's poets, but all
of them *became* children's poets in the second half of the nineteenth
century: people learned "O Captain! My Captain" in childhood, and
its repetition—even in adulthood—reflected, or generated, a "current of childishness."

Certainly a late-twentieth-century critic such as Hall is "right,"
within his twentieth-century horizon of expectations, to see childishness as a limitation: Dickinson's baby talk poems ("'Twas such a little,
little boat / That toddled down the bay!") do not feel as modern, and
are not as appealing to modern readers, as her more elliptical
verses.[15] But nineteenth-century commentators were, by and large,
able to see childishness as a strength, if only a compensatory one. In
1892 the essayist Agnes Repplier noted that the use-value of poetry
had changed; poets were no longer "the unacknowledged legislators
of the world." But if poetry's legislative role was diminishing, Repplier
asserted, its impact was still enormous:

> Yet what matters it, after all, when all around us, on every side, in
> schoolrooms and in nurseries, in quiet corners and by cheerful
> fires, the children are reading poetry?—reading it with a joyous
> enthusiasm and an absolute surrendering of spirit which we can
> all remember, but can never feel again . . . Well might Sainte-
> Beuve speak bravely of the clear, fine penetration peculiar to
> childhood. He knew that, when poetry is in question, it is better
> to feel than to think; and that with the growth of a guarded and
> disciplined intelligence, straining after the enjoyment that per-
> fection in literary art can give, the first careless rapture of youth
> falls into a half-remembered dream.[16]

This passage would seem at first glance like the simple survival of
romantic and sentimental structures of feeling, but I think Repplier's perspective reflects a historical shift rather than the persist-
ence of an earlier sensibility. As I will argue at greater length below,
new cultural discourses were emerging in the later nineteenth century, related to new institutions that purported to value children

above all. Sentimental discourses may have peaked before the Civil War, but the general cultural mania for childhood was just getting under way, and would not reach its apotheosis until the 1880s and 1890s—the era of Fauntleroy suits, the child-study movement, the "Brownies" craze, and the marketing of Emily Dickinson as a wild sprite. Moreover, the definitions of "childhood" and "pedagogy" were in flux, creating a productive tension for poets and readers who engaged with these cultural categories.

Children, who had functioned mainly as a symbolic category for sentimental poets, became the objects of more direct engagement in the latter half of the nineteenth century. Even as the category of "childhood" became more clearly defined, it also became more inhabitable—at least rhetorically—by adults. Identifying a broad cultural pattern that reached beyond poetry, Lewis O. Saum, in his study of private letters and diaries written between 1860 and 1890, has noted that around the time of the Civil War, distinct strains of baby talk crept into adult correspondence. An engaged couple, Delbert Boston and Ella Furney, for example, signed their letters "your own little boy" and "your own little girl."[17] Earlier (romantic, sentimental) generations of adults had turned to children, in poems such as Elizabeth Oakes-Smith's "Sinless Child," for spiritual teaching. But children in the later nineteenth and early twentieth centuries provided more secular therapeutic services, as in this scene from Kate Douglas Wiggin's *Rebecca of Sunnybrook Farm*, (1903) in which Rebecca reads to her aging aunt:

> No one guessed the quiet pleasure that lay hidden in her heart when she watched the girl's dark head bent over her lessons at night, nor dreamed of her joy in it, certain quiet evenings when Miranda went to prayer meeting; evenings when Rebecca would read aloud "Hiawatha" or "Barbara Frietche," "The Bugle Song" or "The Brook." Her narrow, humdrum existence bloomed under the dews that fell from this fresh spirit; her dullness brightened under the kindling touch of the younger mind . . .[18]

Not only does Rebecca physically revive her aunt, but she does so in place of a prayer meeting; the secular ritual of poetry does not supplement the church but actually replaces it, and the promise of heaven is supplanted by the promise of the future as represented by the tableau of a young girl reading poetry.

Later-nineteenth-century Americans were proactive in their approach to childhood: not only did they want to reenter it, understand it, and be revived by it, but they also wanted to "give it" to children so that every child could "have a childhood." Childhood became not so much an assumed condition as a performative option: a way of acting, a way of thinking, a way of reading that was open to all. This expanded accessibility led to some extreme fantasy-work, crossing the border into pedophilia in the case of Eugene Field, who wrote both "Wynken, Blynken, and Nod" and juvenile erotica. But for the most part, children were seen as poetic precisely because they were pure. As Lucy Larcom put it in an 1882 sketch for *St. Nicholas Magazine:*

> The poets who love children are the poets whom children love.
> It is natural that they should care much for each other, because
> both children and poets see things in the same way,—simply, with
> open eyes and hearts, seeing Nature as it is, and finding whatever
> is lovable and pure in the people who surround them, as flowers
> may receive back from flowers sweet odors for those they have
> given. The little child is born with a poet's heart in him, and the
> poet has been fitly called "the eternal child."[19]

There is perhaps a degree of defensiveness in Larcom's characterization: if poets are to be marginalized, then their marginalization can at least be celebrated. But to consign a genre to "childhood" in the later nineteenth and early twentieth centuries was not to render it invisible or irrelevant; rather, to be childlike was to claim a degree of power. The question becomes: how can such juvenile power be described, and what did it do for—or to—popular poetry?

PEDAGOGICAL POWER

To write about children, power, and poetry in the nineteenth century is to build, inevitably, on the notion of sentimentalism, as defined in the pioneering work of Nina Baym, Ann Douglas, and Jane Tompkins. The poems of Longfellow, Whittier, and Riley have sometimes been hailed, and more often dismissed, as "sentimental."[20] And the mode of sentimental writing—with its anti-intellectualism, its sensational emotions, its domestic focus, and its valorization of the weak— certainly informs the schoolroom canon and helped to spark the love that readers felt for this poetry. Mary Louise Kete's *Sentimental Collaboration,* a study that lays much of the antebellum groundwork for my postbellum discussion, traces the sentimental mode through several of its nineteenth-century incarnations. [21] Focusing, refreshingly, on poetry, she moves beyond the familiar question of sentimentalism's subversiveness to consider its specific cultural roles. She argues that in earlier-nineteenth-century America, sentimental poems were, like hair jewelry and black crepe, a way to mourn losses and to forge bonds through mourning: "To grieve was to experience cynicism, discontinuity, isolation. To mourn was to break down the borders of distance or death and to establish the connections through which one could understand and identify oneself."[22] In a compelling reading of an amateur scrapbook of poetry, *Harriet Gould's Book*, Kete shows how sentimental tropes knitted together an intimate New England community of middle-class, but nonelite, adults. Sentimental poems, Kete argues, were collaborations between writers and readers, who engaged in gift-exchange practices (including, but not limited to, the exchange of poetry) in order to build intimate communities based on shared values and common experiences. Kete's evocation of antebellum New England life, so vivid in its specificity, also shows the extent to which sentimental practices of reading and mourning were historically contingent. *Harriet Gould's Book* was the product of a particular antebellum moment defined by evangelical Protestantism, small-scale institutions, local and regional identities, and conventions of mourning that were both extensive and prescriptive.

As she moves the discussion into the postbellum period, however, Kete shifts from the analysis of poetry per se to the analysis of "poetry" as penned by Mark Twain's Emmeline Grangerford in *The Adventures of Huckleberry Finn*. Kete suggests that Emmeline seemed culturally dysfunctional to Twain because, by the latter half of the nineteenth century, sentimental poetry no longer functioned to cement local communities and to maintain rituals quite as it once had. Emmeline, as Kete understands her, marks the corruption and dissolution of sentimentalism as a strategy: her mourning is out of sync with the times, which, although nominally the 1840s, are of course also implicitly the 1880s. What was touching in 1840 was ridiculous by the 1880s. But I want to argue that the Emmeline Grangerford section of *Huckleberry Finn* represents not the decay but rather the transformation of a literary tradition. After all, the imaginary reader of poetry in Twain's scenario is not a sobbing woman (Emmeline herself is dead) but a child, Huck Finn. Huck, not Emmeline, is the reader here—and if Emmeline is the mawkish target of Twain's satire, Huck is the innocent object of his ongoing affection. Huck is Twain's barefoot boy, uncorrupted even as the Emmelines of America descend into farce. Huck is an ideal reader: sincere, responsive (he is inspired to try his own hand at writing), and imaginative. He, not Emmeline, represents the survival of something resembling—but not identical with—the sentimental mode. He is not a sentimental mourner; he is a locus of pedagogy—a pedagogical object, subject to the conflicted discourses of the 1880s.

Sentimentalism was both attractive and repellent to Twain, and this ambivalence has posed a problem for critics of his work. Kete suggests that in his novel *The Gilded Age* Twain "advances a partial solution" to the problem of sentimental morbidity: "If mourning cannot hold the country together and provide a means for it to move forwards, then perhaps hope or speculation could."[23] This comment points to a critical juncture, a shift of focus, between antebellum and postbellum uses of "the heart." The transition that Kete notes, from mourning to hope and speculation, also marks what I believe to be a major shift in how people read poetry and helps to explain the emergence of the child as a pedagogical subject (being celebrated in poetry) and as a pedagogical object (being taught poetry). The functions of sentimental poetry were changing, and changing to such a degree that I think it is misleading to suggest that by the 1890s "The Barefoot Boy" was circulating as a sentimental poem. Even if it began as a sentimental poem in the 1850s, its functions changed over time and as it grew in popularity.

I propose, then, that *the pedagogical* be seen as a distinct literary mode that operated throughout the nineteenth century but became dominant in the period between 1865 and 1917. To understand the power of the postbellum schoolroom canon, it is necessary to read its "best-loved" poems not as sentimental texts but as pedagogical texts, rooted in a culture that speculated on the future even when it appeared to be mourning the past. Pedagogy did not take place just in classrooms but always in actual or imagined *social settings,* involving more that one person in the transmission of thoughts and feelings. This sets pedagogical poetry apart from much twentieth-century verse, which is largely written for, and consumed by, silent individual readers.

Of course, as modes, the sentimental and the pedagogical are intimately related. As Richard Brodhead shows in *Cultures of Letters,* sentimental writing was defined by its disciplinary impulse, as it taught families to curb their children, and communities to control their members, through gentle but firmly normative bonds.[24] In her study of the precocious girl-poetess Lucretia Davidson, Mary Loeffelholz has argued that sentimental poetry, as part of the "domestic-tutelary complex," taught girls to submit to social norms.[25] She shows how poetry, and especially poetry that was performed, demanded and displayed submission even as it appeared to praise freedom, and cloaked the coercive constraints of early-nineteenth-century female education in the language of love. So the sentimental has long had a pedagogical component, and the contrast between the sentimental and the pedagogical modes is one of relative, not absolute, difference, reflecting differences between antebellum and postbellum American culture. Pedagogical practices and texts appeared in the antebellum period (much of Longfellow falls into this category, though his poems are often called sentimental), and conversely, purely sentimental practices and texts continued to emerge throughout the later nineteenth and early twentieth centuries (much of the poetry written to commemorate the First World War dead might be called sentimental). And, indeed, both sentimental and pedagogical poems are still produced today. But broadly speaking, if we assume that popular poems derive their most significant meanings from cultural practices, it is useful to see poetry reading, as practiced in the postbellum period, as distinctly pedagogical: more secular (as opposed to spiritual), more ambitious (as opposed to resigned), more public (as opposed to domestic), and more engaged with children as representatives of the future.

The shift in emphasis, from the sentimental to the pedagogical, can be illustrated through the contrast between the uses of poetry in an antebellum keepsake album (represented by Kete's example, *Harriet Gould's Book*) and the uses of poetry in that direct postbellum descendant of the keepsake album, the school yearbook. *Harriet Gould's Book*, assembled mostly in the 1830s and 1840s, was a collaborative effort, a collection of handwritten poems by family and community members, many of which focused, as did so much published sentimental poetry, on the death of children. The "original" poems in *Harriet Gould's Book* tend to be built from stock phrases, and some are even sometimes copied outright from published sources, so that they signal the writer's (and reader's) participation in a shared system of knowledge and values. Identities are thus constructed not through individual marks of originality but rather through collaboration with a community of like-minded individuals whose like-mindedness is reinforced by their common language. *Harriet Gould's Book*, Kete argues, ultimately uses expressions of mourning to construct a middle-class American self that is sentimentally relational rather than transcendentally isolated. This self is practical, because it constructs and conforms to social norms about the value of family and community, but it is also utopian, because these norms demand that family bonds survive even the grave, so that the most perfect American home (and the most perfect American self) is a literally "heavenly" one.

By midcentury, homemade scrapbooks were being replaced by mass-produced, but still blank, keepsake albums. Then in the 1880s and 1890s, with the rise of both mass education and mass-production technologies, keepsake albums were produced with their contents already pasted in, in the form of high school and college yearbooks. Early yearbooks draw heavily on keepsake album conventions: the photographs appear to be literally "pasted," often at an angle, onto elaborate backgrounds; the students' pictures are accompanied by stock phrases or rhymes, such as might be written in a blank album; and the format is that of a visual bricolage rather than a written narrative. This format has proven highly conservative and will be recognizable to most readers from their own twentieth-century school yearbooks.

One distinctive feature of late-nineteenth-century yearbooks that harks back to *Harriet Gould's Book*, rather than forward to the twentieth century, is the inclusion of a significant amount of derivative amateur poetry. (Here, my use of the word "derivative" is complimentary because it implies "derived from other poems." Yearbooks from, say, the 1980s do feature some poetry, but it is seldom "derivative," because it seldom reflects familiarity with a specific tradition.) Like the poems in *Harriet Gould's Book*, these early yearbook poems are not author centered—they are most often published anonymously—and not concerned with overt originality. The poems in the yearbooks I have seen, mostly from Wisconsin schools in the 1880s and 1890s, take their cues directly from the American schoolroom canon, especially Longfellow, and from a few British authors such as Shakespeare and Tennyson. Longfellow's name is seldom mentioned; rather, the common language that he represents is assumed as student authors construct long, elaborate, and remarkably competent variations on "The Children's Hour" or *The Song of Hiawatha*—indeed, *Hiawatha* parodies are an almost inevitable feature of the yearbook genre. By "competent" I do not of course mean to imply that these amateur yearbook poems deserve a large twenty-first-century readership the way that, say, Emily Dickinson does. They do, however, display an unquestioning command of the schoolroom canon—a cultural competence, or horizon of expectations, that includes an implicit understanding of the ways poetry works and how it can build collaborative identities.

Westside High School's 1898 *Hesper* (Milwaukee, Wis.), for instance, reworks Longfellow's "Psalm of Life" with great precision, mirroring not just Longfellow's prosody but also all of the original's rhetorical devices and its exact number of stanzas. The school football team had apparently been disbanded because the sport was considered dangerous; "A Plea for Football" thus begins:

> Tell me not, in mournful numbers,
> "Football's but a heartless fight!"
> For 'tis not the punching, stabbing,

That it seemeth at first sight.
Football's jolly! Football's manly!
'Tis not wicked as you deem;
"Ye are slugs and ye are fighters!"
Was not spoken of *our* team.[26]

A common experience (losing the team) is wedded to a common language (Longfellow) to produce a poem that in turn produces a consensual "we"—a "we" that includes not just the football team but the whole school. Like the poems in *Harriet Gould's Book,* "A Plea for Football" both invites and coerces its readers to join an affective community, creating a "we" in the second stanza from an "I" in the first stanza, and rallying "us" around a shared value that generates a close bond. The illustration accompanying "A Plea for Football" both evokes the sentimental world of Harriet Gould and signals its distance from that world. In the sketch, a young man, a minister, and a woman in black mourning garb stand crying over a grave, while off to the side stands a headstone that reads "Born 1895 / Died 1897." Like the headstones marking so many of the dead babies of the antebellum era, this headstone marks a two-year times-pan. The sketch might be seen as a parody of sentimental mourning, like Twain's Emmeline Grangerford. And yet the aim of the poem and of the accomanying illustration is not precisely parody. "A Plea for Football" is not directed outward, at literary history, but rather inward, at the institutional history of the school and at the experiences of its individual students. It is not trying to comment on genres or modes; it is using the genre of schoolroom poetry to communicate with a peer group. The poem takes a literary artifact ("A Psalm of Life") and uses it as a cultural artifact, as part of a bonding ritual (yearbook making) and in defense of a bonding ritual (football playing). One reason that later-twentieth-century critics dismissed nineteenth-century popular poetry is that it had a negligible influence on modern and postmodern poetry; it seemed to represent a literary-historical dead end.[27] But, as the poetry in school yearbooks suggests, this dismissal misses the point of popular poetry, which is not to engage with literary history but rather to make social history by forming communities.

While "A Plea for Football" produces a collective "we," conflated with the entire school population, other poems in the yearbook genre single out individuals, as in the following excerpt from the middle stanzas of a long poem about Hiawatha-brand chewing tobacco, written to echo Longfellow's *Song of Hiawatha* and published in the 1890 University of Wisconsin *Badger.*

> Said our Charley McGee Williams
> He of baseball reputation
> "Though I rather would have Spearhead
> I can chew you, Hiawatha."
> Campbell saw no danger to him
> Till his hands became entangled
> Till he found himself imprisoned
> In the snares of Hiawatha.
> Prostrate lay good Daniel Kiser
> At the feet of Hiawatha.
> Johnny Bunn, not one whit wiser,
> Chewed in time with Daniel Kiser.[28]

Even as names are named, though, identities are submerged in the relentlessly normative form of Longfellow's trochees, just as individual yearbook pictures take on a numbing similarity when they are lined up for page after page. My point is not that school diminishes individuality but rather that the rhetoric of yearbook poetry constructs identities determined largely through relationships to others and to a specific institution. Daniel Kiser is defined through Johnny Bunn, and their group experience of Hiawatha (chewing tobacco) and *Hiawatha* (Longfellow's poem) is paramount.

Like antebellum keepsake books, school yearbooks were clearly functioning to help students construct identities that were stable (once the class of '98, always the class of '98) across destabilizing periods of transition. In sentimental texts, this major transition is often the private, domestic experience of mourning; in pedagogical texts, the major transitions are more public and institutional, such as the experience of graduation. Obviously, the currency of these yearbooks was not mourning but hope and speculation; the yearbook's interpretive community was not sentimental but pedagogical. The 1898 Westside *Hesper* stated its goals outright:

> The young boys and girls who form this graduating class will in the next fifty years be the old boys and girls of Milwaukee. We have sometimes wondered how things will look then; possibly some then will wonder how things look now. Accordingly, we print this little book to mark the time and our place in it.[29]

Taken together, "A Plea for Football," "Hiawatha," and the *Hesper*'s 1898 preface participated in the generation of a middle-class American self that was very different from the middle-class self produced through mourning in *Harriet Gould's Book,* although it relied on some

[xxvii]

of the same poetic technologies. This self was tied to large-scale institutions, represented by the city school and by Longfellow—himself a
large-scale institution by the 1890s. The poems are amateur efforts,
but they were professionally printed and financed by "sponsors"
(laundry services, jewelers, liveries) that advertised in the back of the
book. The ties that bound the students at Westside High School
together were those of a cohort, not a family; students imagined that
they were "brothers and sisters" not because of blood ties but because
of generational ties, which were forged through the consumption of
products such as yearbooks, jewelry, chewing tobacco, and popular
songs and poems.

Yearbook poems, unlike their sentimental antecedents, are not
predicated primarily on forms of mourning, but they do implicitly
address historically specific cultural problems—problems of rapid
technological and social change, which required pedagogical, not
sentimental, solutions. The students at Westside High School in the
1890s were, relatively speaking, loosening their domestic ties and circulating in a culture that was, as Alan Trachtenberg puts it, increasingly "incorporated," dominated by larger-scale social systems.[30]
Milwaukee was a city of immigrants, but student ethnicities are submerged in the yearbook, as are rigid gender and class distinctions.
Student pictures are laid out in democratic rows, linked only by
cohort: the sophomores together, the juniors together. The stable
binaries of the earlier nineteenth century, which pitted private
women against public men, are broken down by the yearbook text,
with its uniform photos of both sexes. A great deal of cultural work
went into producing that "we," the "we" of the "Plea for Football"
that does not include just players but all students (boys and girls)
who supported "their" team. But the groundwork was laid, I think,
long before the yearbook was produced, in part through the schoolroom canon, which gave the yearbook's "we" a common experience
of the American language—an experience rooted in both the structural pedagogy of the poems (which often taught overt lessons) and
the institutional pedagogy of the schools that taught these poems.
Rather than sentimental resignation, membership in the school
community required active participation—or submission couched in
the language of action. In yearbook poetry students are implicitly
urged to draw on their common memory of earlier poems and earlier experiences. The resulting interpretive community was bound
together by common tastes, including perhaps a taste for chewing
tobacco or football but also—critically—a taste for Longfellow, and
an easy familiarity with his prosody. This community was both practical and utopian. On a practical level it promoted the progress of

individuals if they learned and followed the rules of engagement, while on a utopian level it also ratified the (apparent if never actual) group consensus through institutional traditions, including the tradition of schoolroom poetry, that seemed both firmly established and inevitable.

READING THROUGH THE BODY

By way of a literary history, then, a transformation can be traced, emerging gradually from the 1850s through the 1890s, as sentimental readings of poetry become pedagogical readings of poetry, mourning is replaced by hope and speculation, and small-scale family or village groups are supplanted by institutional interpretive communities. This transformation has a parallel social history, as readers read poems, not to express or reinforce their resignation as sufferers, but to perform (and perhaps to negotiate) their roles as middle-class strivers who must, in Longfellow's words, be "up and doing." Readers in schools were taught to read poems in specific ways (recalling Olive Dana's disciplinary voice-over), but they were also invited to interpret the poems through acts of repetition. This resulted in an experience of poetry that was highly institutional, grounded in specific incorporated social bodies, but also deeply internalized, grounded in individual bodies and in readers' earliest memories of language-learning. One point of contact between individual bodies and institutional practices was the *McGuffey's Reader* series, through which many students got their first exposure to poetry.

Between 1839 and 1920 the *McGuffey's Reader* series taught more than 116 million children how to read with their voices, how to breathe while they read, and how to use their bodies as vehicles for performance. The *McGuffey's* influence peaked during the Gilded Age as school systems were set up in the Middle and Far West and also in the South, where *McGuffey's* was popular because it seemed (despite a persistent federalist bias) fairly politically neutral. While there are historical accounts, such as Richard Moiser's *Making the American Mind*, that describe these textbooks and their influence, scant attention has been paid to how readers learned to read from them, and how this might help us to interpret the poems that they made famous.[31] The series reached its final form in 1879; the 1879 editions included six levels of readers, titled *McGuffey's First, Second,* and so on through the sixth. The first four readers were designed to help children learn to read, while the fifth and sixth were literary anthologies—and as such, they reached more American readers than any other anthology of the period.

McGuffey's Fifth Eclectic Reader addresses a readership who have learned to read by sounding out, first letters, then one-syllable words with pictorial illustrations.[32] Most nineteenth- and early-twentieth-century American children learned to read using a system that, by 1879, was being called "phonics." In this system, sound took precedence over meaning; what mattered was learning how to read individual sounds aloud, which could then be combined into words. While Americanists have been slow to address this phenomenon, Friedrich Kittler's *Discourse Networks* begins with an analysis of phonetic learning and its relation to later-eighteenth-century Germanic nationalism. Mothers were encouraged to teach their children a nationally standardized system of phonics, and language was thereby experienced as "natural," as an extension of the mother's mouth. To achieve this sense of the natural, though, required training; both mothers and children had to work to produce natural sounds and to connect these sounds to the High German (which could then be experienced as a natural or instinctive language).[33] In the postbellum United States, most children were learning to read in institutional settings, but they were still learning the American language (sometimes as a second language) through *sounds first.* This method of teaching reading produced language as a somatic experience, located not outside the body but within it; language could be figured as a natural part of the self, and that linguistically determined self could in turn be figured as a natural part of a national imagined community.

The *Fifth Reader* assumes that its readers can already read in the sense of "sounding out," but since it equates "reading" with "reading aloud," the literary selections are prefaced by extensive instructions on how to read rhetorically. Rule number one states:

> Before attempting to read a lesson, the learner should make himself fully acquainted with the subject as treated in that lesson, and endeavor to make the thought, and feeling, and sentiments of the writer his own. Remark—When he has thus identified himself with the author, he has the substance of all rules in his own mind. It is by going to nature that we find rules. The child or savage orator never mistakes in inflection, or emphasis, or modulation. The best speakers and readers are those who follow the impulse of nature or most closely imitate it as it is observed in others.[34]

Students are supposed to read naturally, then, and they ought to be able to do so, being children if not "savages." But learning to "read naturally" is not actually assumed to be automatic, even for children; it requires not just Rule number one but twenty-six more pages of instruction on articulation (vocals, subvocals, and aspirates), inflections (rising and falling), accent, emphasis, pitch and compass, and poetic pauses. "Nature" is to be instilled through drills that teach these rhetorical rules until they can be called up instinctively.

The very first selection in *McGuffey's Fifth* reinforces and extends the paradox—that it takes a great deal of training to read naturally—by showing the concrete rewards that can accrue from a convincing performance. Set in the exact time and place—later-eighteenth-century Germany—that Kittler describes as the cradle of phonetic civilization, "The Good Reader" tells the story of how the King of Prussia needed someone to read him a petition. The first page who was called in "did not articulate distinctly": "Every sentence was uttered with a dismal monotony of voice, as if it did not differ in any respect from that which preceded it." The next page, brought in to read the same petition, read tediously, overarticulating and overdramatizing. Finally the King summoned a gardener's little daughter, who happened to have been practicing elocution with great diligence. She read the petition "with so much feeling, and with an articulation so just, in tones so pure and distinct, that when she finished, the King, in whose eyes the tears had started, exclaimed, 'Oh! now I understand what it is all about; but I might never have known, certainly I never should have felt, its meaning had I trusted to these young gentlemen . . .'"[35] The King granted the petition, allowing a widow to take her only son out of the army, and (because the good in *McGuffey's* are generally rewarded on earth, not in heaven) he promoted the girl's father to Head Gardener.

Petitions are not poetry, but the story concretizes the fundamental goals of rhetoric in the *McGuffey's* series. First, expressive reading involves the expression of emotions induced by the text that are nonetheless genuinely felt by the self; like method actors, the readers are expected to submerge their individuality in the emotions of the text and, through those emotions, communicate to others. The meaning lies not so much in words (the King might *not have known* the meaning of the petition had he heard only the pages' readings) but in sounds. The poems in *McGuffey's Fifth* can best be read with this in mind. For example, "It Snows," by Sarah Josepha Hale, works best as a performance piece, allowing the reader to showcase a range of emotions. In five melodramatic stanzas, five social types—the Schoolboy, the Imbecile, the Traveler, the Belle, and the Widow—react to a snowfall; the first stanza begins: "'It snows!' cries the Schoolboy, 'Hurrah!' and his shout / Is ringing through parlor and hall." In every stanza, a different speaker repeats the refrain, "It snows!" In the final stanza,

"It snows!" cries the Widow, "O God!" and her sighs
Have stifled the voice of her prayer;
Its burden yell read in her tear-swollen eyes,
On her cheek sunk with fasting and care.
'Tis night, and her fatherless ask her for bread,
But "he gives the young ravens their food,"
And she trusts till her dark hearth adds horror to dread,
And she lays on her last chip of wood.
Poor sufferer! that sorrow thy God only knows;
'Tis a most bitter lot to be poor when it snows.[36]

At the bottom of the page, *McGuffey's Fifth* includes a "Remark": "Avoid reading this piece in a monotonous style. Try to express the actual feeling of each quotation, and enter into the description with spirit." But where is the "actual feeling" to be found? A silent reader would look for meaning in individual images—in the grimness of the "dark hearth" or in the ambiguity of the biblical reference to Elijah. But *McGuffey's* readers were trained to rely much more on their (learned) rhetorical "instincts," their physical responses, not so much to the pathos of the poem's images, but to its theatrical possibilities. I do not mean to suggest that readers were immune to the poem's tragic images; surely, many of them were touched. But their reading lessons did not demand that they be touched—only that they *sound* touched. The phonetic reader looks, not necessarily for felicitous images, but for the "pitch and compass" of sounds, especially in the repeated refrain, "It snows!" To a silent reader, "It snows!" belabors the obvious, but to a rhetorical reader its repetition offers a key to the poem, a way to make one phrase mean five different things. Far from foreclosing on the poem's ambiguity, the repetition of one phrase opens the poem to a variety of (oral) interpretations.

Hale's goal in writing "It Snows" might well have been to stir up sympathy for poor women; as the editor of *Godey's Lady's Book*, she certainly stood at the center of sentimental culture. But the goal for rhetorical readers of "It Snows" in *McGuffey's Fifth* is not to develop sentimental feelings for the widow. Students are expected to read the piece with "feeling" in order to improve *themselves*—just as the gardener's daughter was able to impress the King, and to achieve a promotion for her father, by reading the widow's petition skillfully. "Actual feelings" in *McGuffey's Fifth* are not necessarily sincere feelings, they are believable feelings. What matters is what students are able to perform. "It Snows" works in this context not because of its sentimental power but because of its pedagogical power: its large cast of characters, mnemonic rhymes, and evocative refrain make it a perfect vehicle for the performance of the self as a competent public citizen.

In the decades following the Civil War, hundreds of school boards adopted the *McGuffey's Reader* series as standard texts. These communities produced readers who knew a few poems very well, and who could recite a poem such as "It Snows" as one measure of the value of education. Unlike novels, which, although they were sometimes read aloud, were mainly for private or even secret consumption, schoolroom poems were taken as templates for interactive pedagogical practices. Their meanings thus proceeded from, and also help to construct, the desires of the communities that taught, learned, internalized, and performed them. Every poem in the schoolroom canon was used extensively as a performance piece, although some, such as *Snow-Bound* or *The Song of Hiawatha*, were mostly mined for excerpts rather than repeated in toto. Performance situations varied, as my chapters will show, but one feature that unites schoolroom poems is a strong sense of sound, of the spoken word, as a basic meaning-producing literary unit. The poem on the page can thus be seen as a script for an oral reading, half-done and finished only when read rhetorically. When readers read poems, then, in youth or in adulthood, they expected them to be conventionally melodious—not just for aesthetic reasons but for social reasons: the poem had to be easy to read, meaning it had to be easy to read *aloud*—meaning, in short, that it had to be convertible to social capital.

SCHOOLROOM CAPITAL

The New England schoolroom poets served many cultural functions—many more than can be summarized in this introductory chapter. But clearly, at least, above and beyond the contents of individual poems, they provided symbolic capital for the educational system and for students within that system. As Pierre Bourdieu has argued, symbolic capital positions people in society, but it also allows them to negotiate the meaning of the capital that they acquire—or more specifically in this case, to negotiate the meanings of the poems they learn.[37] The Russian Jewish immigrant autobiographer Mary Antin registers the difficulty of joining the American consensus, the melting-pot "we," as she describes her school days in Boston in the 1880s and '90s. Antin's identification with American civic institutions—the public library, the public beach, and especially the public schools—is not so much automatic as willed. She sees these institutions as part of herself, the American self that she will make: "The apex of civic pride and personal contentment was reached on the bright September morning when I entered the public school. That day I must always remember, even if I live to be so old that I cannot tell my name."[38] But Antin dates the moment when she really became an American to the day they began to study George Washington in school. She fell in love with Washington and decided to write a poem about him:

> When I had done, I was myself impressed with the length, gravity, and nobility of my poem. My father was overcome with emotion as he read it. His hands trembled as he held the paper to the light, and the mist gathered in his eyes. My teacher, Miss Dwight, was plainly astonished at my performance, and said many kind things, and asked many questions; all of which I took very solemnly, like one who had been in the clouds and returned to earth with a sign on him. When Miss Dwight asked me to read my poem to the class on the day of the celebration, I readily consented. It was not in me to refuse a chance to tell my schoolmates what I thought of George Washington.[39]

Antin, like many children from poor or immigrant backgrounds, concluded that public school offered acculturation as well as knowledge, and the benign America of Washington and Whittier and Longfellow represented an America with which she sought to identify. Her poem echoed the prosody of Longfellow's "Excelsior," and after she recited her poem for the class, and later published it in the newspaper, her teacher rewarded her with a gift volume of Longfellow. The institution of the public school not only taught her the value of Longfellow, it provided a forum for her to produce herself as valuable, in public, *because* of her mastery of poetry.

In addition to the public schools, Antin was also exposed to poetry through church outreach programs that featured "ravishing little girls who stood up in a glory of golden curls, frilled petticoats, and silk stockings to recite pathetic or comic pieces, with trained expression and practiced gesture . . ." Through such performances, Antin writes, she caught a glimpse of a better world, a "world in which the beautiful ladies dwelt with the fairy children and the clean gentlemen."[40] This America was and is a fantasy like "The Barefoot Boy," as Antin's characterization of the scene as a fairy tale implies. But children such as Mary Antin could learn to repeat poetry as a way of learning to act as socially smooth citizens, thus making the fantasy serve their very real desire to succeed. Surely when Antin performed her George Washington poem she was performing her own communicative competence as much as her creative skill. Poetry was part of

Antin's daily life, but it was not therefore quotidian: to her, it was a way to obtain and display cultural capital. As her narrative develops, the American self that she shows to such advantage is predicated on memory (this is a memoir, in which many "pieces" are spoken from memory), and yet it is neither nostalgic nor sentimental. Instead, her childhood self works as a figure for her adult ambition. Rather than functioning as a lost and mourned romantic moment, her early performance of the George Washington poem becomes part of a self that she engages and uses: a speculative, hopeful self.

Antin's individualistic account assumes the shape of a Horatio Alger novel, in which the protagonist rises through luck and pluck. However, Michael Moon has pointed out that, while Alger's stories might appear to celebrate radical individualism, they emerge on closer inspection as celebrations of corporate culture. These are stories about navigating a dense network of urban institutional bonds. They are about fitting into society, not lighting out for the territory.[41] Like the *Badger*'s *Hiawatha* parody, in which individual names are mentioned but submerged into the collective form of the poem, the systems that Antin finds in Gilded Age America discipline her even as they free her. Antin's public school success, begun with the George Washington poem, culminates in a high school graduation scene in which Antin herself speaks two "pieces" (she does not name them) and then, later, another speaker tells an anecdote drawn from Antin's life, sparking an embarrassing scene. When the speaker is finished, Antin is so flattered that she begins to thank the speaker:

> As I rose where I sat, and in a voice that sounded thin as a fly's after the oratorical bass of the last speaker I began:—
> "I want to thank you—"
> That is as far as I got. Mr. Swan, the principal, waved his hand to silence me; and then, only then, did I realize the enormity of what I had done.
>
> My eulogist had had the good taste not to mention names, and I had been brazenly forward, deliberately calling attention to myself when there was no need. Oh, it was sickening! I hated myself . . .[42]

The individualism that she has learned to espouse has its limits; it is not the radical individualism of the earlier-nineteenth-century transcendentalists but rather what might be called the "corporate individualism" of Alger. She must use it to fit in, not "brazenly" to stand up or stand out. Antin's cultural capital is valuable, like paper money, only inside the systems that give it value. If she wants to keep it she must play by the rules, which require individual performances that support institutional as well as personal ambitions.

Paradoxically, Antin's exceptional talents finally enable her to reach her goal of being "normal," subject to the normative shushing of the principal. She is part of a mainstream American public high school class, instead of remaining a marginalized, family-oriented Jewish immigrant like her sister. Strikingly, though, when Antin visits her sister Frieda, what they share is poetry, during the "best time," late at night, when the two are alone in the kitchen:

> I read aloud from Longfellow, or Whittier, or Tennyson; and it was as great a treat to me as it was to Frieda. Her attention alone was inspiring. Her delight, her eager questions doubled the meaning of the lines I read. Poor Frieda had little enough time for reading, unless she stole it from the sewing or the baking or the mending. But she was hungry for books, and so grateful when I came to read to her that it made me ashamed to remember all the beautiful things I had and did not share with her. [43]

To Mary and Frieda, these popular poets do represent not the domestic sphere but rather the public sphere, or rather the institutional sphere in which cultural hierarchies can be established through literary displays—if those displays are in good taste. Antin, here, is sharing what she sees as her wealth—her cultural capital, her "beautiful things." Even as she bonds with her sister over poetry, this very poetry allows her to rehearse, internally and gratefully, her own social mobility and distance from this sister's domestic confines. What she finds in poetry is power: the power not just to rise in the social hierarchy but to speak indirectly (not directly, as she mistakenly did at the graduation) about her own rise by speaking the words of Longfellow, Whittier, and Tennyson. At the same time, *The Promised Land* repeatedly reinscribes the power of specific authorities (Longfellow, Mr. Swan) into a fixed hierarchy that Antin internalizes without question—although not, as any careful reader must sense, without anger.

The self that Antin forges in her memoir—a public, hopeful, speculative, and pedagogical self—is also a self defined in relation to poetry. And poetry, in turn, is defined in relation to a pedagogy rooted in disequilibriums of power. The teacher gives Antin a gift of Longfellow not as a friend but as a mentor; Antin later visits her sister to share some Longfellow verses, taking the mentor's more powerful position as her own. She defends her decision to write an autobiography before the age of thirty by stating that her experience represents that of many immigrants. While Antin is clearly unusual in some ways, her experience of poetry as a powerful and empowering medium was a common one among members—and aspiring members—of the American middle class. Mary Antin's autobiography is informed by her highly individualistic (and yet conforming) ideology; she uses poetry to mark her growing distance both from her immigrant family and from her less successful peers. As Antin intimates, poetry could serve to draw distinctions even as it offered access to all. If middle-class culture was open to many through the public school system, it was nevertheless both homogenizing (in the sense that Antin felt compelled to minimize her Russian and Jewish background to succeed in the melting pot) and racially marked. Antin could become white, if not blonde, and indeed had to identify with white mentors, including Longfellow, whose meters she echoed, in order to become middle class.

The didactic strains of popular poems offered "accessibility," but the ways that they were used regulated that access. This emphasis on access mirrors the aims of the public schools, the institutions that taught most people how to read poetry. On the one hand, the public schools were almost utopian in their insistence on access for all; the whole idea behind the system was to build one unified American community out of heterogeneous materials, as I will discuss at greater length in my chapter on Longfellow. But on the other hand, schools were mostly segregated by race, so that words such as "everyone" and "all" and even "America" could refer more to some than to others. Schoolroom poetry certainly emerged from, and helped to establish, racialized locations, as communities formed based on the perceived social competence of their subjects. As my work on Whittier's "Snow-Bound" will show, the value of "whiteness" was part of what schoolroom poetry established and taught. At the same time, however, schools were places where social boundaries could sometimes be questioned and negotiated even as they were fixed. In 1887 Charlotte Forten Grimké wrote to Booker T. Washington,

> The near approach of the 80th birthday of the poet Whittier suggests to my min a plan in which I would be very glad to have your cooperation. My suggestion is that the pupils of each of the leading colored schools of the South should contribute something towards a birthday present for the venerable poet, as a token of their admiration and esteem, and their gratitude for his earnest, untiring labors on behalf of our race. I presume all the older pupils in the schools know something of his life and his writings, and each action might therefore be confined only to them. I

know the pupils in our schools are poor, but I suppose there are
few who could not contribute the sum of ten cents.[44]

In the later nineteenth century, it became common for students to
contact famous poets, often in search of an autograph or even a
visit. Grimké's decision to offer a gift might seem odd, given the
poverty of her students, but as Marcel Mauss has argued, to give a
gift is always to renegotiate a relationship: when goods are given,
symbolic capital is acquired not by the receiver but by the givers.[45]
To take up a collection was to affirm that the students of "the leading colored schools" represented a distinct community—literal col-
lectivity. Moreover, through gift giving, this community could signal
its power to give charitably (not just to receive charity), and thus it
could claim a measure of equality with Whittier. As Grimké imagined it, the students would establish a relationship to Whittier based
on their knowledge of him, rather than just on his "labors on
behalf" of them. They would both draw on Whittier's "accessibility"
and negotiate the terms of their own access. Like Mary Antin,
Grimké's students were producing themselves not just as readers
but as citizens with demonstrable public value, through their mastery of a schoolroom poet.

CONSTRUCTING GENEALOGIES

In 1895 construction began on James Russell Lowell Elementary
School in Missoula, Montana. The building was a two-room wooden
structure serving grades one to four; for grades five to eight, students
transferred to John Greenleaf Whittier School, a larger building that
served all of Missoula's growing west side. Of the four "core" schoolroom poets—Longfellow, Whittier, Holmes, and Lowell—Lowell's
ubiquity is the least explicable, although in all four cases their connections to families of "sterling worth," as one critic put it, increased
their public value.[46] Longfellow and Whittier made sense as role models because their work (or at least some of their work) was highly
accessible and thus well known among middle-class teachers. And
even Holmes (a much less obviously appealing figure than Whittier
or Longfellow) had written a few "hits," including "The Chambered
Nautilus" and "The Last Leaf," that made him memorable to readers.
But Lowell's reputation as a poet was mixed even in his lifetime; as
Littell's Living Age put it in a generally positive review, "[W]e are not
prepared to place Mr. Lowell in the first rank even of American
poets . . . He is not *thoroughly* inspired, and constantly suggests a fal-
tering towards something prosaic."[47] The only Lowell piece that was

very widely repeated by schoolchildren was a section from "The Vision of Sir Launfal" beginning, "And what is so rare as a day in June?" So what was Lowell doing in Missoula?

The short answer to this question would be that Lowell was in Missoula because he was almost everywhere: naming an elementary school the "James Russell Lowell School" was simply a convention by 1895, signaling the school board's basic cultural competence and acknowledging the authority not so much of Lowell's poems as of his name. Textbooks and periodicals tended to stress the schoolroom poets' distinguished genealogies; for instance, Leon Vincent's 1906 high school textbook *American Literary Masters,* notes: "The Lowells of New England are descendants of Percival Lowell, a prosperous Bristol merchant who came to America in 1639 and settled at Newbury, Massachusetts. The family had been distinguished through its various representatives for public spirit and business acumen as well as for a devotion to letters."[48] Lowell's specific genealogical authority was bolstered by the rising didactic authority of New England, which I will discuss at greater length in my chapter on Whittier's "Snow-Bound." Beginning with the 1876 Centennial and continuing through the turn of the century, the colonial revival promoted New England, not so much as a region, but as the locus of all things truly American. As Joseph Conforti puts it in his study *Imagining New England,* "[For] many colonial revivalists, Old New England represented a repository of traditions that needed to be preserved and invoked to revitalize Anglo-Puritan descendants, assimilate immigrants, and redress the perceived excesses of modern America."[49] Such goals—assimilation and reform—dovetailed with the goals of many school systems, and the New England past, as represented by the New England schoolroom poets (along with the Pilgrims), became "everybody's" past, the heritage that all children, regardless of background, were supposed to claim. Lowell's very status as a New England poet made him a national, or even nationalist, icon. Thus, paradoxically, while Lowell's distinguished pedigree set him above almost all of his readers, this same New England background made his name a common one among schoolchildren. He represented a tradition that was not so much exclusive as coercively inclusive: elementary school had become compulsory in Montana by 1895, and children had to learn the version of America's past that the James Russell Lowell School was teaching.

But as is clear from the Wisconsin yearbook parodies, readers who were taught the schoolroom poets as part of their national heritage then read them (and rewrote them) in ways that served their local interpretive communities. It should not be surprising, then, that the most popular new poet of the later nineteenth century,

James Whitcomb Riley, was a westerner who posited himself not just as a writer but also as a reader—a member of the interpretive community for which he wrote. This community was defined in part through its knowledge of schoolroom poetry, a knowledge that constituted a kind of genealogy that made people feel as if they had something visceral in common. In the introduction to his definitive *Complete Works,* Riley (who was always working to build a homespun persona) is quoted:

> There was but one book at school in which I found the slightest interest: McGuffey's old leather-bound Sixth Reader. It was the tallest book known, and to the boys of my size it was a matter of eternal wonder how I could belong to "the big class in that reader." When we were to read the death of Little Nell, I would run away, for I knew it would make me cry, that the other boys would laugh at me, and the whole thing would become ridiculous. I couldn't bear that. A later teacher, Captain Lee O. Harris, came to understand me with thorough sympathy, took compassion on my weaknesses and encouraged me to read the best literature. He understood that he couldn't get numbers into my head. You couldn't tamp them in! History I also disliked as a dry thing without juice, and dates melted out of my memory as speedily as tinfoil on a red-hot stove. But I was always ready to declaim and took natively to anything dramatic or theatrical.[50]

Despite his slightly roguish tone, Riley is signaling not an eccentricity but a commonality with his readers. His literary genealogy can be traced, not just to a book, but to a form of life, characterized by exchanges with peers and "dramatic or theatrical" readings. Many of Riley's poems are simply glosses on the schoolroom tradition: "The Other Maude Muller" reprises Whittier's "Maude Muller" as a comedy, in the manner of yearbook parodies, while "The Old-Fashioned Bible" repeats the exact form, and many of the exact phrases, from another schoolroom standard, "The Old Oaken Bucket." Riley's text begins, "How dear to my heart are the scenes of my childhood," a quote from "The Old Oaken Bucket" that, he assumes, he does not have to frame as a quote because it is common knowledge. He then continues, "The old-fashioned Bible— / The dust-covered Bible— / The leathern-bound Bible my grandfather read," echoing the *McGuffey's* refrain, "The old oaken bucket— / The iron-bound bucket— / The moss-covered bucket that hung in the well."[51] Riley relied on the collective memory of his / readers to make his poems doubly effective: his *form,* as well as his words, invoked childhood. But my broader point is that

Riley was successful because he did what everyone did: he used the conventions of his interpretive community to make schoolroom poetry fit his needs and the needs of his readers. Riley and his readers shared the same expectations and the same desires; the "fit" was perfect. "The Old Oaken Bucket," like the name "James Russell Lowell," was not a fixed artifact; rather, its wide circulation made it open to appropriation and redeployment by readers with their own agendas.

Rewritings and parodies are only the most traceable evidence of what I take to be the widespread practice of using poetry to fit into the social order. Institutions provided readers with symbolic capital in the form of poetry, and individuals used this capital to perform versions of themselves externally and also, perhaps (although this is difficult to document), to define themselves internally. The exact ways that readers defined themselves socially through poetry is one of my major points of inquiry, and versions of this question are addressed in every chapter. On one level, as Mary Antin's strategies suggest, schoolroom poems helped to form what Bourdieu calls an aristocracy of taste. But this function was unstable, precisely because the schoolroom poets were so popular. When Lowell's name graced a muddy schoolroom in Missoula, the schoolroom may have gained a little prestige but Lowell also lost a little. Moreover, although the Gilded Age was a period of heightened class awareness, class identification was not the only way, or even necessarily the main way, that people situated themselves socially. Pedagogical poetry was just as frequently deployed to bind cohorts (of students in a yearbook, for instance) or to imagine national communities; in these cases, it became an intimate performance that helped to incorporate readers into social systems not based on class (although such systems may have had a vested interest in masking class distinctions). Certainly, to describe the pedagogical institutions of the later nineteenth century is to describe systems of discipline and domination, in which children and adults were subject to forces beyond their control. At stake in every one of my chapters is the question of how popular poetry perpetuated, but also helped its readers to negotiate, these large-scale systems.

The New England schoolroom poets (Longfellow, Whittier, Lowell, Holmes) made the western schoolroom poets (Riley, Field) possible, creating a widespread, albeit limited, understanding of what poetry was and what it could accomplish. And all the poets I examine, including Emily Dickinson, can be called "schoolroom poets" because they appeared regularly in school readers and textbooks. This signals a certain degree of public acceptance since by the 1880s textbooks (and, increasingly, graded curricula) were set by districtwide committees. However, I do not focus exclusively on schoolrooms, because a poet's appearance in the schoolroom is as much an effect as a cause of his or her popularity. Therefore, after my initial chapter on Longfellow (whose presence was ubiquitous in schools) I investigate other cultural locations, to see how popular poetry became popular and why adults, as well as children, valued it.

Popular poetry was promoted by institutions that were, at times, disciplinary in structure and function, including schools, museums, theaters, newspapers, and magazines. These institutions depended on, and maintained, imbalances of power between adults and children, producers and consumers, middle-class people and those perceived as deficient by reason of race or nationality. But it is difficult to see the effects of poetry itself as purely disciplinary. To learn a poem was also to gain access to powers, not just of repetition, but of interpretation—and even (in the case of rhetorical reading) to gain access to powers of interpretation *through* repetition. Such power is not sentimental power, based on self-abnegation; it is pedagogical power, based on learned social competence. And this competence can be displayed through quoting—a practice of repetition that does not simply repeat but rather forces lines of poetry into new contexts, giving it new use-values. Let me return briefly, by way of illustration, to "The Barefoot Boy," as he appears in a poem written by the western regional poet Ellen Atherton in 1884. "Kansas, the Prairie Queen" appeared in a volume titled *Walls of Corn* that was printed in Hiawatha, Kansas, translated into German, and distributed throughout Middle Europe as an advertisement for immigration:

> The country boy with the bare, brown feet,
> Tripping to school with his books and slate,
> May climb some day to the highest seat—
> In some great crisis may save the state.
>
> Little he thinks, at his books or play,
> While the warm blood mantles his "cheek of tan,"
> Of the work of the years that stretch away;
> Yet the careless boy is the coming man.[52]

Whittier's "barefoot boy with cheek of tan" thus becomes not just an emblem of the lost New England past (although the quote would evoke that heritage for the poem's American readers) but also an emblem of hope and speculation. The repetition of "cheek of tan" posits the boy as part of a community that is at once local (rooted in a Kansas cornfield) and national (the Barefoot Boy could be president!). Atherton's poem is thus a gloss on Whittier's "Barefoot Boy," drawing on the national schoolroom tradition to picture an "old acquaintance," with "cheek of tan," who is cast in powerfully mnemonic meters that both preserve and transform his memory.

*   *   *

SCHOOLROOM POETRY represents America's usable literary past, if by "usable" we mean "most frequently used." Memorials of the school-room poets still dot the landscape, from the Whittier Glacier in Alaska to the Riley Children's Hospital in Indianapolis. My claim for their work is not simply that it was popular; rather, I want to argue that, because it was popular, schoolroom poetry deserves to be read, and read closely, with its audiences in mind. However, by "audiences" I do not mean statistics or groups drawn from library records, although this would be one way to establish the presence of historical readers. Instead, throughout this book, I use anecdotal evidence, drawn from sources (photographs, newspaper reports) that cite *particular* communities, although they often reveal very little about the readers themselves. The reason for this focus on communities is my sense that while every single reading of a popular poem (or indeed of any text) is to some degree a new reading, its meanings are always directed and limited (although not absolutely determined) by its social context.

This problem of dealing with obscure readers is exacerbated if we consider the ways in which popular poems constructed not just social performers but also internal forms of subjectivity. Robert Pinsky has written about the way that poems can be simultaneously public and private, arguing that "poetry as breath penetrates to where the body recognizes the stirring of meaning. Poetry mediates, on a particular and immensely valuable level, between the inner consciousness of the individual reader and the outer world of other people."[53] It is worth asking, however, how the "inner consciousness of the individual reader" is constructed, and how this consciousness (perceived as internal) might stem from the reader's (external, empirical) historical moment. In the chapters that follow I will not, for the most part, venture too far into the subjective interiors of nineteenth-century readers. However, especially in my discussion of Eugene Field, I will gesture toward the form of internal selfhood that the recitation of poetry, and specifically the infantilization of American poetry, may have helped to produce. That is, while I will not claim to know what readers were thinking, I will begin to outline the shape of the self as it was popularly represented (and thus perhaps constructed) by Field in the transitional decade of the 1890s. Of course poetry did not *determine* the ways that people understood their own interior selves, but in

[XLIII]

an age of mass memorization, it surely had some influence on the ways they remembered themselves as children—and in turn constituted themselves through memory.

The cultural historian Carolyn Steedman has made this argument in her study *Strange Dislocations: Childhood and the Idea of Human Interiority, 1780–1930*:

> The figure of the child, released from the many texts that gave birth to it, helped shape the feelings, and structure feeling into thought. Raymond Williams came close to describing this process when he wrote of the 'activation of specific relations' when poems are read, stories told, plays enacted and watched. What takes place in those moments, he claimed, are 'real processes . . . physical and material relational processes.' And he goes on to describe 'the poem first "heard" as a rhythm without words [. . .] as a moving shape inside the body.' These movements of relationship, between people and things (entities visualized, phonemic patterns given a name) are means of cognition, ways of thought. One of the problems, on the historical plane, is that the process described here is always individual, as well as often collective, not just the activation of pre-existing networks of understanding and belief and relationships, but a means of bringing them into being as well. The idea of the child was the figure that provided the largest number of people living in the recent past of Western societies with the means for thinking about and creating a self: something grasped and understood: a shape, moving in the body . . . something *inside*, an interiority.[54]

Childhood, in other words, became a way for adults to essentialize themselves as human subjects, constituted specifically through the body. Steedman's study focuses on prose texts, but her idea of the human interior as a child-figure is especially applicable to schoolroom poetry. A poem such as "The Barefoot Boy" could be memorized, and thus internalized, to become part of the child and ultimately part of the childhood self—the miniaturized self—that adults had come to feel defined them. "The Barefoot Boy" could help to construct a version of the adult's "essential" self—a self that, despite its seemingly essential qualities, was composed of historically specific discourses and assumptions.

Schoolroom poetry sometimes figured the self as a child, as in "The Barefoot Boy." But even when it did not make this explicit connection, as in "The Vision of Sir Launfal," it was still learned in childhood and became a constitutive part of what people understood "childhood" to be. By the later nineteenth century, as I will argue in my chapters on Field and on *St. Nicholas Magazine,* rhyme and meter were beginning to sound childish, albeit appealingly so, to adult ears. This led to a surge in the production of children's poetry while also incidentally laying the groundwork for the modernist revolt against formal prosody. Many of the most popular poems of the 1880s and 1890s, such as Riley's "Raggedy Man," were children's poems that found an appreciative adult audience, precisely because they were accomplishing what readers expected: they were shaping childhood through poetry and poetry through childhood. Emily Dickinson, who was marketed through children's magazines and presented as a childlike prodigy, charmed some readers in the 1890s (while infuriating others) for related reasons. Her poems seemed to be (mis)shapen, recalling but also distorting the rhymes and meters that adults knew from childhood—and that they saw as part of their essential selves. Reactions to Dickinson's verses were visceral because readers had a specific horizon of expectations for what poetry was supposed to sound like and what it was supposed to do, and if their *McGuffey's Readers* had succeeded, then these expectations felt instinctual to them.

The self, as constituted through schoolroom poetry, was both a product of institutions and a ballast against them. In her study *On Longing,* Susan Stewart uses the miniature as a metaphor for "the interior space and time of the bourgeois subject": "The miniature, linked to nostalgic versions of childhood and history, presents a diminutive, and thereby manipulatable, version of experience, a version which is domesticated and protected from contamination."[55] As a miniature art form—unlike the sprawling realist and romantic novels of the postwar scene—popular poetry could be experienced, like the nostalgic version of "childhood," as an uncontaminated retreat from large-scale social forces. And yet it was the presence of those social forces—educational, historical, theatrical, journalistic—that made poetry available, and useful, to readers in the years between the Civil War and the First World War. Moreover, to perform schoolroom poetry, as I have shown, was not to reject society but to join it. A poem such as "The Barefoot Boy" presents itself as a pastoral enclosure, but in practice it was "contaminated," and energized, by voices and bodies: Olive Dana's voice, for instance, and her costumed student's "barefoot" body. Readers turned Whittier's poem into a pedagogical text, a text predicated on social exchange and social transmission. Popular poetry ultimately offered, not an escape from literary and social conventions, but an escape *into* them—and *into* the simultaneously nurturing and disciplinary communities that poetic performances helped to construct.

SCHOOLROOM POETS

CHAPTER ONE

Reading America: Longfellow in the Schools

In 1882, Henry Wadsworth Longfellow's seventy-fifth birthday inspired hundreds of fans, mostly teachers and schoolchildren, to send their greetings, often accompanied by thinly veiled attempts to obtain his autograph. A few even sent original poems inspired by his benign persona:

> O Longfellow! Lover of children!
> You truly are happy this day
> For a million young hearts send you greeting
> And with innocent trustfulness pray
> That the God of the poet may keep you
> And ward far away the sad time
> When your life may cease to remind us
> That we, too, may live "lives sublime."
> Every schoolroom today is a temple
> Every child is a worshipped small
> And they bow, as unto a fetish
> To your picture which hangs on the wall.[1]

As with much of the mail that Longfellow received, the idolatrous tone of this writer must be taken with a grain of salt. Still, the jumble of sacred and secular imagery does capture the role that Longfellow played in later-nineteenth-century public schoolrooms. As American public education became widespread and systematized in the decades following the Civil War, solid, tax-supported, multiroom brick buildings began to supplant one-room schoolhouses. These buildings had names that reflected their ambitions to make every life "sublime": there were Washington schools and Hamilton schools, Lowell schools and Whittier schools. After the turn of the century, there were even a few Whitman schools. But most commonly—or rivaled in popularity only by Lincoln and Washington schools—there were Longfellow schools. Longfellow schools were usually primary schools, and even today thousands of American schoolchildren—in Tacoma, Washington; in Wheaton, Illinois; in Portland, Maine—spend their formative years walled in, as it were, by Longfellow.

Longfellow's stature in schools—a stature that remained strong even as his critical reputation weakened—bears examining, especially in light of his self-professed romantic nationalism. Nineteenth-century debates about the function of public schools often centered on the relationship between the student (the citizen, or citizen-to-be) and the nation. Liberals wanted schools to promote social progress, while conservatives wanted them to promote social control; all agreed, however, that school lessons, including poetry lessons, should teach children how to be Americans and how to practice "civic virtues," although the exact definition of "civic virtues" was in question. Longfellow stood at the center of this debate over freedom versus control, seeming to defuse it with his benign authority; whatever their differences, educators and students could unite in matters of taste, since "everyone" could learn to love Longfellow. Students read his work, committed it to memory, performed it for their teachers and parents, and remembered it as adults. And yet, his most commonly taught poems—*The Song of Hiawatha* (1855), "Paul Revere's Ride" (1860), and "A Psalm of Life" (1839)—raise the very issues that his persona defused, asking students to negotiate (rather than simply to learn and repeat) national narratives that included them as active reading subjects. Virtually all the recent critical work on Longfellow assumes that he is worth studying because of his extraordinary cultural impact; given this, it seems essential to read Longfellow as he was construed by a postbellum public school system that "worshipped, as unto a fetish," his poetry and his picture. His institutional role also leads to a larger question, implicit in my analysis: how can the term "schoolroom poet" be recruited, not just as a descriptive label but as an analytical tool, a way to make sense of the power that schoolrooms gave to—and took from—poetry?

Longfellow's creative output peaked in the 1850s, and recent critical evaluations of his work locate him in the antebellum era, most frequently as a male sentimentalist who soothed his readers' anxieties. Eric Haralson argues that Longfellow's popularity at midcentury resulted from his feminization; even as he urged readers to make their lives "sublime," his use of the word "blurred the gendering as well as the social valences of a Romantic 'sublimity' centering on the male isolato," replacing the rugged hero with a milder model. Matthew Gartner makes a similar point, arguing that Longfellow's public persona was that of a "humanized father figure" whose patriarchal power was tempered by domesticity. And Virginia Jackson, focusing not on gender roles but on Longfellow's power as a popularizer, a "faux-bard," teases out the dynamics by which he offered his readers access to an imaginary common language rooted not in words but in pictures. Jackson points to the reassuring functions of such verbal pictures, which demanded only superficial reading while offering a sense of mastery.[2] All three critics refer to his waning popularity in the later nineteenth century, but it is at this historical juncture that we encounter a curious fact: while Longfellow may have become less popular, he remained (unlike, say, Lydia Sigourney) just as "known," and even became *increasingly* well known, because by 1900 his work was taught in almost every school in America. Catholic as well as public school textbooks reprinted him; African-American teachers streamed out of normal schools such as Hampton armed with Longfellow lesson plans; and school ceremonies drew on his work to add solemnity and authority to the occasion. Thus I begin my analysis, not in the antebellum period when Longfellow wrote most of his poems, but in the postbellum era when his work became, like schooling itself, not merely popular but compulsory.

Six months after Appomattox, Frances Wayland, president of Brown University, told the National Teachers' Union that the Civil War had been caused by "a diffused and universal education in the North and a very limited education of the South . . . the Civil War was a war of education and patriotism against ignorance and barbarism."[3] "Barbarism" took different forms in the imaginations of later-nineteenth-century educators: "barbarians" might be the urban poor, the Catholics (who had their own school systems, thought to be controlled by Rome), the southern freedmen, or foreign immigrants. Certainly, however, the mandate for public schools was a staggering one: not only were they to educate children, but they were to remake them, so that the next generation could build a united America unfettered by sectional, ethnic, or racial conflict. What had been a disorganized, local, practical task—the education of children—took on utopian dimensions, as educators and politicians began building schools that were framed as utopian spaces where children would be changed: their own history (seen as a liability if "ethnic") would be replaced by a reductive Anglo-Saxon version of American history, and "civic virtue" would soon efface any religious or cultural eccentricities. In other words, schools were expected not to reflect social problems but to solve them—and to solve them by producing competent citizens. Among Longfellow's popular poems, a few emerged as "schoolroom standards," including *The Song of Hiawatha,* "Paul Revere's Ride," and "A Psalm of Life." Each of these poems offers a specific form of social competency to readers: *The Song of Hiawatha* makes learning to read a process of assimilation into American culture, "Paul Revere's Ride" locates readers in a national community by giving them a common history, and "A Psalm of Life" posits and celebrates the civic virtue of the (assimilated, American) reader. Taken together, these poems teach lessons that register the national ambitions of the educational institutions that promoted them as classics.

HIAWATHA AND THE SUBJECT OF CIVILIZATION

In school systems concerned with the eradication of what Frances Wayland called "barbarism," *The Song of Hiawatha* might seem like an odd choice. And yet Longfellow's book-length Indian narrative was one of his most widely excerpted and taught texts. In faux-primitive trochaic tetrameter (lifted from the faux-primitive Finnish national epic, the *Kalevala*), Longfellow's poem tells the life story of Hiawatha, a supernatural Ojibway chief. Hiawatha teaches people to grow corn, to write "picture-language," and to worship the Great Spirit Gitche Manito; he marries the maiden Minnehaha (who dies in an extended sentimental deathbed scene); and he ultimately paddles his birch canoe into the sunset just as the white missionaries arrive. *Hiawatha's* initial popularity as an adult text is well known; when it was released in 1855 it quickly became the most popular book-length poem of the American nineteenth century. As Richard Stoddard recalled, "It was eagerly read by all . . . who suddenly found themselves interested in the era of flint arrow-heads, earthen pots, and skin clothes. Everybody read the *Song of Hiawatha*."[4] Stoddard's description registers the sense of national simultaneity that, according to Benedict Anderson, is generated by print culture and mass literacy. And yet the poem itself is specifically preliterate, depicting an archaic America without a written language or a written history. Located on the cusp between oral and written language, *The Song of Hiawatha* became a popular text for children who were just beginning to read.

After the Civil War, graded schools began to replace one-room schoolhouses, and education became more systematic. Teachers sought texts that were suited to particular developmental stages. Selections from *Hiawatha* had been used as rote schoolroom recitations beginning in the 1850s, but toward the end of the century the poem became extraordinarily popular among progressive educators as an interactive reading text for elementary schoolchildren. In the wake of evolutionary theory (Darwin, Spencer), and also following the older tradition of romantic racialism (Herder), young children were believed to recapitulate earlier stages of civilization. John Dewey, the most influential educator of the Progressive Era, wrote in 1897:

> I believe that knowledge of social conditions, of the present
> state of civilization, is necessary in order to interpret the child's

powers. The child has his own instincts and tendencies, but we do not know what these mean until we can translate them into their social equivalents. We must be able to carry them back into a social past and see them as the inheritance of previous race activities.[5]

Hiawatha was recruited to carry children "back into a social past" where they could work at their own level. The aims of developmentally sensitive educators were practical: they wanted children to learn to read via relatively easy (but not vulgar) texts. But the effects of using *Hiawatha* were also nationalist and utopian, as the poem promoted bonds of kinship by depicting a preliterate national past that "everybody" (to use Stoddard's word) could access and share.

In this way, Longfellow's story mirrors one of the ur-narratives of American education: oral savages (bound together by their common prelinguistic origin) become literate citizens who nevertheless remain bound by the savage past they share. Like Hiawatha, American students moved from orality to literacy and from barbarism to social competence culminating in a (graduation) ritual. *Hiawatha*'s prologue begins with a dialogue that represents an oral exchange:

> Should you ask me, whence these stories?
> Whence these legends and traditions,
> With the odors of the forest,
> With the dew and damp of meadows,
> With the curling smoke of wigwams,
> With the rushing of great rivers,
> With their frequent repetitions,
> And their wild reverberations,
> As of thunder in the mountains?
> I should answer, I should tell you,
> "From the forests and the prairies,
> From the great lakes of the Northland,
> From the land of the Ojibways . . .
> I repeat them as I heard them
> From the lips of Nawadaha,
> The musician, the sweet singer."[6]

The very first lines, then, posit a pedagogical scene: the reader is a questioner, and the speaker, the "I," has all the answers, drawing on the natural authority of the landscape. The stories themselves, the speaker asserts, actually emanate not from Nawadaha but from birds, beavers, bison, and eagles. Like birdsongs, they are repetitive because they are wild, and the storyteller can only report them verbatim, without interpretation or embellishment.

While his readers are still auditors—and thus on an equal level with Nawadaha, the sweet singer, participating in his oral culture—Longfellow makes a sentimental case for the Indian subjects' value, if not quite their equality, appealing to "Ye whose hearts are fresh and simple":

> Who have faith in God and Nature
> Who believe that in all ages
> Every human heart is human,
> That in even savage bosoms
> There are longings, yearnings, strivings
> For the good they comprehend not,
> That the feeble hands and helpless,
> Groping blindly in the darkness,
> Touch God's right hand in that darkness
> And are lifted up and strengthened;
> Listen to this simple story,
> To this Song of Hiawatha!
>
> (*H*, 3)

The Indians, then, are embryonic humans, still at the earliest stage of development, like infants in the darkness of the womb. They have emotional but not intellectual faculties. Thus far the readers, too, have been addressed as de facto babies, prepared to read the poem through emotional rather than intellectual appeals. The story, the speaker announces, will be told "in tones so plain and childlike / Scarcely can the ear distinguish / Whether they are sung or spoken." The conceit of the poem is preliterate: everyone is in darkness together, listening. No one can read.

The final section of the prologue, then, comes as something of a jolt, as a reader (not an auditor, not in darkness) intrudes on the scene—just as the missionaries will intrude in canto 22, at the end of the poem. Longfellow addresses this reader:

> Ye who sometimes in your rambles
> Through the green lanes of the country,
> Where the tangled barberry-bushes
> Hang their tufts of crimson berries
> Over stone walls gray with mosses,
> Pause by some neglected graveyard,
> For a while to muse, and ponder

> On a half-effaced inscription,
> Written with little skill of song-craft,
> Homely phrases, but each letter
> Full of hope and yet of heart-break,
> Full of all the tender pathos
> Of the Here and the Hereafter;
> Stay and read this rude inscription,
> Read this Song of Hiawatha!
>
> (*H*, 3–4)

Who is this antiquarian, rambling through the green lanes and stone walls of what appears to be the New England countryside? The collective, infantile audience has suddenly become an adult poring over half-effaced inscriptions on tombstones. In breaking the prehistoric temporal frame, Longfellow also shatters the illusion that the poem is oral; now it is an inscription, and one specifically compared to a series of *letters,* a text written in English. Why call attention to the artificiality of his "natural" Indian language? The rambler never reappears as a character; the rest of the poem inhabits the world of the Ojibways as Longfellow imagines them. But this rambler is important because he marks the ultimate end point of this narrative of Manifest Destiny: he is an adult, he is enlightened, and—crucially—he can read. This makes him powerful: unlike the earlier childlike auditors, he is not meekly asking questions; instead, he is being implored to stay awhile—to take a breather from his walk to listen to the stories of a people whose original power he has eclipsed.

By the turn of the century most people were encountering *Hiawatha* in lower elementary school, through anthology primers or through such specialty publications as Florence Holbrook's *Hiawatha Primer* (1898); the *Deutscher Hiawatha Primer* (1899), also by Holbrook; or Mary Proudfoot's *Hiawatha Alphabet* (1902). Proudfoot's *Hiawatha Industrial Reader* (1915) asks children to read selections from *Hiawatha* and then to do concrete, connected activities: "Let us be fairy Indians and go out into this forest and cut poles for a wigwam."[7] Instructions are then given for fashioning tabletop wigwams out of sticks and leaves. Like Longfellow's prologue, Proudfoot's *Hiawatha* woodcrafts are designed to help readers withdraw—temporarily—from the abstract realm of print, concretizing their experience of the text and connecting it back to the natural "odors of the forest."

And yet Proudfoot's aims are ultimately precisely the opposite: children must pass through the fairy-Indian, wigwam-building stage so that they can become competent readers. The child must move from nature to culture, from preliterate singing to literate reading, from an Indian state of mind to an American (but not American Indian!) state of mind. The stakes are made very clear in a lesson from the 1912 *Davis-Julien Reader*. A grandmother is speaking to her three grandchildren:

"What makes the rainbow, Grandma?"
"Shall I give you the Indian reason, children?"
"Please do, Grandma," said they, and she told them the story:

> At the door one summer evening
> Sat the little Hiawatha . . .
> Saw the rainbow in the heaven,
> In the eastern sky the rainbow,
> Whispered: "What is that, Nokomis?"
> And the good Nokomis answered,
> 'Tis the heaven of flowers you see there;
> All the wild flowers of the forest,
> All the lilies of the prairie,
> When on earth they fade and perish,
> Blossom in that heaven above us.'

"I wish I could be like Hiawatha," said Ben, "and learn the language of all beasts."
"I think, Ben," was Grandma's reply, "if you learn your own tongue, that will prove more useful. However, vacation will soon be here, and when you and the girls go up into the mountains, you can be Hiawatha."
"Oh, that will be fun," said all three together.[8]

Like the rambler at the end of Longfellow's poem, Ben is instructed to play Indian while he is on vacation, but to keep evolving in real life. Natural languages—like those spoken by Hiawatha, who can talk to squirrels—are too concrete to be useful to grown people. Boys, especially, must learn to read and write English, the universal, if not precisely natural, language of success.

Children who encountered *Hiawatha* in elementary school often returned to the poem later in life, as Indian-themed summer camps became popular and costume pageants (often performed at camp) also enjoyed a vogue. Beginning in 1900, the Canadian Pacific Railway Company promoted a "Hiawatha" pageant at a summer resort at Kensington Point, Desbarats, Ontario, catering to prosperous New York and Chicago vacationers. Families rented tents for eight dollars per week and were able to live out the fantasy articulated by Ben in the *Davis-Julien Reader.* The pageant—which was staged every year for over thirty years, until the Great Depression felled it—was performed entirely by Ojibway Indians using artifacts borrowed (or so the brochure claimed) from the Smithsonian Institution.[9] The implication—that civilized people can take a fun trip "back to nature" with real Indians—suggests that frontier texts such as *Hiawatha* were understood as depicting earlier versions of the American self: less civilized, but offering a healthy respite for exactly that reason.

The cultural work of *Hiawatha* was thus embedded in daily-life activities: children not only read the text together in school but also encountered the poem in performance contexts. In the poem itself, oral performances sacralize the past by bringing it vividly to life in the present. At Hiawatha and Minnehaha's wedding feast, the old storyteller Iagoo tells a chapter-long tale, "The Son of the Evening Star," about two lovers, Osseo and Oweenee. The story takes place near the beginning of time, "When the heavens were closer to us / And the Gods were more familiar."[10] Osseo is an old and ugly man, but the lithe Oweenee, sensing his inner beauty, consents to marry him. The rest of the story depicts a series of Ovidian transformations: Osseo passes through an oak tree to become a young man again; Oweenee just as suddenly withers into an old woman; and a group of aunts and uncles who laugh at the couple are turned into birds. Finally, at the end of the story, the spell is broken: Osseo and Oweenee are again both young and perfectly matched, and the relatives turn from birds back into people. Only they are not fully grown adult people but rather curiously timeless little creatures:

> "Then the birds, again transfigured,
> Reassumed the shape of mortals,
> Took their shape, but not their stature;
> They remained as Little People,
> Like the Pygmies, the Pug-Wudjies,
> And on pleasant nights of summer,
> When the Evening Star was shining
> Hand in hand they danced together
> On the island's craggy headlands,
> On the sand-beach low and level."
> Still their glittering lodge is seen there,
> On the tranquil Summer evenings,
> And upon the shore the fisher
> Sometimes hears their happy voices,
> Sees them dancing in the starlight!"
>
> (*H*, 84)

Iagoo's tale not only makes the past metaphorically present, through vivid images, but also tells the literal story of a past—smaller and more childlike than the present—that persists in the "glittering lodge" of the Little People. Moreover, the effect of the story is to produce bonds of kinship among the wedding guests, in addition to cementing the new kinship between Hiawatha and Minnehaha:

> All the wedding-guests delighted
> Listened to the marvelous story,
> Listened laughing and applauding,
> And they whispered to each other:
> 'Does he mean himself, I wonder?
> And are we the aunts and uncles?
>
> (*H*, 91)

Here Iagoo uses his oral skills to create a sense of kinship among auditors who may or may not be literal "aunts and uncles" but who bond through their role as listeners. Moreover, the bonds he depicts may be ancient, set in a time "near the beginning," but they are also figured as eternal, as the Little People dance forever in the starlight; they work as a common focal point for Iagoo's spellbound audience. To sacralize the past is to make it a concrete (visible, audible) part of the present, while allowing it to retain its prehistoric authority and power.

As the sociologist James Brow has argued (drawing on Benedict Anderson), constructing and sacralizing the past helps to maintain the nation-state:

> Tradition typically composes a version of the past that not only binds the members of the nation to one another, by proclaiming their shared descent and / or common experience, but also associates the nation as a whole with a particular territory that—maintaining the domestic imagery of the family—is its homeland.[11]

Through the schools, *The Song of Hiawatha* made the American homeland visible and audible to students—not as a map or a chart but as an archaic point of origin that could never be changed or defiled, and that could always be revisited through repetition.

Like the "natural" state of childhood, the landscape of Longfellow's poem is sacred partly because it is assumed to stand outside of history, reflecting an organic order that nonetheless underwrites and validates a national history. In the poem's final canto, "Hiawatha's Departure," Hiawatha encounters "Black-Robe" missionaries (whom he calls "my guests") and decides to paddle into the sunset:

> "I am going, O my people,
> On a long and distant journey;
> Many moons and many winters
> Will have come, and will have vanished,
> Ere I come again to see you.
> But my guests I leave behind me;
> Listen to their words of wisdom,
> Listen to the truth they tell you,
> For the Master of Life has sent them,
> From the land of light and morning!"
>
> (*H*, 159)

Hiawatha leaves behind a message of assimilation that carries traces of ambivalence. While, on the one hand, "every human heart is human," on the other hand Hiawatha himself is essentially choosing to die rather than to merge with the white man. So are the Indians supposed to fade away, or are they supposed to join the dominant culture of the coming Europeans?

In most school contexts the question was moot, because the poem was not really functioning as a text about Indians at all; rather, it was aimed at children's own preoccupations (with themselves) and at helping them to connect concretely to their own immediate past. Thus one 1898 textbook summarizes "Hiawatha's Childhood" for very little children by involving them in the material history of cradles:

> Nokomis made a little cradle for Hiawatha.
> It was made of wood and skins.
> She put moss in it, too.
> The moss made it soft.
> Nokomis put Hiawatha into his cradle.
> She tied him into it.
> He did not cry.
> She hung the cradle on a tree.
> The winds would rock him.
> The birds would sing to him.
> The squirrels would talk to him.
> How do you like Hiawatha's cradle?
> Would your baby brother like it?[12]

The notion of taking Hiawatha out of his own cradle and substituting a (presumed white) baby brother cuts both ways: it is both a fantasy of universal humanity (all babies like to be rocked) and an allegory of Manifest Destiny (whites replace Indians). But the ultimate aim of

[11]

a text such as this is to introduce the reader to a famous American poem that "everybody" knows, so that he, too, can feel like part of this "everybody." *Hiawatha* can produce these feelings because it is a text about the prehistory of the nation that could also be seen as part of each child's personal prehistory: ontogeny recapitulates phylogeny.

It should be obvious that, despite its romantic celebration of Indians, *The Song of Hiawatha* is finally a text that indeed replaces Indian babies with white ones. As numerous critics have pointed out, Hiawatha is a distinctly nineteenth-century American hero, and his progress through life ultimately bears a suspicious resemblance to the popular Prang chromolithograph that depicts the life stages of (white, Victorian) Man.[13] *Hiawatha*'s cultural work as a nationalist text is made especially clear, and ironic, in those recorded cases when it was used to help assimilate Indians into the American educational system. It was perhaps inevitable that the poem would become a fixture in Bureau of Indian Affairs schools, and by 1890 the Sioux and Fox Agency school, Indian Territory, was celebrating Longfellow's birthday. But certainly one of the longest-running examples of a Native American *Hiawatha* pageant was initiated by a teacher, Cora M. Folsom, at Virginia's Hampton Institute (originally a Freedmen's Bureau normal school) in 1881. For the next thirty-five years, according to Folsom, Indian students performed *Hiawatha*, at Hampton, in "the summer hotels and gardens of New England," and ultimately at Carnegie Hall.[14] An article in the *Cleveland Gazette* described one such performance on the Hampton campus:

> Last night these Indian students gave an exhibition at Virginia Hall, before a cultured audience. It was a set of tableaux, illustrating Longfellow's poem of Hiawatha, and acted out as it was by genuine Indians, was a curiosity indeed. . . The tableaux were excellent. The scenes were accompanied by the reading of Longfellow's lines relating to them by an Indian boy of fifteen, who tapped a bell as he finished a description, and the curtain was then drawn, disclosing the scene. We had the childhood of Hiawatha—his visit to Minnehaha—how he wooed and how he won her. How he took her to his wigwam, and his wedding with the beggar's dance of Paupaukeewas and the song of Chibiabos. A half dozen or more such tableaux followed, all genuine Indians in genuine Indian costumes with the tents, bows and arrows.[15]

When the *tableaux vivants* were first organized, they were a fund-raising effort to buy a stained-glass window depicting Pocahontas for St. John's Episcopal Church in Hampton. The window, still a major

tourist attraction in the town, depicts Pocahontas kneeling to be baptized. Similarly, in *Hiawatha,* a Jesuit missionary delivers Christ's message to Hiawatha, sparking both his conversion (he instructs other
Indians to listen to the message) and his immediate, euphemized
departure "to the portals of the sunset," "to the land of the Hereafter." In a classic Manifest Destiny move, he fades into nature so that
nature can be subdued by the stronger force of the white man. In the
stained-glass window, Pocahontas kneels to be baptized, and in so
doing she too "fades away," not literally into nature but figuratively
into European culture: she assimilates, just as her form is incorporated into the European form of the stained-glass window, and just as
Hiawatha's "Song" is incorporated into a form taken from European
(specifically Finnish) prosody. This process echoes the educational
process at Hampton, which sought to incorporate Indians into the
school with the express purpose of making them less Indian and
more American. Booker T. Washington, who worked as a tutor in one
of the Indian dormitories at Hampton, reminisced with his characteristic blend of anger and resignation: "The things they disliked
most, I think, were to have their long hair cut, to give up wearing
their blankets, and to cease smoking, but no white American ever
thinks that any other race is wholly civilized until he wears the white
man's clothes, eats the white man's food, speaks the white man's language, and professes the white man's religion."[16] In order to grow up
into civilization, the Indian students were expected to grow up and to
stop being Indian, or at least to stop acting like Indians.

And indeed, it is safe to say that in the *Hiawatha* tableaux, the
Indian students were not acting like Indians; they were acting like
white people acting like Indians. This may explain a surprising audience reaction, noted by the *Cleveland Gazette* writer who visited Hampton. It should be mentioned that, while Longfellow's poem spawned
many parodies and burlesques, when the original text was performed
it was generally received with the respectful solemnity that its oracu-
lar tone commands. Nevertheless, the *Gazette,* having described the
Hiawatha tableaux, goes on to report:

> Among the audience were several rows of Indian boys and girls,
> from full-grown men to boys of ten, and from women to little
> girls, and it was as interesting to watch these as the stage itself.
> Throughout the play, as the scenes of their Western savage life
> passed before them, they became wildly enthusiastic, chattered
> to each other in Indian language, and clapped their hands while
> they roared and laughed. Talk about the Indians having no sense
> of the humorous! Last night these young Indians laughed more

than any white audience I have seen, and I am sure they have enjoyed themselves thoroughly.[17]

What the earnest Ohio reporter read as scenes of "genuine Indians in genuine Indian costumes" the genuine Indians themselves appear to have read as low comedy. The divergence between the reporter's perspective and the Indians' perspective is not a divide that *The Song of Hiawatha* wishes to acknowledge. The poem's message is that, in the time before written history, everyone spoke the same language ("with the odor of the forest") and could communicate perfectly, heart to heart. But the only way to gain access to this sacred homeland of the past is to learn to read and write English, the language of American history, American bureaucracy, the American school system, and *The Song of Hiawatha*.

"PAUL REVERE'S RIDE" MAKES HISTORY

On February 27, 1880, the Cincinnati public schools celebrated Longfellow's birthday with a districtwide celebration; one schooll child, Max Loeb, faced an audience of his teachers and peers to declaim:

> Listen, my children, and you shall hear
> Of the midnight ride of Paul Revere,
> On the eighteenth of April in Seventy-five;
> Hardly a man is now alive
> Who remembers that famous day and year.[18]

If *Hiawatha* gave children a common past, linking their own preliterate experiences to the "childhood" of the nation," Paul Revere's Ride" offered them access to history, beginning with a solid date: April 18, 1775. And yet, as Benedict Anderson has pointed out, people care about national history not (or not just) because it provides names and dates but because it connects them to one another, and to an idea—the nation—that ultimately exceeds history:

> If nation-states are widely conceded to be "new" and "historical,"
> the nations to which they give political expression always loom
> out of an immemorial past, and, still more important, glide into
> a limitless future. It is the magic of nationalism to turn chance
> into destiny.[19]

As a schoolroom poem, "Paul Revere's Ride" could link the mundane reality of Max Loeb's classroom in Cincinnati to nothing less than the sublime force of destiny. Its historical narrative succeeds precisely because it is energized by a streak of magical thinking that knits the local to the national, the temporal to the timeless, and the living to the dead. The mechanisms that this poem uses are so precise, and mirror so closely the technologies of nationalism as Anderson describes them, that a very close reading of the poem is required to see how it works.

"Paul Revere's Ride" was, and to some extent remains, an uncannily familiar poem. John Van Schaik, for instance, breaks the detached critical voice of his 1939 study to remark, "Like many thousands of American boys and girls, the writer used to recite the poem at school exhibitions. No lines come more readily to mind than 'Listen my children and you shall hear . . .' "[20] The poem spurred mass secular pilgrimages to the Old North Church, as Charles Gettemy's 1912 biography of Revere confirms, reverting to mass pronouns:

> Upon how many thousands of schoolboys who have declaimed the stirring lines of Longfellow's description of Paul Revere's Ride, and upon how many thousands, too, of their elders, has the picture drawn by the poet left its indelible impression? Certainly it is the sum and substance of all their knowledge of the subject to hundreds of visitors who, every summer, wander through those old, narrow streets of the North End of Boston and gaze with reverence upon the graceful spire of Christ Church. The stone tablet placed in the wall of the tower by order of the city government in 1878 tells them that THE SIGNAL LANTERNS OF PAUL REVERE DISPLAYED IN THE STEEPLE OF THIS CHURCH APRIL 18, 1775, WARNED THE COUNTRY OF THE MARCH OF BRITISH TROOPS TO LEXINGTON AND CONCORD.[21]

Christ Church, then, became a relic in the foundation of American memory, a relic authenticated by Longfellow's poem, which furnished, as Gettemy points out, the only account of Paul Revere that schoolchildren (and adult tourists, because of their schooling) were likely to know.

As "Paul Revere's Ride" became a classroom staple, and one that was often taught in conjunction with Revolutionary War history, exasperated historians began to point out (to little avail) that Longfellow's narrative is wrong. Helen Clarke commented in 1913, "So convincing is it ["Paul Revere's Ride"] that even grown up historians repeat its inaccuracies as bona fide history. No less a man than

John Fiske was sadly mixed about the famous beacon lanterns and, in all seriousness, relates that Paul Revere watched for them himself from Charlestown." But, Clarke notes, Revere's actual historical record is so bland that "[n]o one who compares Revere's own circumstantial and unilluminated account of his ride with Longfellow's ballad will be but thankful to the poet."[22] In other words, to quote the title of a recent best-selling history book (a title that claims to quote Warren G. Harding), "I love Paul Revere, whether he rode or not."[23] The persistent problem, here, is remarkable: the poem dramatizes the power of the nation through its history so effectively that the facts of history cease to matter.

"Paul Revere's Ride," like the figure of the poet Longfellow, circulated easily through the American public school system because it seemed to offer patriotism cleansed of politics, although of course school curricula were engaged with the political project of assimilation. In 1888 *Forum* magazine launched a series in which the leading educators of the day were asked to contribute essays addressing the question "What shall the public schools teach?" The resulting series, stretching over a full year, is a microcosm of late-nineteenth-century educational discourses. While opinions vary on virtually everything else, one point of consensus emerges: schools must teach children how to be Americans. As Abraham Isaacs (author of "Stories from the Rabbis" and an inveterate preserver of Jewish-American heritage) puts it in his *Forum* contribution, "The growing sentiment of American nationalism, sacred now after war and struggle, which is permeating all classes and creeds, demands that our schools be made the guardians of American ideals, to give them that strength and sanctity which the nation requires." Isaacs suggests that Longfellow in particular, "the gentle poet who never strikes a harsh chord," can help with the "moral education of America's youth"—an education that must be rooted in civics, not religion.[24] It is in this context—in the context of a secular classroom with a mandate to strengthen the Union—that "Paul Revere's Ride" became an important American poem.

When the poem first appeared (in 1860 in the *Boston Transcript*, in 1861 in the *Atlantic Monthly*, and finally in 1863 as part of *Tales of a Wayside Inn*), it was understood to be a Civil War poem, making the familiar move of invoking the founding fathers to support the Union cause. This historical context was quickly forgotten, however, and I have never seen a mention of the Civil War in critical discussions of the poem produced after 1865. Just as the poem made the real events of 1775 irrelevant, so too was its original cultural work as a Civil War poem quickly forgotten. But if "Paul Revere's Ride" does not provide an accurate account of Revolutionary War history, and if it shed its original links to Civil War history, then what kind of history does it teach?

The first lines of the poem establish a pedagogical relationship between the speaker and his auditors: "Listen, my children, and you shall hear / Of the midnight ride of Paul Revere . . ." (*FP,* 43). These lines mimic the forms and functions of an oral culture, much like the opening of *Hiawatha.* But Longfellow departs from folkloric conventions that set oral narratives in timeless times; instead he specifies a date: "On the eighteenth of April in Seventy-five; / Hardly a man is now alive / Who remembers that famous day and year" (*FP,* 43). This first stanza locates "Paul Revere's Ride" in a calendrical past tense that can be represented by dates and geographical locations. Anderson has argued for the significance of this very modern construction of time: "The idea of a sociological organism moving calendrically through homogeneous, empty time is the precise analog of the idea of the nation, which is also conceived as a solid community moving steadily down (or up) history."[25]

A narrative poem, even more visibly than a novel, can move through homogeneous stanzas like a clock, ticking at regular intervals. Longfellow presses the point as he charts Revere's progress at regular intervals throughout the poem: "It was twelve by the village clock / When he crossed the bridge into Medford town"; "It was one by the village clock / When he galloped into Lexington"; "It was two by the village clock / When he crossed the bridge into Concord town" (*FP,* 46). This device heightens the suspense, but it also gives the reader a sense of the common link between these towns. The purpose of telling time in the poem is to show how Medford, Lexington, and Concord are moving, together, toward one fatal moment when "the shot heard 'round the world" (itself a remarkable conflation of aural immediacy and print media) will begin the Revolutionary War.

"The fate of the nation," as Longfellow puts it, depends on Revere's ability to transmit news across a wide geographical area, a mandate that also underwrote the expanding public school system of the later nineteenth century. In another reply to *Forum*'s question of 1888, "What shall the public schools teach?" Benjamin T. Harris argues that the fate of the nation, as an idea and as a body of competent citizens, depends on "spreading the news":

> I speak of the newspaper as the symbol of modern civilization because it is an emblem of the democratic spirit which insists on the removal of every obstacle to the participation of each in the good of all . . . Education should fit individuals for this

[17]

interchange of all with all. Each must learn the indispensable means for intercommunication. A simple reference to this principle which rules our civilization, and to which the newspaper points as a symbol, suffices for the justification of a public school system.[26]

Interchangeable parts had made Northern factory systems incredibly efficient during and after the Civil War, and here the principle is extended to public schools. If "Paul Revere's Ride" is seen as one of those parts—usable in every school, suited to every curriculum—then one aspect of its efficacy becomes clear. Unlike an actual newspaper (likely to be controversial) the "news" that the poem spreads is a fait accompli, not subject to debate, although like a newspaper it gives students that sense, described by Anderson, of contiguity and horizontal community which is so crucial to national identity.

And yet to produce a sense of kinship through these events, "Paul Revere's Ride" must not so much efface history as link it to larger forces. The poem's initial focus on calendrical time allows the reader to see himself or herself as the logical culmination of a historic chain of events. "Paul Revere's Ride" builds its suspense link by link:

> He said to his friend, "If the British march
> By land or sea from the town tonight,
> Hang a lantern aloft in the belfry arch
> Of the North Church tower as a signal light—
> One if by land, two if by sea;
> And I on the opposite shore will be,
> Ready to ride and spread the alarm
> Through every Middlesex village and farm,
> For the country folk to be up and to arm."
>
> (*FP,* 43)

Paul Revere could not be more rational and explicit. As if offering a history lesson (and indeed, the poem's pedagogical frame suggests that such a lesson is in progress) the poem charts its hero's movement from town to town, using a modern measure of time (a clock) and a modern sense of space as empty and yet connected, like stops on a railway journey. In schools the poem was literally mapped and also linked to historical sites and monuments, as exemplified by a 1911 teacher's guide: "['Paul Revere's Ride'] can be taught most effectively if a map of Massachusetts is hung on the wall and Paul Revere's route carefully traced out. Pictures of Paul Revere, of his Boston home, and of the Old North Church should also be shown."[27]

Remarkably, though, after Revere has issued his instructions, he shoves off from solid ground into a realm that is not defined by rational causes and effects: a realm of physical and temporal distortion, disembodiment, and the undead:

> Then he said "Good night!" and with muffled oar
> Silently rowed to the Charlestown shore,
> Just as the moon rose over the bay,
> Where, swinging wide at her moorings lay
> The Somerset, British man-of-war;
> A phantom ship, with each mast and spar
> Across the moon like a prison bar,
> And a huge black hulk, that was magnified
> By its own reflection in the tide.
>
> (*FP*, 44)

Revere has begun the process of dissociating himself from Britain, so that things British now appear to be infused with stunting limitations, like a prison, or monstrous magnifications, like the *Somerset*. But he has not yet become American, either, because the country's borders have yet to be drawn. This liminal state between colonial and national subjectivity (which echoes, in fact, the liminal state of the *state*) offers no set "accounting system," no fixed standards for measurement or proportion.[28] This lack of standard measurements signals a break from the poetically and calendrically measured chain of events that Longfellow established earlier in the poem. It marks Revere's passage from modern to archaic time—from bureaucracy to blood—and from official history into the realm of a civil religion.

When the narrative switches back to Revere's friend, who is waiting for him on solid ground, it does not regain its footing in clock-regulated history. Instead, it switches into present tense: "Meanwhile, his friend, through alley and street / Wanders and watches with eager ears" (*FP*, 44). For the rest of the poem, Longfellow will disrupt the border between past and present by mixing verb tenses, sometimes even in a single sentence. Tenses become muddled because Revere is adjudicating between the colonial past and his American revolutionary moment, while the poem's frame pulls both colonial and revolutionary time forward into a "present" that contains all times, making dates irrelevant because they are all part of the same capacious national moment.

This odd passage through simultaneous time zones leads to an uncanny graveyard:

> Beneath, in the churchyard, lay the dead
> In their night-encampment on the hill,
> Wrapped in silence, so deep and still,
> That he could hear, like a sentinel's tread,
>
> The wrathful night-wind as it went
> Creeping along from tent to tent,
> And seeming to whisper, "All is well!"
> A moment only he feels the spell
>
> (*FP*, 45)

The wind, like a naturalized version of Revere (who will himself later be borne on the wind), spreads news to the dead, who are recruited, here, as a supernatural backup unit for the national cause. Time seems to move in both directions as the wind (oddly wrathful and yet reassuring) turns the dead into sleepers who might awake.

When Longfellow wrote birthday greetings to the schoolchildren of Cincinnati in 1880 he also conjured an army out of non-military materials:

> I can only send you my Christmas and New Year's greeting to the grand army of your pupils; and ask you to tell them, as I am sure you have often told them before: to live up to the best that is in them; to live noble lives, as they may in whatever condition they find themselves; so that their epitaph may be that of Euripides: "This monument does not make thee famous, O, Euripides! but thou makest this monument famous."[29]

The link between Longfellow's letter to Cincinnati and his ideological work in "Paul Revere's Ride" is direct: in both instances, an army is made timeless through an emotional appeal. The churchyard and the schoolroom are rendered, not as practical necessities, but as grand inevitable conflagrations of Americans, whose value is not just timeless but monumentally timeless. School thus takes on the weight of an experience—like military service–that forges national consciousness through intimate bonds rooted not in calendrical history but in destiny.

As Revere begins his ride, he too is figured in the present tense as part of an eternal landscape:

> And beneath him, tranquil and broad and deep
> Is the Mystic, meeting the ocean-tides;
> And under the alders that skirt the edge,

> Now soft on the sand, not loud on the ledge,
> Is heard the tramp of his steed as he rides.
>
> (*FP*, 45)

Revere is riding against time constraints ("It was one by the village clock"), but he is also skirting the edge of timelessness and of a more "mystic" point of national origin. His horse's hoofbeats, as they merge with both the landscape and the present tense, become part of an archaic natural history.

The poem's story line unfolds from midnight into twilight, but its people and objects never solidify in the broad light of day. A chicken swims in the moonlight, an empty building is haunted, and Revere's own body becomes, like the British man-of-war, "a shape in the moonlight / a bulk in the dark":

> He saw the gilded weathercock
> Swim in the moonlight as he passed,
> And the meetinghouse windows, blank and bare,
> Gaze at him with a spectral glare,
> As if they already stood aghast
> At the bloody work they would look upon.
>
> (*FP*, 46)

The meetinghouse windows are not just personified; they are prophetic. However, they are prophetic not because of their institutionalized authority but precisely because the meeting-house's power to organize or control people has been lost. The meetinghouse stands "aghast," which implies not only fear but specifically fear of the dead, if we recall that *aghast* is derived, as Longfellow the philologist would have known, from the Old English word for ghost. The prophecy-producing principle here is not the state. Rather, Longfellow is rooting American origins in a sacred moment that is legitimated by blood:

> And one was safe and asleep in his bed
> Who at the bridge would be first to fall,
> Who that day would be lying dead,
> Pierced by a British musket-ball.
>
> (*FP*, 46)

Here, then, is the poem's unknown soldier. Anderson stresses the importance of the moment: "No more arresting emblems of the modern culture of nationalism exist than cenotaphs and tombs of unknown soldiers. The public ceremonial reverence accorded these monuments, precisely because they are either deliberately empty or no one knows who lies inside them, has no true precedents in earlier times."[30] The magic of nationalism that turns, in Anderson's words, "chance into destiny," is anchored by "one" whose whole story is his American death, pierced by a British musket ball.[31]

In the poem, the sleeping martyr's death is no accident; it is part of the destiny that "Paul Revere's Ride" makes both timeless and inevitable. Following this logic, the unknown soldier who is "first to fall" makes a sacrifice "at the bridge" between colonial and national history, but his sacrifice engenders not history but rather a spirit, a soul. The soldier's anonymity signals a vanishing point on the imaginary national horizon: he does not have a name or a birthday because he is not modern but ancient: he is more ghost than man, and he is memorable precisely because he cannot be remembered as a historical, calendrical figure.

Revere never completes his journey toward a more stable and stationary state of American citizenship; the poem leaves him in medias res. His transitional status reinforces history by standing outside of it; he acts as a disorderly, unaccountable precursor to textbook accounts of battles, dates, and presidents. Paul Revere's liminality extends also to his social status; he does not have a fixed class position. In fact, he barely has a visible body. Revere's dangerous qualities—his dark, half-dissolved body, his polluting associations with blood and the dead—signify his status not as a citizen but as a citizen-to-be. Like the schoolchildren who repeated his story, Revere is in the process of becoming American. He traverses Middlesex as a medium, spreading news that is modern (clocks, calendars) and yet ancient (ghosts, prophecies). As its name suggests, Middlesex works as a middle ground, a fulcrum of transformations that ultimately result in clear boundaries being drawn. And yet, like Longfellow himself, Revere's persona is ambivalent, or "wavering," akin to the Walter Scott heroes admired by George Lukacs in his work on historical narrative. For Lukacs, narratives centering on a mediocre hero create a neutral ground on which extreme social forces (like those encountered in public schools) can be brought into contact, and, through this contact, historical changes are not just registered but negotiated.[32]

Nevertheless, the poem postulates that "the people" will solidify into a community—a common body that structurally echoes the horizontal community of children at the beginning of the poem. And these people will feel borne (or reborn) on the night winds of the past because Revere has made history not legible but palpable:

> For, borne on the night-wind of the Past,
> Through all our history, to the last,
> In the hour of darkness and peril and need,
> The people will waken and listen to hear
> The hurrying foot-beats of that steed
> And the midnight message of Paul Revere.
>
> (*FP*, 47)

The hoofbeats are compelling, like the hypnotic meter of the poem itself. But they are not telegraphic—they offer no specific message, only the audible sense that the nation has a message that is like a heartbeat, a rhythm not linked to any one thought or idea.

This visceral sense of the nation as more cyclical (like a heartbeat) than historical was integral to the promotion of patriotism in the public schools. In an 1890 article in *Arena,* the educator E. B. Andrews described how patriotism, like poetry (and like the heart), must be internal:

> As the mere wearing of the cross cannot constitute one a Christian, simply to fly the national emblem over our schoolhouses will never, by itself, make us staunch devotees of this nation's weal. Not the stars and stripes, but what the stars and stripes stand for: liberty, union, rights, law, power for good among nations—these are the legitimate spurs to our enthusiasm as citizens.[33]

"Paul Revere's Ride" was recruited to give students an internal identification with its hero and thus implicitly with America's roots. Margaret Haliburton gave the following advice to turn-of-the-century teachers of the poem: "The emotions felt by the actors (suspense, ghostly dread, impatience, etc.) must each in turn be felt by the pupils who read, and back of these emotions must be a genuine admiration for the actors themselves."[34] Revere's authenticating function demands that students not merely perform his journey but also internalize it. Simply repeating Longfellow's lines verbatim is like simply flying the stars and stripes; it is not enough. To use the language of the *Cincinnati Enquirer*'s "Birthday Celebration" report, "souls" must be "fired."

"Paul Revere's Ride" was used to promote nationalism in the public schools, and as my reading has shown, it narrativizes and produces a national spirit that underwrites national history. In the schools, public recitation was understood to be an act of interpretation based not in analysis but in identification. A 1907 *Boston School Superintendent's Report* summarizes what was then the common view:

To express a noble thought nobly and sincerely is a great spiritual experience, for genuine warmth of feeling for what is pure and good results in the creation of high ideals, and the possession of high ideals is the first step toward the formation of character. Good reading, then, is an accomplishment worthy of earnest cultivation. "Of equal honor with he who writes a grand poem is he who reads it grandly," Longfellow has said, and Emerson, "A good reader summons the dead from their tombs and makes them speak to us."[35]

What is interpreted are the feelings behind a poem, not the ideas raised by a poem. And those feelings are supposed to mirror those of the poem's author; the reader summons the dead and speaks for the dead.

"Paul Revere's Ride," then, works as a blueprint for the nation as an imagined community, mapping out the space and time of the nation, and giving readers access to a version of American history that they can all experience together, simultaneously. Like Hiawatha, Revere represents the nation's past. But unlike Hiawatha, who must die (in order that civilization can overtake North America), Revere is perpetual. To recite "Paul Revere's Ride" as Max Loeb did was to tap into a force that appeared to dissolve social tensions, replacing them with the bond of a common history. This history was not just a string of dates (although it was that) but also an affective, mysterious experience—the experience of hearing Revere's hoofbeats across the centuries, or the experience of hearing "Paul Revere's Ride" repeated on Longfellow's birthday. Such experiences could be felt and remembered as simultaneously local and national, internal and external, and historical and timeless— like the patriotic spirit that the schools promoted.

THE MAN WITHOUT QUALITIES

When students read *The Song of Hiawatha,* "Paul Revere's Ride," or indeed any Longfellow poem, their readings were invariably mediated by the monumental presence of the poet himself. In many cases his white-bearded portrait stared down from the classroom wall, and his poems were usually taught as the representative works of a great American. Julia Colby, a teacher whose career stretched from the 1880s to the 1910s, composed the following verse to help her students keep their important February dates straight:

> The 22nd is the birthday of Washington and Lowell,
> Our honored and loved Lincoln the 12th,

> While for Longfellow in memory we keep 27th,
> Their greatness more precious than wealth.
> Washington and Lincoln each presidents great
> Who are loved by our people so well;
> The others are poets—four links in the chain—
> Washington, Lincoln, Longfellow, Lowell.[36]

To reduce Washington, Lincoln, Longfellow, and Lowell to "four links in a chain" may be an effective mnemonic device, but it also signals a certain vagueness, an interchangeability, between these biographically diverse figures. Clearly, Colby is advancing Longfellow as an exemplary American citizen, with "greatness more precious than wealth." But what constitutes this greatness, exactly? Colby's vagueness is not just a function of her clearly limited poetic talent; such vagueness pervades almost every popular representation of Longfellow: he is "great," "ideal," or "sublime." How could such sweeping terms help students learn anything? What were they supposed to learn?

To examine the cultural work performed by "Henry Wadsworth Longfellow" as a figure, it is helpful to turn away from his historical-narrative poems and look instead at a lyric poem whose speaker was very closely identified with Longfellow himself. "A Psalm of Life" was one of Longfellow's early "hits," and it proved enduring. In nine muscular stanzas, framed as "what the heart of the young man said to the psalmist," the speaker states his ambitions: "Tell me not, in mournful numbers / Life is but an empty dream!" The speaker goes on to instruct readers: "Life is real! Life is earnest! / And the grave is not the goal," and so we must all work to progress, to be "a hero in the strife," to "Act—act in the living present!" to learn from the "lives of great men," to "make our lives sublime," and to leave "footprints on the sands of time" as an inspiration to others. Finally, the last stanza commands:

> Let us, then, be up and doing,
> With a heart for any fate;
> Still achieving, still pursuing,
> Learn to labor and to wait.
>
> (*FP*, 2–3)

This poem, even more explicitly than "Paul Revere's Ride" or *The Song of Hiawatha*, seems to embody the values of Longfellow the schoolroom poet, commanding young people to take the "great men" of the canon as role models and to work within the established American social structure to achieve measures of success as conventional as the poem's own measures. It was, from its earliest inception, a schoolroom recitation; before he published it, Longfellow reportedly recited it to his class at Harvard following a lecture on Goethe. Its continued pedagogical function was cemented when it appeared in *McGuffey's Sixth Eclectic Reader* (1879), thereby ensuring its distribution to millions of schoolchildren across the nation and across generations. The poem's relative brevity, its unshakably mnemonic rhyme and meter, and its didactic structure made it an especially popular "memory gem," a piece that children were compelled to recite and that adults were likely to recall later in life.

However, the central paradox of "A Psalm of Life," a poem that reads like a string of straightforward statements, rests in the ambiguous subject-position that it generates. At the beginning, the speaker seems to be a young man speaking only for himself: "Tell me not in mournful numbers . . ." But by the fourth stanza the speaker has become some sort of collective: "Art is long, and Time is fleeting / And our hearts, though stout and brave, / Still, like muffled drums are beating . . ." The imagery is martial, commanding a form of heroism rooted in a group effort. The reading subject is at one point exhorted to "Be a hero in the strife!" but it is unclear what heroes are supposed to do and what kind of battle they are fighting. Like Julia Colby's vision of a "greatness more precious than wealth," the exact nature of the speaker's actions (and his instructions to the reader) are elusive. The poem begins as an assertion of individualism, but it is a peculiar form of individualism, as the poem moves from "I" to "we" and from a firm subject-position (identified with one man, and implicitly identified with Longfellow) toward a murky plurality of voices.

"A Psalm of Life" thus presents the same interpretive problem as "Henry Wadsworth Longfellow": it represents something worth emulating, but it is vague on the details. This, I think, is the key to its success. Mary Louise Kete uses the term "collaborative individualism" to describe a model of American identity opposed to "possessive individualism." A "greatness more precious than wealth" is a greatness not owned but shared. The collaborative self "does not exist unless in an ongoing, reciprocal relationship with an other in which the boundaries between self and other, past and present, alive and dead are constantly being negotiated."[37] And yet the terms of this negotiation are limited in advance by the poem's conventional structure: unlike, say, Walt Whitman's experimental collaborations, "A Psalm of Life" invites readers to participate in a reading experience based on conventional expectations of prosody and performance. Public schools were organized to produce collaborative individuals: people who were individualistic (inspired by "great men," inclined to work hard and prosper) but who played by very definite rules. Fitting in to the larger imagined community of the nation began by fitting into the local community of the school; identifying schools with national figures was a way to accomplish both and, through this, to provide a way for students to build a sense of themselves as collaborative individuals. The school song for the Frankford, Pennsylvania, Longfellow School tells its students how to feel as they sing together:

> With One Accord this song we sing,
> Our tributes in our hearts we bring,
> And full of love for her fair name—
> Her good shall be our aim.
> Hurrah, hurrah for the Longfellow School!
> Hurrah, hurrah for the Longfellow School![38]

This is an early example of what would come to be called "school spirit," an expression of kinship based on emotional ties to an institution. Longfellow's poems, as I have argued, provide in both their forms and their contents the raw materials for collaborative individualism, by offering readers a sense of kinship with one another and with the "spirit" of the nation. Longfellow's persona embodies the form of subjectivity that one accord might produce. To make one accord, individual eccentricities must be minimized in favor of a conventional, univocal "hurrah."

One thing is clear: Longfellow was very appealing to teachers, who were only marginally professionalized in a rapidly professionalizing America, and who were motivated to promote certain forms of cultural capital. Teachers were unevenly educated and badly paid, and they had to market their own value, and the value of education in general, to parents and taxpayers through exhibitions and public programs. As Sarah Pearson of Youngstown, Ohio, wrote to Longfellow, "Living in a busy manufacturing town we teachers do not find in society very much interest in, or knowledge of literature and are on the alert to seize upon any means of awakening such an interest in the minds of the young and cultivating a taste for the pure wells of thought found in the works of our best authors."[39] Longfellow and the other schoolroom poets occupied a peculiar place in American literary history at the end of the nineteenth century. He offered instant access to the world of his house, Craigie House, which was pictured in chromolithographs and school gift-cards. By the 1890s the Perry Company was manufacturing postcards of Craigie House and selling them in bulk to teachers to give as prizes. The Perry pictures represented a prized world of genteel East Coast civilization, not too money oriented, not too mass cultural, but not too intellectual either, or at least intellectual only in the sense of the "public intellectual." These values contrast not only with the heterogeneous values of new immigrants but also with the values of the new postbellum power elite: the robber-baron rich, the sensationalist newspaper magnates, and the specialized social-scientific intellectuals. Collaborative individualism offered teachers and students a sense that they could have access to and share "a greatness more precious than wealth."

What is striking, though, about the "pure wells of thought" is that Pearson stresses, not any particular idea, but the purity of Longfellow's thought in general. Longfellow *makes* thought pure; his *person* is somehow at the root of his value. This emphasis on personality indeed purifies thought, in the sense of ridding it of any specific ideas. Longfellow was part of a star system of schoolroom poets maintained—like the Hollywood star system as Richard Dyer describes it—by fans who did not have the power that they ascribed to their idols, but who derived some sense of power from an intense identification with them. For Dyer, the difficult-to-define quality of "charisma" is culturally determined, and the most charismatic figures are infused with the tensions of their era. Longfellow's magnetism perhaps derived from the way that he embodied contradictions: he was genteel but accessible to all classes; he was an "establishment" figure and yet not exclusive; he was scholarly and yet suitable for beginning readers; he represented a lofty "ideal" and yet his image was determinedly unexceptional. His persona was in some ways an impossible synthesis, finessed only because its contradictions were glazed over with idealizing language.

American schools were also in some sense an impossible synthesis, dependent on local communities for funding and direction but linked to a larger national agenda. Louis Althusser has called the public school system an "ideological state apparatus," and this makes clear sense in France, where schools were and are run by the central government, with national requirements and national tests. What is extraordinary about the American system is how American schools—despite their radically decentralized organizational structure—managed to create an ideological apparatus capable of promoting specific forms of nationalist ideology without recourse to any federal bureaucracy. All over the country, tiny district systems worked in sync to produce a national educational experience and to help children imagine themselves as part of a national community. They did this not by deferring to an actual federally appointed national school leader (there was no such person) but by electing to promote national figureheads such as Longfellow. The advantage of this, of course, was that Longfellow could not make policy; he could only make feelings—and therein lay both his power and his useful limits. Longfellow represented a stable America that school systems (with their many local controversies) could not otherwise agree to produce.

Ironically, Longfellow represented a stable America precisely because his persona was so negotiable. On the one hand, teachers could appropriate him as a normative standard against which students could be measured, thereby adopting the controlling assumptions behind his (white, male, born-in-America) neutrality. In 1899, a children's class in Deadwood, South Dakota, composed of poor immigrant students wrote letters to Longfellow's daughter Alice describing their studies. These formulaic letters show how Longfellow was understood as a model of (Anglo-Saxon, American) civic virtue. Cecil Gandolfo's is typical:

> We have been reading about Longfellow's life in a little book. We read about his home and where he went to school when he was a boy. Henry Longfellow wrote a letter to his father. His father wrote a pleasant letter in return. Mr. Longfellow was educated. Henry shot a robbin [*sic*] and cried, and never went hunting again. I have herd [*sic*] the Village Blacksmith, the Children's Hour, and Paul Revere. I like Paul Revere best of all. On our door we have several pictures of Longfellow. Cecil Gandolfo.[40]

On Cecil Gandolfo's letter the teacher has penciled, presumably without Cecil's knowledge, some information about him for Alice: ("Italian French"). Indeed, on each of the letters, the teacher's handwriting identifies the child's background: Sarah Blumenthal ("A little German girl who speaks very broken English"), Jackson Ammons ("His father is a saloon-keeper—and worse"), Robert Cohen ("German Jew parentage—a miserable home"). The teacher apparently wants to show Alice Longfellow how her father's exemplary poetry and life are helping to mitigate the children's "broken" and "miserable" backgrounds by exposing them to an Anglo-Saxon middle-class culture based on taste. Illustrating the contradictions that Longfellow masked without resolving, this teacher covertly locates her students in the social hierarchy while overtly offering Longfellow as a poet who can dissolve social difference by acting as a civilizing force.

But Longfellow's promise of access to middle-class conventions also inspired marginalized people to assert themselves through his work— to ask that the promise of kinship and community be fulfilled. In Emma May Buckingham's female bildungsroman, *A Self-Made Woman;*

or, Mary Idyl's Trials and Triumphs (1873), Mary Idyl's supposed "diary" recounts her rise from rural poverty, her schooling, her teaching career, her travels in the antebellum South, and her eventual marriage. Buckingham's preface emphasizes her book's own didactic aims:

> The story of Mary Idyl is true in the main. Its aim is to encourage those of my sex who are struggling up towards a higher moral and intellectual life, to urge them to persevere until the end is attained . . . If this story shall assist one of my sex in the work of self-instruction—of taste and heart-culture—I shall not regret the weariness and effort which it has cost me.[41]

Buckingham closes her 342-page "diary" with an account of Mary Idyl herself. We see Mary agreeing to allow the author to publish the diary, and echoing the author's preface, but also insisting that the text end not with her words but with Longfellow's:

> "If it shall prove a beacon to one of my sex, and stimulate her fainting energies to renewed exertion, I shall not regret the hours I have spent in recording my own experience. Stay;—close it with Longfellow's stirring 'Psalm of Life.' I will copy it here for you," and she went to her writing-desk. As she bent over her task, I thought that I had never seen a more interesting face than Mary Idyl Willington's.[42]

The story is then capped by all nine stanzas of "A Psalm of Life," although without the original subtitle, "What the Heart of the Young Man Said to the Psalmist." The omission is telling, because Buckingham is integrating Longfellow's poem, not just into an educational story, but into a woman's account of her own education, enshrining it as something absolutely personal, and gendering it female. Mary Idyl's desire to "prove a beacon to one of my sex, and stimulate her fainting energies to renewed exertion," reads like a paraphrase of "A Psalm of Life." Or, put another way, "A Psalm of Life," written out in Mary Idyl's hand and placed at the end of her diary, becomes a précis of her story, and the poem's "us" refers in this context to "women." "A Psalm of Life" thus functions as a "psalm" of early feminism, a paean to women's self-education. The poem would have been familiar to Buckingham's readers, but this does not mean she is telling them something they already know when she quotes it. On the contrary, the whole point of her narrative is that women must force their way—autodidactically—into the "us" that must be "up and doing," and into a nation that limits women's ambitions even as it frees men to live as if they had no limits. By inserting Longfellow's text into her own, she is not just recopying but rewriting it explicitly to include herself and her readers.

D. J. Jordan makes an analogous move in his "Philosophy of Progress," published in the *African Methodist Episcopal Church Review* in 1893. Jordan, an educator who went on to serve as president of Edward Waters College, argues that progress is inexorable and natural: "Throughout immensity there is no such thing as rest or inactivity." After a fairly lengthy disquisition on the nature and inevitability of progress and on the importance of education, Jordan concludes:

> Permit me to say, in conclusion, that despite all adverse circumstances:
>
> > Let us all be up and doing,
> >   With a heart for any fate;
> > Still achieving, still pursuing,
> >   Learn to labor and to wait.[43]

Is his substitution—"Let us *all* be up and doing," instead of "Let us, *then*, be up and doing"—a mere accident, or is it an unconscious or perhaps even conscious bid for inclusion as part of the American subject-position epitomized by Longfellow? Jordan's gloss on Longfellow's quote suggests the latter; after quoting Longfellow, he exhorts his African-American readers, "Do not be discouraged. America is ours, and we must prove it." Like Buckingham, Jordan is not quoting Longfellow because Longfellow is "news." He is quoting Longfellow to perform his linguistic competence as an insider, a reader who knows how to repeat what he has read, and to make it newly powerful through repetition.

Hans Jauss uses the term "double misunderstanding" to describe how texts always open a gap "between the intention of the writer, the finished work, and its significance for the observer. In this way the constitution of meaning may be seen as a never-ending process between the production and reception of the work."[44] This so-called "misunderstanding" is not a failure but rather a productive process of social meaning-making. Jordan's iteration, with a slight change, of an otherwise familiar phrase—"let us, then, be up and doing"—signals that he is receiving the text, not as a monological, transcendental pedagogical transmission, but as a poem that he can use—that he can make his own. Longfellow's most firmly fixed poem—fixed in the sense of cleaving to convention, unfolding predictably, and appearing with an almost dreary frequency in essays and novels—is still an unfixed poem, in the sense that its reception, and hence its meaning, varies depending on who reads the text and why.

I do not mean to suggest that Buckingham and Jordan are reading "A Psalm of Life" subversively. Far from it: they are reading Longfellow for his explicit messages about self-making and self-construction and for the sense of national belonging that he inspires, and they are still largely enclosed (I am tempted to say trapped) in the horizon of expectations that his work allows them. The culture through which the poem circulated advocated ambition for all while undercutting the ambitions of many; the poem solves this problem by keeping its ambitious sensibility intact while expunging virtually all concrete historical markers from the poem: there are no national boundaries of any kind; there are only "lives sublime," which are figured as lives overwhelmed with feeling. Since reading poetry was seen by educators like Sarah Pearson (the Ohio teacher concerned with "pure wells of thought") as an accomplishment in itself, to repeat "A Psalm of Life" was already to be "up and doing." It is both an announcement of ambition and an ambition fulfilled; it gives its readers both the desire to succeed and a measure of success. There is no need to go outside the poem for a feeling of mastery. This is what makes "A Psalm of Life" so utopian: it is a perpetual-motion machine that generates both ambition and a sense of accomplishment without recourse to historical or national limitations. The poem frees the speaker to be, or to do, anything: its promises are thus both compelling and utterly grandiose.

To venture outside the utopian lyricism of "A Psalm of Life"—to go into the world armed with the poem, as the poem itself suggests its readers do—was to encounter systems (including educational systems) that were neither free nor fair. The poem's "us" might expand to include everyone, but when it was recited as part of the 1880 Longfellow Day celebrations in Cincinnati, it was recited in segregated schools. Indeed, the problematic aspects of Longfellow's apparent accessibility are in retrospect almost too obvious to enumerate; like the equally problematic "melting pot" ideology, the notion of Longfellow as a role model for all is limited by his class, race, and gender. His strongly embodied and monumentalized presence (his photo was almost as common as the American flag in the classroom) is always already grown up, middle class, and white. Noting his profuse whiskers, William Dean Howells took to calling him "the White Mr. Longfellow."[45] This nickname can serve to remind us of the compartmentalizing, hierarchical, and segregationist practices that flourished behind the access that Longfellow (like the public schools themselves) seemed to promise. Sarah Blumenthal of

Deadwood, South Dakota, was not and could not be like Longfellow in her ethnicity, class, and gender—and the value system implied by his canonization meant that Blumenthal's own qualities (immigrant, working-class, female) could be read only as liabilities to overcome. Students' horizons of expectation were partly (if not wholly) determined by educational institutions that promoted assimilation and nationalism. At the same time, Buckingham and Jordan (admittedly, adult educators rather than young students) suggest that Longfellow was open to at least a degree of interpretation. Jauss's notion of double misunderstanding can be applied to education as well as to reading. It is safe to say that even young students like Cecil Gandolfo were not just machines or parrots, no matter what his rather condescending teacher may have assumed. There is always a gap (and often a "productive gap") between what teachers offer and what students receive.

Under most circumstances, however, students' internal reactions to Longfellow are not recoverable (although this does not mean they are unimportant): even when students wrote personal responses to his work, these responses seem conditioned by institutional expectations and teachers' demands. Longfellow was for the most part a poet of public display, not of private dissent. On the occasion of Longfellow's centenary, *The Little Chronicle* (a self-described "clean, complete, nonpartisan weekly news magazine for Boys and Girls and Busy People") published this telling (if slightly defensive) assessment of his achievement:

> All critics are disarmed before Longfellow's lofty character and uplifting verse. There is no other source of happiness than the true, the beautiful, and the good. All the writers who have ever lived have taught us no more, and Longfellow has taught us nothing less. More than that, he brought the philosophy of virtue and happiness down to the common plane of understanding. He taught us, not the penalties of sin and selfishness, as do those who are accounted the greatest poets, but he taught us to choose, and to want to choose, the best, to the find the highest, not in exceptional talents and opportunities, but in common human experiences and duties; not in money and fame and unique pleasures, but in nature and home ties and ready sympathy and spiritual aspirations.[46]

The value of fitting in, of assimilating rather than seeking "unique pleasures," was central to the project of American public education between 1865 and 1917. Longfellow's poems offered narratives of kinship, national "spirit," and collaborative individualism that readers could use to demonstrate their own social competence as students and as citizens. The *Little Chronicle* article ends by comparing Longfellow to Lincoln: Lincoln, the writer asserts, "made poetry of the duties of citizenship," while Longfellow "turned citizenship into poetry." Again, as in Julia Colby's heuristic poem, the historical particularities that distinguish Lincoln from Longfellow are suppressed in favor of their commonalities: they are two "links in the chain," inspiring precisely because they are great and yet not *too* great to be conventional role models. American schools made Longfellow fit into their wider pedagogical agenda, presenting him as a model of collaborative individualism, who could—as Benjamin T. Harris put it—prepare students for "the interchange of all with all." His work "turned citizenship into poetry," teaching students such as Max Loeb how to read—and to feel—like Americans.

CHAPTER TWO

Learning to Be White: John Greenleaf Whittier's Snow-Bound

John Greenleaf Whittier's 1866 poem *Snow-Bound* offers some of the same pleasures as a house-museum, full of period furniture and roped-off rooms. The house depicted in *Snow-Bound*, the Haverhill homestead, became a museum in 1892, so that visitors could see the Whittier family hearth with its andirons intact. By the later nineteenth century, Massachusetts was dotted with abandoned farmhouses (including Whittier's) that seemed to symbolize the fading away of a more innocent rural America. Like the many local museums that sprang up both to teach people about fading folkways and to commemorate those ways as irreparably past, Whittier's poem expresses and elicits nostalgia through a catalogue of vanished artifacts and practices, opening the walls of his childhood home and showing his readers a safe domestic space. A three-day snowstorm rages outside, but inside the old-fashioned New England family (circa 1820) roasts chestnuts, spins wool, and tells stories around a wide-mouthed fireplace in a tableau that came to signify "New England childhood" for many of the poem's readers.

Published as a book-length volume, second in popularity only to Longfellow's *Song of Hiawatha*, *Snow-Bound* established Whittier's benign postbellum reputation, went through multiple editions (especially Christmas editions) well into the twentieth century, and remains a staple in teaching anthologies such as the *Norton Anthology of American Literature*, although it is not as widely read as it once was.[1] Early critics, such as James Russell Lowell, saw the poem as an affectionate rendering of rural child-life; later the "New Critics" understood it as a romantic meditation on the passage of time; and, following Ann Douglas, James E. Rocks has reevaluated it as a celebration of women's domestic sphere.[2] Given its fame and popular longevity, however, the poem has generated little recent critical interest. And for a long time, I confess, I found this poem difficult to read critically; it struck me as simply nostalgic: accessible, neutral, and obvious. But to appear accessible, neutral, and obvious is in itself to stake out a particular position, and I have come to believe that these very qualities point to the poem's central concerns, concerns that have remained critically underarticulated but that account for the poem's enduring cultural power. Whittier's *Snow-Bound,* published by an abolitionist writer on the eve of Reconstruction, works—consistently if not always self-consciously—as a poem about *whiteness.* It is a poem about being surrounded by the literal whiteness of a snow-storm, but it also describes a family defined by its whiteness, and it shows how the poet learned to act "white," and to assume the privileges of whiteness, while also questioning those privileges. This final point is key: the meaning of whiteness is very much a *question* for Whittier, and although his poem begins with a series of black and white binaries, by the end emerging shades of gray signal the poet's distinctive vision of the nation's multiracial potential.

The poem's late-nineteenth-century reception did not focus—at least not explicitly—on its mediation of whiteness. Instead, its sustained visibility in American culture was underwritten by the larger discourse of colonial revival—a movement propagated through museums, schools, fairs (which often featured "colonial kitchens"), and the new interest in antique collecting. The colonial revival relied on a master narrative of American history that is still so familiar it barely needs repeating: focusing exclusively on New England, it begins with the Pilgrims landing at Plymouth Rock and conflates the history of Massachusetts with the history of America. Most Americans were introduced to *Snow-Bound* in school, where it was presented as an exemplary historical artifact. The introduction offered by the *Buckwater Fifth Reader* is typical; Geoffrey Buckwater explains to his fifth-grade audience that, while Whittier's poems lack the "literary finish" of Longfellow's, they have their own rough charm:

> they concern the life of his countrymen, are truly American, and
> are the natural expression of his individual genius in his own
> simple, nervous, native speech. "Snow-Bound" gives a picture of
> a frugal, refined, and devout family in a New England country
> home in the first part of the nineteenth century.[3]

Readers' responses were conditioned by such relatively neutral introductions, and this might suggest that the very project of reading *Snow-Bound* as a poem about whiteness is anachronistically rooted in current theoretical concerns. And yet, as Steven Mailloux has pointed out, horizons of expectation are never stable; they are constantly—and sometimes painfully—in the process of renegotiation, and through this struggle new meanings emerge.[4] The colonial revival invented a tradition—a normative, white "American heritage"—but this master narrative unfolded, *as Whittier understood,* against the backdrop of an increasingly heterogenous nation. And even though *Snow-Bound* became an urtext of the colonial revival, its author had been a fervent abolitionist, steeped in the very racial anxieties that the colonial revival suppressed. To read *Snow-Bound* as a poem about whiteness is to explore what readers saw—but also what they did not or could not see—in the text, exposing a historically specific late-nineteenth-century struggle over America's past and how it should be remembered.

RECONSTRUCTING WHITTIER

The first and most influential review of Whittier's *Snow-Bound* was published by Lowell in an 1866 issue the *North American Review.* Lowell values Whittier's text as a record of a vanishing era:

> It [*Snow-Bound*] describes scenes and manners which the rapid changes in our national habits will soon have made as remote from us as if they were foreign or ancient. Already, alas! even in farmhouses, backlog and forestick are obsolescent words, and close-mouthed stoves chill the spirit while they bake the flesh with their grim and undemonstrative hospitality. Already are the railroads displacing the companionable cheer of crackling walnut with the dogged self-complacency and sullen virtue of anthracite.[5]

As objects enter collections they shed their original practical functions to take on new uses and new significance, and as they are recontextualized they also tell new stories. Collections, in other words, are always also narratives. The words and objects in Whittier's poem are already working, in Lowell's review, as antiques, narrating the story of their own obsolescence. Their value lies in the fact that they are no longer used; they represent a past that cannot be recovered except through the imagination. Their job, then, is to spark that imagination, not so that readers can return to the past but so that they can remake it as an object of nostalgia. In Lowell's case, what the fireplace helps him remember is an intimate community—a community that was cheerful and "companionable" and that reflected *national habits.* The narrative that he imposes on the poem is thus one of nostalgia for a lost America that everyone remembers and everyone mourns. "The past" thus replaces the fire as a locus of community: the memories of the backlog and forestick can constitute "us," because they represent a past that "we" hold in common.

The past, as read by Lowell, is authenticated by the survival of artifacts such as those described by Whittier's poem. What could be more neutral, and more objective, than artifacts? Late-nineteenth-century

Americans—especially those connected to old East Coast families, or those who wanted to claim such connections—developed a mania for collecting. The colonial revival, which was inspired by the 1876 Centennial celebrations and then grew in scope and influence through the end of the century, set off a new interest in artifacts from the colonial and early republican periods. Alice Morse Earle, the most popular author affiliated with the movement, wrote a series of books reconstructing the material culture of early New England. Her *Home Life in Colonial Days* (1898) is organized into chapters according to artifactual categories; there are chapters on spinning wheels, jack-knife industries, and hand weaving, among others. The "Kitchen Fireside" chapter unfolds in a charmingly miscellaneous way, describing gridirons, plate warmers, turnspits (and turnspit dogs), and smoking tongs. The way that these items were being revalued by 1898 is suggested by her discussion of warming pans: "The warming-pan has been deemed of sufficient decorative capacity to make it eagerly sought after by collectors, and a great room of one of these collectors is hung entirely around the four walls with a frieze of warming-pans."[6] Morse ends her kitchen chapter with a nod to Whittier:

> To me the true essence of the old-time fireside is found in Whittier's *Snow-Bound*. The very chimney, fireplace, and hearthstone of which his beautiful lines were written, the kitchen of Whittier's boyhood's home, at East Haverhill, Massachusetts, is shown in the accompanying illustration. It shows a swinging crane. His description of the "laying of the fire" can never be equaled in any prose:
>
> > We piled with care our nightly stack
> > Of wood against the chimney back—
> > The oaken log, green, huge, and thick,
> > And on its top the stout back-stick;
> > The knotty fore-stick laid apart,
> > And filled between with curious art
> > The ragged brush; then hovering near,
> > We watched the first red blaze appear,
> > Heard the sharp crackle, caught the gleam
> > On whitewashed wall and sagging beam,
> > Until the old, rude-furnished room
> > Burst, flower-like, into rosy bloom.[7]

Like the warming-pan frieze, Whittier's poem, in this context, functions ornamentally, as symbolic capital—signaling both its own value and the worth of its "collector." For Earle, both the quoted poem and the antiques provide an instant kind of genealogy, a tangible link, to a prestigious version of the past. Few people collected immigration trunks or slave manacles; the point was to display objects that revealed (or manufactured) a *native-born* history, and the older the better. Earle's writing is infused with the sense that she and her readers are preserving "their" heritage; in the chapter "Old-time Flower Gardens," for instance, she confides that "[o]ur mothers and grand-mothers came honestly by their love of gardens. They inherited this affection from their Puritan, Quaker, or Dutch forbears."[8]

By the late nineteenth century, the economic power of New England, and the communities it fostered, was fading. The demographic record shows that the productive center of the country shifted continually westward. Technology and immigration, meanwhile, had radically transformed towns like Haverhill. Joseph Conforti makes this point in his historical analysis of New England's colonial revival:

> In many ways, the colonial revival and commemoration of Old New England provided an imaginative escape from the disloca-tions of the present—a historical refuge where the native-born could indulge their nostalgia for simpler times. In its most insid-ious expression, the celebration of Old New England encour-aged cultural retaliation against "swarthy" foreigners . . . But for many colonial revivalists, Old New England represented a repos-itory of traditions that needed to be preserved and invoked to revitalize Anglo-Puritan descendants, assimilate immigrants, and redress the perceived excesses of modern America.[9]

As Conforti points out, one popular manifestation of this new nostal-gia was "old-time" kitchens, hearths like the one from *Snow-Bound* that were reconstructed at fairs and fund-raisers, often staffed by women in period costume. For instance, in 1881 Mary Vincent Holmes of Cleveland, Ohio, wrote to Whittier asking for the exact measurements of the Haverhill kitchen for an "author's carnival." Whittier replied, "I certainly never dreamed when writing 'Snow-Bound' and making a pen picture of the old house at Haverhill that it could be worthy of a 'counterfeit presentation,' but if it can aide [*sic*] a good cause I have no objection."[10]

In the cultural climate of the colonial revival, it was perhaps inevitable that the Haverhill homestead itself would be restored as a museum, with the old-time hearth as its central attraction. In 1891 Alfred A. Ordway was commissioned to oversee the project, assisted by the aged Whittier:

> The armchair that Whittier and his father and his grandfather
> had used was found in the woodshed. The simple, round, bandy-
> legged kitchen table was taken from the attic. The poet told him
> [Ordway] minutely where everything belonged. There was the
> desk of Whittier's grandfather at which the early poems were
> written . . . On it now rests a large guest book.[11]

The guest book was for the hundreds of visitors, many of them on
summer holidays or fall foliage tours, who might wish to leave their
signature behind. With their signatures, visitors registered both their
distance from the past and their desire to be bound together by that
past. The intimate community that Lowell mourned in his early
review was gone, but in its place was a newer, more far-flung, imagined community of literary pilgrims.

The Whittier Family Homestead aroused visceral, even possessive,
responses from visitors. As Harriet Prescott Spofford described it, "Little boxes and paperweights are made from the boards of the garret
floor of the Whittier homestead . . . but the whole house would have
to go to lathe to meet the demand generally, for this is the old farm
house celebrated by 'Snow-Bound,' our national idyll, the perfect
poem of New England life."[12] Like Alice Morse Earle, it seems that
many early visitors to the Whittier Homestead were bitten by the collecting bug; they wanted to take home pieces of the physical property,
perhaps as souvenirs, but perhaps also as a means of owning that version of the past which the house represented. By leaving their names
behind and taking "little boxes and paperweights" away, visitors recontextualized the house—and the poem that made it famous—turning
both into figures for their own dislocation and longing. *Snow-Bound*
thus functioned as a museo-logical narrative—story that produced a
"replica" of a lost way of life—so that New England folkways could be
mourned even (or especially) by people who had never lived on farms.

Spofford's conflation of "New England life" with national history
was of course common in the later nineteenth century and contributed to the tourism industry by helping to promote "Whittier-
Land" (as hotel brochures called the area around Haverhill) as an
American heritage site. Whittier was widely considered the vox pop-
uli of New England and therefore America's poet. More specifically,
he was figured as the "American Burns," America's rustic poet, a kind
of artifact in his own right. The critic and anthology editor Edmund
Clarence Stedman discussed this dynamic in *Century Magazine.*

> Here again we confront the statement that the six Eastern states
> were not and are not America; not the nation, but a section—the

> New Englanders seeming almost a race by themselves. But what
> a section! And what a people, when we take into account, super-
> added to their genuine importance, self-dependence ranking
> with that of the Scots or Cascons. As distinct a people, in their
> way, as Mr. Cable's creoles, old or new. Go by rail along the East-
> ern coast and note the nervous, wiry folk that crowd the stations
> . . . This hive of individuality has sent out swarms, and scattered
> its ideas like pollen throughout the northern belt of our states.
> As far as these have taken hold, modified by change and experi-
> ence, New England stands for the nation, and her singer for the
> national poet. In their native, unadulterated form, they pervade
> the verse of Whittier. [13]

Visitors to the Whittier Homestead museum were offered a scene
from America's past embodied not by people but by antique furniture, metonymic representatives of old New Englanders, a "race by
themselves" who nonetheless stood for America's past. Through an
image of pollinating bees, Stedman suggests that this isolated "race"
can be claimed by everyone. Whittier's house and its furniture were
accessible as an imaginary domestic space onto which visitors could
project nostalgic longings for "self-dependence."

At the same time, however, the museum's accessibility as an object
of nostalgia was limited by its unspoken racial location, for if the
boundaries of American regions could be easily crossed (both literally
and imaginatively), the boundary of American race—the so-called
color line—was if anything rigidifying in the later nineteenth century.
The museum was managed by the Haverhill Whittier Club, which had
incorporated in 1886 to "honor Whittier by bringing together his
friends and admirers."[14] Like the Daughters of the American Revolution, the Whittier Club was an exclusive (and, as went without saying,
exclusively white) social organization. Admission was by nomination
only, and limited to the "most prominent citizens" of the area, who
met in formal evening attire. The Whittier Club had much to preserve, since the area was rich in history; as a travel-magazine article
put it, "Whittier-Land" exerted a mysterious power over residents and
visitors alike: "The swash and swell of the waves on its beautiful coast
lisp only the fragments of a secret. Its ever-winding country roads and
wild-flower perfumed lanes whisper, 'It is not in us.' Those wondrous
nerve-centers, that Anglo-Saxon race stock, sturdy and liberty-loving—there is the core of the matter."[15]

The "core of the matter" posed a problem, however: the Whittier
museum represented at once the "liberty-loving" democratic traits
of the New Englander and his white, native racial stock, although

whiteness is so often deployed as a privilege that undermines the practice of true democracy. As Matthew Jacobson has argued in his work on the political history of whiteness, many Americans in the later nineteenth century linked whiteness to the issue of fitness for self-government. "White" immigrant groups (Swedish Protestants, for instance) could contribute to the health of the body politic, while it was feared that nonwhite groups ("swarthy" Italians, for instance) might join forces with African-Americans to hasten the decline of the republic. Even as he celebrated the communal virtues of Whittier's New England fireside, Lowell was also warning of how outsiders were incapable of assimilating those virtues; in an 1884 essay titled "Democracy," he asserts that the governments of large cities are being overtaken by "the most ignorant and vicious of a population which has come to us from abroad, wholly unpracticed in self-government and *incapable of assimilation by American habits and methods*" (italics mine).[16] As it turns out, then, Lowell's notion of American identity—his notion of who should gather around the fire—stems from the assumption that some people are naturally unfit to be American. It is not just a matter of "national habits" after all, but a matter of "race stock."

Ruth Frankenberg has called whiteness a "location of structural advantage," a place that white people occupy that depends on boundaries, on the existence of "others" against whom this place is defined.[17] This location derives its power in part from being "invisible in plain sight," by positing itself as the center, the unarticulated norm, the home of the unmarked American subject. While Frankenberg, as a sociologist, understands "location" to mean "social location" (rather than physical space), physical space can also play a part in defining and defending a social "location of structural advantage." As Valerie Babb has persuasively argued, world's fairs, settlement houses, museums, and public schools tended to idealize whiteness as a desirable social norm and to link whiteness with American democracy.[18] Nineteenth-century visitors to the Whittier Homestead encountered precisely that: an ideal American space that was also a white space, representing a desirable social norm and a microcosm of American democracy. Explicit references to Whittier's interest in racial politics were effectively erased from the homestead, at least until 1927, when, as Donald Freeman, a local Whittier Club historian, writes, "the colored citizens of Haverhill asked for and received permission to place a bronze commemorative plaque by the front entrance of the Birthplace."[19] Permission was granted by the Whittier Club, among whose ranks the "colored citizens of Haverhill" were not represented.

If we understand meaning to be a function of popular reception, then *Snow-Bound* was primarily a nostalgic poem, expressing, like the museum that memorialized it, longing for a simpler, more rustic, more intimate, more democratic, and whiter America. As Jean Pickering and Suzanne Kehde put it, "In times of change or crisis, nations look to the past and infer a narrative that erases all confusion or contradiction, which is not presented as history but as a figuration of essential . . . Americanness . . . a mythic national identity that, Platonic fashion, has always existed."[20] As I have suggested, to read the poem as a collection of artifacts is to encounter a narrative that cannot be confusing or contradictory because it is all surface: its most important "contents" are physical objects (the forestick, the backlog, the andirons), and its story is one of loss but also of progress: through their memories of the past, Americans are equipping themselves for citizenship. Given this narrative, it should not be surprising that Whittier's *Snow-Bound* became a classroom favorite as schools attempted to teach children how to act American.

Whittier's postbellum reputation thrived as his abolitionism (which had defined his adult life and much of his artistic output) was not forgotten but rather framed as quaint, as an "antique" virtue with no postbellum social consequences. In 1903 John Buckham asserted, "It is difficult to connect the Whittier of later years with the editor, legislator, agitator of earlier years . . . and [yet] the calm of after years was only the more golden for the noble strife and activity of early manhood."[21] In an evaluation for the mammoth *Library of the World's Best Literature*, George Carpenter is blunter, dismissing Whittier's abolitionist writings as inferior because they are not "national" enough: "They were all efficacious, but they were militant in quality, instruments in a transient struggle, the product of discord and sectional feeling, and hence hardly destined to live in the national memory."[22] Most notable here is the notion, which seems to have been the driving force behind the production of "Whittier" as a national icon, that history must be suppressed to produce "national memory." By reading *Snow-Bound* artifactually, as a museum catalogue, readers could transform the most ideologically challenging of the popular American poets into what might be described as the ideal white subject: neutral, reassuring, and transparent, inhabiting and enforcing cultural norms and boundaries so efficaciously that they became invisible (except to those who were excluded). "Neutral" objects and artifacts could be recruited to tell a nostalgic narrative about American history that could not be refuted—a narrative that celebrated the "Anglo-Saxon race stock" of New England through its material culture.

But I want to suggest that, in the case of *Snow-Bound*, to read the poem as a nostalgic narrative is to read it through a horizon of expectations that suppresses more than it reveals—like a collector picking and choosing only the "best" (most neutral, most comforting) images. The marks of history, and the history of race as a construct, remain visible in the text of Whittier's poem, even if—like whiteness itself as a condition—they are not visible to all readers at all times. The poem was certainly used to manufacture American memories, functioning as a nostalgic narrative of national (i.e., New England) identity, but it also struggles with contradictions not present in the empty museum rooms that memorialize and simplify its story. I do not want to suggest that the popular readings of *Snow-Bound* were simply wrong; on the contrary, the poem's cultural use-value as a museum catalogue, and as a specifically white social location, shows precisely what was at stake, and how much readers were willing to overlook as they sought a "figuration of essential" American identity.

WHITENESS BEFORE APPOMATTOX

Whittier's relation to figurations of essential American identity was both helped and hindered by his Quakerism. Colonial revival enthusiasts loved Quakers, just as many modern antique-collectors love the Amish. As revivalists imagined them, Quakers used picturesque language, lived a quaint and simple lifestyle, and tended to come from old East Coast families. But practicing Quakers such as Whittier were not so easily contained; they also tended to agitate for discomfiting causes, taking positions (on African-American and female suffrage, for instance) that were considered extreme. Whittier's own postbellum emergence into the pantheon of white-haired schoolroom poets belied his early reputation as a destabilizing force. He began *Snow-Bound* at a moment of transition: the Civil War was over, and the main battle of his life, the fight to end slavery, was won. Just as the nation was reconstructing itself, abolitionists too were reconstructing their public and private identities in the context of a nation without a clear and present enemy.

Whittier, as a career abolitionist, had long been forced to engage with the discursive construction of whiteness, the extent to which whiteness stood for purity, and the question of whether whiteness should be in any way preserved or defended. White abolitionists held a range of conscious and unconscious racial prejudices, a problem that Whittier recognized and tried to combat, even as he sometimes expressed ambivalent racial attitudes himself. In the 1830s he publicly supported William Lloyd Garrison's fight to eliminate a Massachusetts law that prohibited marriage between whites and blacks. "Come, thou sagacious discriminator of skins," Garrison wrote in the

Liberator as this issue was being debated by state legislators, "define thy boundary line!"[23] Whittier, in a letter to the *Amesbury Chronicle* that was reprinted in the *Liberator,* asserted that the old marriage law was a vestige of slavery and that slavery in Massachusetts would never be fully eradicated until "cruel and anti-Christian prejudice" was also gone.[24] In language familiar to anyone who has read antiabolitionist rhetoric, Garrison, Whittier, and their female supporters were accused of being "amalgamationists," advocates of miscegenation who personally lusted after black lovers.

White abolitionists' racial identity was constantly under attack by opponents who accused them of being somehow nonwhite (and who assumed they would find this insulting). Whittier parodied this in a topical poem celebrating the election of the Whig abolitionist John P. Hale to the Senate; the verses are supposedly spoken by the proslavery Democrats' leader:

> We're routed, Moses, horse and foot
> If there be truth in figures
> With Federal Whigs in hot pursuit,
> And Hale, and all the "niggers."[25]

By "niggers," Whittier means himself and the other Hale supporters. (He was well aware of the term's rudeness, and his published poems and letters never use it to describe actual African-Americans.) Later in the poem, a venerable old rock formation's head turns mysteriously black, as the speaker reports:

> We thought the "Old Man of the Notch"
> His face seemed changing wholly—
> His lips seemed thick, his nose seemed flat;
> His misty hair looked woolly . . .
>
> *(PW,* 326)

If the "Old Man of the Notch" represents New England folk tradition, then this tradition is a white tradition—but one that Whittier is parodying here. Or, more precisely, Whittier is parodying the racist hysteria that sees white traditions as threatened. And of course, in parodying this hysteria, Whittier is also defending the legendary rock by showing the absurdity, the impossibility, of ever turning a white heritage into a black one.

In many ways Whittier's abolitionist struggle can be framed as a symbolic battle over purity. If antiabolitionists, equating whiteness with purity, were quick to levy charges of sexual deviance and even "blackness" against Whittier, Whittier maintained, in poem after poem, that race prejudice and slave holding were the true pollutants. In "The Panorama," he describes a white slave-owner's dwelling:

> Of ampler size the master's dwelling stands,
> In shabby keeping with his half-tilled lands;
> The gates unhinged, the yard with weeds unclean,
> The cracked verandah with a tipsy lean.
>
> . . . .
>
> There, all the vices, which, like birds obscene,
> Batten of slavery loathsome and unclean,
> From the foul kitchen to the parlor rise,
> Pollute the nursery where the child-heir lies,
> Taint infant lips beyond all after cure.
>
> (PW, 326)

Images of decay, "plague-spots," viruses, and filth pervade Whittier's abolitionist verse. Rather than see the North as pure and the South as impure, or whites as pure and blacks as impure, these pestilential images suggest that, like the germs from the kitchen that rise to the nursery, the wrongs of slavery are bad precisely because they permeate every boundary. No state can be pure until all are pure. This discourse is so marked in Whittier's writings that it even spawned a 1933 psychodramatic biography, *Quaker Militant,* that uses Freud to pathologize Whittier's preoccupation with cleanliness.[26]

But what were the politics of Whittier's viruses and "plague-spots"? Toni Morrison has called the "power of blackness" in American literature "a fabricated brew of darkness, otherness, alarm, and desire that is uniquely American."[27] In Whittier's abolitionist poetry, blackness as a trope is projected not onto slaves but onto racially white slaveholders who are framed as "others," often—curiously—in orientalist terms that stress their indolence. An example of this is Whittier's poem "The Hashisch," which equates cotton with smoke from a hookah:

> O potent plant! so rare a taste
> Has never Turk or Gentoo gotten;
> The hempen Haschish of the East
> Is powerless to our Western Cotton!
>
> (PW, 316)

Whittier, then, often displaced the standard practice of maintaining whiteness against Africanism with an equally racialized, but less

specifically antiblack, rhetoric. "The Cable Hymn," for instance, celebrates the telegraph as an instrument of enlightenment:

> Through Orient seas, o'er Afric's plain
> And Asian mountains borne
> The vigor of the Northern brain
> Shall nerve the world out-worn.
> From clime to clime, from shore to shore
> Shall thrill the magic thread;
> The new Prometheus steals once more
> The fires that wake the dead.
>
> (*PW*, 256)

Here whiteness is grafted, Frankenstein-style, onto the darker parts of
the world, resulting in one living body that may be multihued on the
outside but that has a white, Northern brain. My point in analyzing
these verses is to show how Whittier maintained whiteness as a primary and positive identity, even as he questioned aspects of white
privilege. By 1866, then, he was in a unique position to rethink whiteness as a form of identity, because for thirty years the whiteness of
Whittier's heritage, skin, and mind had been the subject of both
pride and anxiety. Unlike the other schoolroom poets, whose mild
involvement with abolition was well within the bounds of respectable
Boston society, Whittier's abolitionism had defined and delimited his
entire public identity for decades. *Snow-Bound* was the poem that soft-
ened Whittier's reputation, easing him into the more politically neutral category of an "American Burns." As a collector, Whittier was
attuned to the folklore and material culture of rural Massachusetts.
But he was also attentive to storytelling, and it is through Whittier's
storytellers that more conflicted discourses about the racial boundaries of the poem's image of Haverhill homestead begin to emerge.

WHITENESS VISIBLE

Snow-Bound can be read as a poem about being buried in whiteness,
about learning to act white, and about negotiating the meaning of
whiteness. Whittier begins his poem outside, in the gathering storm,
then moves inside, stressing the contrasts between outside and
inside. One of the visual paradoxes of the poem is that the snow that
whitens the entire landscape is figured as dark, and made to carry
the metaphorical weight of darkness, otherness, and savagery. One
of Whittier's opening epigraphs, from Cornelius Agrippa, makes
this explicit:

> As the Spirits of Darkness be stronger in the dark, so Good Spir-
> its, which be Angels of Light, are augmented not only by the
> Divine light of the Sun, but also by our common Wood Fire: and
> as the Celestial Fire drives away dark spirits, so also this our fire
> of the Wood doth the same. (*PW*, 399)

The white snow is coded as dark, so that, from the very beginning of
the poem, categories of light and dark, black and white, are explicitly
constructed through cultural discourses rather than being figured as
natural. As children, Whittier and his brother are intrigued by the
dark world outside their New England farmhouse. The narrator
describes how, on the second day of the storm, "we looked upon a
world unknown / On nothing we could call our own":

> The old familiar sights of ours
> Took marvelous shapes; strange domes and towers
> Rose up where sty or corn-crib stood,
> Or garden-wall or belt of wood;
> A smooth white mound the brush-pile showed,
> A fenceless drift what once was road;
> The bridle-post an old man sat
> With loose-flung coat and high cocked hat;
> The well-curb had a Chinese roof;
> And even the long sweep, high aloof,
> In its slant splendor, seemed to tell
> Of Pisa's leaning miracle.
> (PW, 400)

The outside is not just wild nature, against which domestic culture
can be defined; it has a culture all its own, albeit a fascinatingly jum-
bled one of marginal people and exotic architecture. But as the storm
progresses, the outside gets less inviting and more sinister:

> All day the gusty north-wind bore
> The loosening drift its breath before;
> Low circling round its southern zone,
> The sun through dazzling snow-mist shone.
> No church-bell lent its Christian tone
> To the savage air, no social smoke
> Curled over woods of snow-hung oak.
> A solitude made more intense
> By dreary-voiced elements,
> The shrieking of the mindless wind,
> The moaning tree-boughs swaying blind,

And on the glass the unmeaning beat
Of ghostly finger-tips of sleet.

(*PW,* 400)

I quote these passages at length to show how Whittier frames solitude as a specifically cultural or even racial isolation: there are voices outside; they are just not part of the family, not part of what "we could call our own." The snow takes the shape of outsiders, Italians and Chinese, and then veers into a sheer savagery that is unassimilable in its otherness. The sleet's rappings are indecipherable, like a foreign language, and the boys' home feels more Christian, more "light," and more civilized by contrast.

The postbellum American scene was itself a world unknown, peopled by immigrants (including large populations from China and Italy), freedmen, and former Southern rebels. While I do not want to argue that Whittier is deliberately allegorizing here, it seems clear from contemporary reviews that part of the appeal of *Snow-Bound* was its withdrawal from the haunted and illegible landscape of postwar America into what was seen as a more innocent domestic time and place. As Kate Gardner wrote, in an early review,

> As the weapons of strife are thrown aside, and while the campfires are being lighted, and the sentinels pace to and fro, weary after the cares of the day, a holy quiet steals even over the battlefield, and in this dreamy, weary silence, memory carries the stern warrior back to boyhood days, so in the battle of life, when weary with fighting for Freedom and the Right, trusting in God for the future, a holy quiet steals over the soul, and in this twilight of life's troubled days, home scenes are pictured by memory's fancy, and beautiful visions "weave their bright hues into woof," "Snow Bound" steals from the poet's pen, and comes to us, even "As the benediction / That follows after prayer."[28]

Certainly the house is a place of reassurance and meaning making, or specifically tradition making.

While the outside is a savage place, the fire is situated on the border between outside and inside (the chimney must be open, after all, to let the smoke out). The family piles wood in the fireplace, lights it, and waits "until the old rude furnished room / Burst, flower-like, into rosy bloom":

While, radiant with a mimic flame
Outside the sparkling drift became,
And through the bare-boughed lilac-tree

Our own warm hearth seemed blazing free.
The crane and pendant trammels showed,
The Turks' heads on the andirons glowed;
While childish fancy, prompt to tell
The meaning of the miracle,
Whispered the old rhyme, "*Under the tree,*
When fire outdoors burns merrily,
There the witches are making tea."

(*PW,* 400)

Curiously, Whittier devotes the vast majority of the first 180 lines of
the poem to setting margins, as it were, rather than establishing a specific picture of the Haverhill homestead kitchen or its inhabitants.
The fire, held back by Turks' heads, beats "the frost-line back with
tropic heat," suggesting a particular geography. The extremes of hot
(fire) and cold (storm) also represent cultural extremes, or margins:
dark Europeans, Asians, and American witches, all of whom are outsiders compared to the climatologically and culturally "temperate"
Yankees who gather in the kitchen. This centering of the kitchen as a
white space defined by dark margins reprises a basic cultural complex
that has been discussed by Ruth Frankenberg, who writes, "Whiteness
and Americanness seemed comprehensible to many only by reference to the Others excluded from these categories," so that inde-
pendence is defined by dependent others, freedom by unfree others,
and normalcy by exotic others.[29] Minute attention to margins defines
the center, which needs less articulation since it is, culturally and nar-
ratologically, a subject-position; it is the place where Whittier sits, and
where we, as readers, are invited to sit. The center, posited as the
Haverhill kitchen, is a place of normalcy, a place of light, and an
implicitly white, as opposed to dark or exotic, place.

Within this circle of light, stories will be told and lessons will be
learned. What is at stake here is Whittier's own education: How will
the center define him? How will he take the pieces of his heritage—
as offered through characters in the poem—and combine them to
make a coherent self-defining narrative? The bulk of *Snow-Bound* is
devoted to pedagogical exchanges that serve to teach the young Whittier who he is, and how he should locate himself as a good person and
a good citizen. Although the Haverhill homestead is posited, in the
opening scene, as a racially white location (against a dark and savage
outside), the characters that teach Whittier range from very light
(indeed, dead white) to very dark (or "pard-like"). The characters
can be divided into three categories: those who are wholly white,
including the aunt, the uncle, and the two dead sisters; those who

patrol the borderline between whiteness and blackness / darkness, including the mother and father; and those who engage in actual or imaginative border-crossing between races, including the Whittier boys, the schoolteacher, and the visitor Harriet Livermore. Although *Snow-Bound* makes only passing allusions to abolition, it is a poem about race—blackness as well as whiteness—and how racial categories incite the speaker's imagination, his desires and his fears.

ABSOLUTE WHITENESS

If the Haverhill homestead is represented as "typical," a representative farmhouse, then within its walls Whittier also describes two Yankee "types," his uncle and his aunt. His uncle is a romantic, grown-up "Barefoot Boy," and his aunt is a long-suffering spinster. These are folk characters, closely allied with the natural and cultural landscape of New England. Neither recounts a real story, a chronological narrative; instead, both offer paradigmatic descriptions of antebellum folkways. The uncle lives closer to nature than to culture, but unlike the "savage" storm outside, the uncle's nature is ultimately tame almost to dullness:

> Our uncle, innocent of books,
> Was rich in lore of fields and brooks,
> The ancient teachers never dumb
> Of Nature's unhoused lyceum.
>
> (*PW,* 402)

Indeed, the uncle's genealogy (or at least his spiritual genealogy) reaches back to ancient Rome, the first Western civilization to perfect the pastoral form. The uncle understands Nature: "her voices in his ear / Of beast or bird had meanings clear, / Like Apollonius of old" (*PW,* 402). There are no outsiders in the uncle's world, which is perfectly legible to him despite his illiteracy. This "simple, guileless, childlike man" lives a self-sufficient life that seems a model of self-government. And yet Whittier is quick to point out his limitations; the uncle is "Strong only on his native grounds / The little world of sights and sounds / Whose girdle was the parish bounds" (PW, 402). Far from being a celebration of nativism, the uncle's portrait functions as a gentle critique of the nostalgic notion that New Englanders in their "native, unadulterated form" are uniquely fit to lead the nation. On the contrary, the uncle's provincialism limits him to a perennial childhood—hardly the model for an ideal democratic citizen.

The aunt is also situated as a New England character type: the spinster. She remembers "the huskings and the apple-bees" of her youth, and Whittier describes even her language as a form of handwork: "Weaving through all the poor details / And homespun warp of circumstance / A golden woof-thread of romance." But the aunt's weaving is limited, like the uncle's strength, by parish bounds. Both the uncle and the aunt are "local characters," but they are also isolated and static. Not only are they unmarried and unfruitful, but the accounts they give of their lives are circular and "typical," not based on any chronological national or even local events. These are the two living characters in the poem that have no contact with "others": no slaves, no freedmen, no Indians, no immigrants. In this sense, they are the most perfect representatives of the white utopian New England that Alice Morse Earle found at the Whittier Family Homestead. And yet they are limited, repetitive, and static.

The sense of stasis intensifies as the two Whittier sisters (who do not tell their own stories) are sketched as self-sacrificing, generous, truthful models of nineteenth-century maidenhood, in portraits that meld the Yankee-republican culture of 1820 with the narrator's more literary sentimental outlook of 1866. Whittier's sister Elizabeth, who lived with him for most of her adult life, had died just before Whittier began writing *Snow-Bound*, and she is rendered in the language of nineteenth-century sentimental nostalgia as Whittier addresses her directly:

> I cannot feel that thou are far,
> Since near at need the angels are;
> And when the sunset gates unbar,
> Shall I not see thee waiting stand,
> And, white against the evening star,
> The welcome of thy beckoning hand?
>
> (*PW,* 403)

To note the whiteness of that hand seems almost facile, since it reflects only the entrenched conventions of representing nineteenth-century angels of the house, both living and dead, as pale beauties. But Whittier's apostrophe to Elizabeth, in the context of *Snow-Bound*, links her affectively to the household that created her. She represents that household in its dead white form—as a pure object to be longed for but never again touched. Her white body is timeless (shorn of history), chaste (she beckons only her brother), and passive (it offers no counsel, no stories), as it stands waiting for the speaker to cross over into death. Such a concentration of purity is enervating; it literally stops the narrative, forcing it into lyric mode.

[52]

I have suggested that the Haverhill homestead is a white location of structural advantage, but within its walls the whitest characters are not shown to any great advantage: they are static, unfruitful, and metaphorically or literally dead. Toni Morrison argues that an Africanist presence defines "Americanism" in many literary texts, that without an "other" the self is paralyzed: "Whiteness, alone, is mute, meaningless, unfathomable, pointless, frozen, veiled, curtained, dreaded, senseless, implacable."[30] The uncle and aunt can amuse the children, but they have little to teach them; certainly, they cannot offer them any kind of future. And the sisters are even more static, stuck in the world of the sentimental apostrophe and reaching out from the grave with their chilly white hands.

BORDER PATROLS

The father's and mother's stories are by contrast actual narratives: less static, less "bounded," and more national. Indeed, as pedagogical narrators, they seem intent on helping the children understand their family's American identity. The father speaks first:

> Our father rode again his ride
> On Memphremagog's wooded side;
> Sat down again to moose and samp
> In trapper's hut and Indian camp;
> Lived o'er the old idyllic ease
> Beneath St. Francois' hemlock trees.
>
> (*PW,* 401)

Memphremagog, a lake on the border between Vermont and Canada, works as a margin like the snow-covered yard and the Turk's-head hearth. When evoked in the context of storytelling, the lake helps to consolidate a "center," a community of Yankees whose household property lines echo the national property lines drawn (and transgressed, but also thereby strengthened) by the father.

Reinforcing these borders, the mother's recollections begin:

> Our mother, while she turned her wheel
> Or run the new-knit stocking heel,
> Told how the Indian hordes came down
> At midnight on Cocheco town,
> And how her own great-uncle bore
> His cruel scalp-mark to fourscore.
>
> (*PW,* 401)

The mother, like the aunt, is spinning a tale as a form of handwork. But unlike the aunt's story, this one is fruitful—and has some momentum—because it involves contact with racial others. Not only is the Yankee integrity of the town threatened in the mother's story, but the very body of her great-uncle is violated by "hordes" that open it, leaving a red mark on white skin. The great-uncle, unlike the Indians, is individuated but not defeated by his experience. Indeed, the very presence of the Whittier family tableau underlines the eventual triumph of the white settlers at Cocheco.

But the next part of the mother's narrative modifies the implication that white civilization has triumphed—and must triumph—over savage "others." She reads from "Chalkey's Journal, old and quaint— / Gentlest of skippers, rare sea-saint!" The story tells how Chalkey's ship was stranded, so that "cruel, hungry eyes pursued / His portly presence mad for food" (*PW*, 401). The sailors discuss casting lots about whom to eat, and Chalkey volunteers himself. But just as he is about to be killed and devoured, porpoises appear, so the crew eats them instead. This, then, is the story of white cannibals preparing to eat a Quaker. The story of the scalping—a barbaric violation of whites by Indians—is trumped by an even more barbaric scene, with Anglo-Saxons in the role of barbarians. The notion that there is some innate connection between race and civilization—a notion central to so many assumptions about whiteness in the later nineteenth century—is undercut by the mother's account. The mother reminds us that martyrdom—at the hands of whites as well as Indians—was central to the experience of Quakers in early America. Even as the Haverhill homestead is posited as a culturally central white space, the mother opens the meaning of whiteness to negotiation.

BORDER CROSSING

The three most formative moments in the text—moments that provoke passionate responses from the young Whittier—involve direct confrontations with African or Africanized subjects. I take as axiomatic Morrison's claim that an Africanist presence defines white American subjectivity in many "classic" American texts, including schoolroom poems. And as I have discussed, this was especially true for Whittier, whose literary production was shaped by the problem of slavery. Whittier's account of his own education begins with an African:

> We sped the time with stories old,
> Wrought puzzles out, and riddles told,

Or stammered from our school-book lore
"The Chief of Gambia's golden shore."

(*PW*, 401)

The line that Whittier "stammers" is from Sarah Wentworth Morton's poem "The African Chief," which appeared in Caleb Bingham's early American schoolbook *The Colombian Orator*. The full text of the poem describes a slave rebellion on Haiti, prefiguring the Civil War that would be so central to Whittier's adult experience. As a figure within this poem, though, the "Chief of Gambia's golden shore" brings color and exoticism to the fireside: he is not himself American, although he highlights the virtuous American Quakerism of the Whittier family. Like the Turk's head in the fireplace, he stands in a "tropical" location (Haiti) that defines the "temperate" moral landscape of New England by contrast. But he does not change or challenge the family's values as he is admitted to their circle as an honorary member: on the contrary, he reinforces the abolitionist beliefs that are already a part of the family's Quaker background, implicitly strengthening the rightness of their moral and cultural centrality. Moreover, his unfreedom works to make the freedom of the Whittier family more palpable. He stands at the beginning of the storytelling cycle and serves in many ways to introduce the Whittier family; in this way, he might be seen as what Morrison has called an Africanist "surrogate and enabler," a "vehicle by which the American self knows itself as not enslaved, but free; not repulsive, but desirable; not helpless, but licensed and powerful; not history-less, but historical; not damned, but innocent; not a blind accident of evolution, but a progressive fulfillment of destiny."[31] From this perspective, the African Chief is not really an African at all but rather a figure against which Whittier's own self can be constructed, since binaries of light versus dark and civilization versus savagery organize the space that his family—a free, powerful, and innocent group of Yankees on the right side of history—inhabits.

But the poem does not rest in such simple binaries. The African Chief does not just reinforce the "parish bounds" of the cozy farmhouse scene. Indeed, he ultimately disrupts them, as Whittier breaks from his pastoral mode to look forward in time:

How often since, when all the land
Was clay in Slavery's shaping hand,
As if a far-blown trumpet stirred
The languorous sin-sick air, I heard:
"Does not the voice of reason cry,
    Claim the first right which Nature gave,

From the red scourge of bondage fly,
Nor deign to live a burdened slave!"

(*PW*, 401)

When this image appears in the poem, the narrative flashes forward to envision an active response to bondage, a response that might serve to break down the racialized black/white binaries on which the poem's "location of structural advantage" depends. In this way, the white space of the house is stable (safe, innocent, white) only insofar as it is read nostalgically. Break the structure of nostalgia by looking to the future, and a "storm" of uncertainty seeps through the cracks—a storm of demands from the past and responsibilities to the future, incompatible with mere nostalgia.

Moreover, the Chief is urged to "fly" from the "red scourge," an image that aligns him with the great-uncle fleeing the Indians; both are working for the establishment of Enlightenment ideals in the New World. As John Saillant has pointed out, representations of the black male body dominated much abolitionist discourse. He suggests that these images, "black and masculine" (as opposed to victimized or feminized), invited an experience of bodily likeness, a cross-racial identification among men, that precipitated "a new, liberal ethos of race relations."[32] Obviously, such a "new ethos" never fully caught on, even in abolitionist circles. Still, the lesson that the African Chief teaches is not one of condescending pity toward the slave but rather one of admiration for the power of his "avenging hand."[33] The poem compares the Chief to William III and George Washington, thus bringing the slave rebel into European history on the winning, revolutionary side. This sets up a counterdiscourse within the poem's narrative, as invoking "others" such as the African Chief becomes a way not just to draw boundaries but also to redraw them, thereby rendering the "black and white" terms of the color line as at least theoretically open to questioning. If the outside storm is savage, the African Chief is civilized on at least two fronts: he is aligned with civilized leaders, and he is admired by Yankees who are themselves set up as admirable. In this way, the boundaries that the tropical Chief marks are also at least potentially destabilized by him: he elicits reflection on the future, not just a restoration of the past.

As a schoolroom poet, Whittier was often taught—along with Longfellow, Lowell, and Holmes—as a representative white American to be emulated. As I have discussed, schoolroom poetry was framed as ideologically neutral, even as it was used by schoolteachers to promote the tradition of New England/America. *Snow-Bound* also features a schoolteacher who teaches Whittier and his brother about the uses of tradition. The "master of the district school" is portrayed as a laughing and energetic young man who tells amusing tales of Greece and Rome adapted to the New England landscape, so that Aracthus becomes a millbrook and Olympus a huckleberry hill. In this way, the family's Yankee heritage is linked to the best of world history, strengthening the value and cultural centrality of the New England Yankees. But this narrative, rather than simply establishing New England's past, becomes the basis for a different kind of future:

> Large-brained, clear-eyed, of such as he
> Shall Freedom's young apostles be,
> Who, following in War's bloody trail,
> Shall every lingering wrong assail;
> All chains from limb and spirit strike,
> Uplift the black and white alike;
> Scatter before their swift advance
> The darkness and the ignorance,
> The pride, the lust, the squalid sloth,
> Which nurtured Treason's monstrous growth.
>
> (*PW,* 404)

Images of pollution and filth, familiar from Whittier's abolitionist verse, reemerge here, culminating in the specter of a monster borne of darkness. But again, the darkness is not equated with racial blackness, as Whittier predicts that men such as his schoolteacher will refute "the cruel lie of caste":

> A schoolhouse plant on every hill,
> Stretching in radiate nerve-lines thence
> The quick-wires of intelligence;
> Till North and South together brought
> Shall own the same electric thought,
> In peace a common flag salute,
> And, side by side in labor's free
> And unresentful rivalry,
> Harvest the fields wherein they fought.
>
> (*PW,* 404)

Again, rather than simply indulging in nostalgia, rather than trying to reinstall the white New England rural world that has been lost, Whittier imagines a character fortified by this tradition who nevertheless helps to move it beyond its "parish bounds." As in "The Cable Hymn," northern "intelligence" is figured as a telegraph wire, benignly freeing "black and white alike." Not only does the technology of the telegraph reduce distances, but the schoolteacher himself folds from the past into the future tense, so that his character is a catalyst for change rather than, or in addition to, being an object of nostalgia. In this way, he is identified with the African Chief: both are pedagogical figures, inspiring the boys to use their heritage, not to defend their position as self-governing New Englanders, but to go out and promote liberty for all people.

It is worth pausing to consider, though, what these "black and white" southerners are at liberty to do. According to the dominant logic of Snow-Bound, they are free to become more like New Englanders: to identify with the teachings of the many Yankees, like Whittier's own niece, Lizzie, who traveled south to teach during Reconstruction. Whittier wrote approvingly to his friend Harriet Pitman: "Lizzie got well on to Camden, S.C. where she is teaching. She has 65 scholars—she and two other teachers have rooms in the dwelling of a colored man, and take their meals in another."[34] The boundaries of New England, and the unpolluted spaces that those boundaries are supposed to create, are not so much broken here as expanded: the utopian "electric thought" shared by blacks and whites has its origins in New England. And, as Robert Morris points out in his history of Reconstruction and education, it is true that as northern teachers streamed south, they tended to adorn their classrooms with portraits of three northern "intelligences": William Lloyd Garrison, Wendell Phillips, and Whittier. [35] The images in the schoolmaster's section ultimately reinforce the virtues of white people as teaching and learning subjects. If the schoolmaster's counterparts travel south, as Whittier hopes they will do, they will bring "electric thoughts" of liberty from New England, where freedom is nurtured in farmhouses like the Haverhill homestead. But what about their African-American students? How do they fit in?

Harriet Livermore, the final character that Whittier depicts, is a white New Englander, and yet she brings a distinctly Africanist presence to the text: she represents what happens when borders are not just expanded (to include more honorary New Englanders) but truly broken or blurred. James Rocks, who sees Snow-Bound as a sentimental and domestic text, reads her mainly as a foil, a negative example against which the more conventional angels of the house (male and female) can be praised.[36] Many signals in the poem, however, point to Livermore's importance—and Whittier devotes more lines to Livermore than to any other individual in Snow-Bound. She is a marginal figure who stands neither fully "outside" nor "inside" and who reprises, while threatening to collapse, all the boundary lines that the poem draws elsewhere:

> Another guest that winter night
> Flashed back from lustrous eyes the light.
> Unmarked by time, and yet not young,
> The honeyed music of her tongue
> And words of meekness scarcely told
> A nature passionate and bold
> Strong, self-concentrated, spurning guide,
> Its milder features dwarfed beside
> Her unbent will's majestic pride.
> She sat among us, at the best,
> A not unfeared, half-welcome guest.
>
> (*PW*, 404)

If the pleasures of *Snow-Bound* are the pleasures of a museum full of self-evident artifacts, then Livermore is disconcerting partly because she is not transparent: her "honeyed tongue" suggests gentleness (also sexuality, of course), but her "nature" belies her actions, and that nature is not the benign Arcadian version of nature experienced by the uncle. Like the storm outside, Livermore's nature is hard to read and thus invites unease.

As a figure in a nostalgic poem, this character is notable for being "unmarked by time and yet not young": she embodies the notion, or fear, that time and memory are not homogeneous and collective (a prerequisite for national nostalgic narratives) but rather idiosyncratic, unfinished, and debatable. Both of the Whittier sisters are presented as dead and mourned, whereas this woman lives in the present tense and to some extent hijacks the poem; indeed, she even outleaps the poem itself. In response to an outpouring of public interest in her, Whittier included an extraordinary headnote in the 1888 Riverside edition of his poems, explaining that the "not unfeared guest" was "Harriet Livermore, daughter of Judge Livermore of New Hampshire, a young woman of fine natural ability, enthusiastic, eccentric, with slight control over her violent temper, which sometimes made her religious profession doubtful." The headnote describes this woman's eccentric belief systems, her travels in Europe and Asia, and her friendship with Lady Hester Stanhope, "a woman as fantastic and mentally strained as herself." What Whittier neglects to mention, but which Rebecca Davis points out in *Gleanings from Merrimack Valley*, is that Livermore, "by permission of President Jackson, . . . gave one of her religious addresses to an assembled Congress, being the first female who had ever spoken publicly within its halls. [She also] spoke under three other administrations, viz.: Martin Van Buren's, John Tyler's, and John Quincy Adams's. A pioneer, truly, in female speaking!"[37]

This pioneer in female speaking does not address the assembled group at Haverhill. Instead, she offers her distinctive physical presence:

> A certain pard-like, treacherous grace
> Swayed the lithe limbs and drooped the lash,
> Lent the white teeth their dazzling flash;
> And under low brows, black with night,
> Rayed out at times a dangerous light;
> The sharp heat-lightnings of her face
> Presaging ill to him whom Fate
> Condemned to share her love or hate.
> A woman tropical, intense
> In thought and act, in soul and sense,
> She blended in a like degree
> The vixen and the devotee.
>
> (PW, 404)

Livermore, then, is like a leopard, a wholly black animal whose darkness lends her a certain sensuality, whose teeth gleam white, and whose brow (like the brows of Africans in pseudoscientific phrenological texts) is low and "black with night." And yet the problem with Livermore—or one of the problems—is that she does not have a clear racial identity:

> Nor is it given us to discern . . .
> What mingled madness in the blood,
>   A life-long discord and annoy,
>   Water of tears with oil of joy,
> And hid within the folded but
> Perversities of flower and fruit.
>
> (PW, 404)

As an amalgamation of animal and human, black and white, flower and fruit, this woman offers a compressed catalogue of anxieties about the problem of making a united nation of out racially and geographically heterogeneous materials. At one point, Whittier calls her soul "debatable land," as if the state of civil war were a continuous feature of Livermore's peculiar constitution.

And yet she is attractive. No character in the poem is more fully physically embodied, and few characters in Whittier's oeuvre are as discomfitingly sexual. As "a woman tropical, intense," Livermore stands on the erotic borderline defined by the African Chief, the witches making tea, and the Turk's-head andirons. Nostalgia and sexual desire are an odd mix, like water and oil: if nostalgia strains for purity and stasis, sexual desire produces a narrative thrust—the desire for procreation, not reconstruction. If Whittier's vision of a Reconstruction schoolhouse where black and white, North and South, all "own the same electric thought" is a hopeful image, it is also an image of control, of peace through reeducation and integration. And his prediction that blacks and whites will "harvest the fields wherein they fought" displaces the issues of mixing and fruition onto the safely asexual plane of a farmer's field. As Edward Pierce wrote, in the journal of the New England Freedman's Aid Society, "Our schools and teachers [have had] a most important influence in restoring social order."[38] Livermore is problematic because she breaks down the social order, a social order represented by the Haverhill fireside and by the museum that it inspired. The collectors' narratives that the poem inspired assumed that "old" New England was orderly and pure—but Livermore is neither. Her whiteness is counteracted, not by her heritage (which is solidly New England—based, as Whittier's headnote asserts), but by her nature, her passions, and her outspokenness. She does not offer a pale, dead hand from beyond the grave; rather, she offers eroticism and unsafe questions about the centrality of the fire, since (although she sits with the family) she does not seem to need it—she generates her own "self-concentrated" energy.

This woman represents a fault line in the liberal white circle around the fire, not by being simply racially black, but because she fails to be simply racially white. She exposes whiteness, especially white womanhood, as a complicated performance, maintained by certain behaviors she spurns; and she indicts Whittier's liberalism as a potential instrument of control, since she is unsettling to him precisely because she is beyond his control. Whittier ends his portrait of her with an oddly passive-aggressive expression of pity for her unstable "frame":

> But He who knows our frame is just,
> Merciful and compassionate,
> And full of sweet assurances
> And hope for all the language is,
> That He remembereth we are dust!
>
> (*PW,* 405)

This woman, "the warm, dark languish of her eyes" and her "tapering hand and rounded fist," must be physically dissolved, reduced to dust, in order to become an object of pity. Her body is a problem that cannot be solved as long as it arouses such ambivalent feelings of desire and fear, and it arouses those feelings because it brings the outside inside. In other words, this body mediates not the triumph of New England as a figure for America but the emergence of America as a multicultural and multiracial society. This society cannot be simply refigured as one ever-expanding family circle anchored by a New England fireside, no matter how pure and how sure of their moral fortitude the New Englanders themselves may be.

And yet, ironically, "eccentricity" was one of the standard cultural exports of the region: Whittier, like other romantic regional writers, generated a cottage industry of charming eccentrics such as Skip Ireson and Maude Mueller. The difference with Livermore is how hard she pushes it: across lines of gender and race. Her character finally implies that "perversities of flower and fruit"—far from being tropical, exogenous weeds—are in fact indigenous to Haverhill; that the egalitarian values espoused by Sarah Morton, Whittier's mother, and Whittier himself might not lend themselves to boundaries at all but to the pushing of limits, the breakdown of conventions and taboos. Here we come, then, to an impasse that characterizes both *Snow-Bound* and Whittier's abolitionist poetry: on the one hand, the work draws on a New England identity based on purity and moral rightness; on the other hand, if part of being morally right is being egalitarian and reform-minded, then everyone must be admitted to the circle around the fire. However, if there are no boundaries between the family and the outside (with its Italians, witches, and Africans), then what kind of chaos might result? What desires might be released? How might New England, and indeed the nation, be changed?

The poem's strikingly different depictions of Elizabeth Whittier and Harriet Livermore express profound ambivalence about whiteness as a hedge against change. Elizabeth, as the pale sister, embodies whiteness, but she also carries the pallor of death: she literally stands in heaven, beckoning the narrator to join her. If the narrator is nostalgic for an America defined by New England values, if he engages in the culture of collecting and preservation, he also understands the whiteness he yearns for to stand at the end of history, in a shadowy realm that is finally dark with death and stasis, just as the white snow outside is paradoxically figured as dark. When the narrator lapses into nostalgic musing, his images sheer off into the grave:

> Green hills of life that slope to death
> And haunts of home whose vistaed trees
> Shade off to mournful cypresses
> With the white amaranths underneath!
>
> (*PW,* 406)

Amaranths are mythical white flowers that bloom forever, uncontaminated by life but therefore also oddly unaffected by it. Livermore, as the dark other, embodies amalgamation, blending "in the like degree / the vixen and the devotee," but she also mirrors the narrator's own fascination with her, his desire to move beyond the isolation and safety of his whiteness as emblematized by his snowbound house. Moreover, as Livermore mediates nonteleological history through her ambivalently black and white body, she mediates the fragmentary plots of a nation that cannot be reconstructed in the image of New England, if only because New England itself is shown to be irreducible to a single physical type. Livermore's powerful presence underscores the body's—or at least her body's—irreducibility to neutral representative status. Instead, she registers conflicts, between flower and fruit, war and peace, vixen and devotee, black and white, that suggest that power (for surely she is the most powerful figure in the poem) comes not from stable identities but from ongoing contacts between people, even across the color line, and even if those negotiations destabilize the Yankee norm.

Moreover, Livermore bears a family relationship to the angel that closes the poem:

> Clasp, Angel of the backward look
> And folded wings of ashen gray
> And voice of echoes far away
> The brazen covers of thy book;
> The weird palimpsest old and vast,
> Wherein thou hid'st the spectral past.
>
> (*PW,* 406)

Although we might at first see this angel as a piece of Victorian funeral statuary, she is not a reassuring or legible figure; she is also neither black nor white, though she comes at the end of a poem nominally defined by these binaries. This angel does not offer a legible, teleological, collection of pictures or artifacts but rather a "weird palimpsest" that is not obvious or transparent but requires interpretation. Her "backward look" is not an escape but a challenge, the challenge that comes from acknowledging that the text of American history is difficult to read.

From this perspective, it makes sense that the angel is not simply white (unlike the angel Elizabeth, invoked earlier), because postbellum America was not simply white. Whittier lived through a period in American history in which the racial identity of the nation was in flux. Like Livermore, the "angel of the backward look" is a disorienting force that demands not a retreat into utopian projections of purity but rather an admission that the past, like the angel's body, is a gray area: it is not just black and white, and it is far from simple. *Snow-Bound* is a complicated poem, and a great many "gray areas" had to be suppressed in order for readers to see it as a simple nostalgic narrative. And yet suppress they did: my reading of the poem is less a reception study than a study of messages that readers were not prepared to receive.

SNOW-BOUND IN SCHOOL

Snow-Bound is a poem that comes out firmly against slavery but that remains ambivalent about the ways that white and black people might mix. It dreams of educating "black and white alike" while expressing anxieties about racial amalgamation. This same attitude—a moral certitude about slavery (now that it was over) coupled with a great deal of ambivalence about race—pervaded late-nineteenth-century schools, including Freedmen's Bureau schools. In 1899, Miss Frances B. Johnston took a photograph of a classroom at the Hampton Institute, the former Freedmen's Bureau school that counted Booker T. Washington among its alumni.[39] The photograph shows a room full of upright, uniformed African-American men, listening to another student who is standing on a podium reading aloud. Next to the podium, propped on an easel, is a portrait of Whittier. And behind Whittier, on the blackboard, are chalk drawings of the Haverhill homestead and of the hearth scene from the 1887 edition of *Snow-Bound*. This photograph was part of a group that was eventually sent to the Paris Exhibition as part of the Negro Exhibit, emphasizing "the importance placed by the institute on the training of the Negro in the arts that pertain to home and farm life."[40] At the Paris Exhibition, the photos were to be arranged in pairs that contrasted the backwardness of rural blacks with the enlightened lifestyles of Hampton graduates; thus, as the school newsletter, the *Southern Workman*, put it, "The old-time one-room cabin and the old mule with his rope harness, just tickling the ground with a rusty plough, will be contrasted with the comfortable home of the Hampton graduate."[41]

Frances Benjamin Johnston (1864–1952). *Literature—Lesson on Whittier.*
Middle Class. 1899, plate from an album of Hampton Institute. 1899–1900.
Platinum print, 7 1/2 x 9 1/2". Gift of Lincoln Kerstein. The Museum of
Modern Art, New York, NY. Digital Image © The Museum of Modern
Art / Licensed by SCALA / Art Resource, NY.

The underlying narrative of the Paris Exhibition collection was
meant to show the success of the "Hampton Idea" of Black Reconstruction, which stressed self-reliance and moral development as pre-
requisites for political and economic enfranchisement.[42] It might
seem paradoxical that a poem celebrating rural primitivism would be
held up as a model to students trying to escape rural primitivism. But
not all primitive pasts are alike; or, at least, all did not carry the same
cultural baggage in 1899. As I have discussed, New England represented America's "heritage," something everyone should embrace and
preserve as a source of value, whereas the black rural South was
expected to fade away in the wake of progress. As a didactic text in its
own right, the photo exhibit attempts to narrativize the process by
which African-Americans could supposedly become nonmarginal
Americans, fit for self-government, if they adopted the dominant New
England qua national narrative epitomized by *Snow-Bound*.

And yet, of course, throughout the nineteenth and early twentieth centuries the color line barred African-Americans from joining

even an imagined community of American middle-class readers. While lynch mobs and the courts patrolled the line with violence, genteel New Englanders did so more euphemistically, by celebrating a heritage that was by most definitions open only to those who could visibly assimilate. The discourses of the colonial revival helped to construct white New England as a location of structural advantage, representing it as the most authentic and valuable version of the American past. And clearly *Snow-Bound* was used to advance this master narrative. The photo, in its serial context, produces a horizon of expectations that reads *Snow-Bound* as part of an ideal to which all should aspire. Its function at the Paris Exhibition, like the function of the Whittier Homestead museum, was to produce a narrative that linked New England values with moral virtue and fitness for self-government. Ironically, the "party line" at Hampton (which not everybody agreed on, even then) was that African-Americans should not demand the vote too quickly; first, they needed to prove that they were capable of self-government. Equality, at Hampton, was not a right; it was something that had to be proven (over and over) with concrete evidence such at the photo of the *Snow-Bound* lesson. As the Hampton photos show, the ideal of whiteness was a powerful ideological force. Even if *Snow-Bound* questions New England hegemony, it was still used (at Hampton and elsewhere) to promote New England hegemony. Its meanings were determined by the institutions through which it circulated, and those institutions (the Whittier Homestead museum, the Hampton Institute) promoted specific readings rooted in nostalgia, nationalism, and normative whiteness.

So did *all* Whittier's early readers read *Snow-Bound* reductively, as a text that promoted New England hegemony? In closing, I want to look briefly at one more Hampton text. The Hampton Leaflets were a series of cheap paper leaflets, designed to offer lesson plans to African-American primary-school teachers in rural areas. The preface to one leaflet titled *American Authors' Birthdays* gives a sense of the conditions under which teachers worked:

> These programs are meant to be suggestive. The aim is to give to those teachers in the South whose salaries are too small to allow them to spend much money for books, and who do not have access to libraries, a "bowing acquaintance" with the author, so that their pupils may get from them a few of the best selections for programs and memory gems. It is supposed that the teachers have been saving clippings from newspapers and magazines to supplement the work outlined here.[43]

The authors, whose writings are arranged into programs meant to commemorate their birthdays, include Eugene Field, James Whitcomb Riley, Joel Chandler Harris, James Russell Lowell, Henry Wadsworth Longfellow, Booker T. Washington, Paul Laurence Dunbar, and John Greenleaf Whittier. The Whittier program includes standard "memory gems" such as "The Barefoot Boy" and "Barbara Frietche," as well as the Christmas hymn that Whittier wrote for the "contraband" scholars at St. Helena Island during the Civil War. It also contains a brief Whittier biography, written by the African-American educator Emily Harper Williams.[44] Williams notes that "Whittier's poetry falls into three classes, poems on religion, freedom, and country life. The latter are perhaps now the most popular . . . 'Snow-Bound' is the most faithful picture of our Northern winter that has yet been put into poetry." In *Snow-Bound* and in his other country poems, she asserts, Whittier "sang of the joys of childhood in the country and the beauty of love before which all are equal."[45] Did some teachers follow Williams's lead and teach *Snow-Bound* as a poem about equality? Did students feel included in, or excluded from, the past that the poem depicts? Such questions cannot be answered, because these rural primary-school students and teachers are silent: their opinions as readers were not recorded, or if they were recorded they were not saved in any of the archives that I have found. Their silence—the effacement of their readings and experiences—is perhaps also part of the story of American schoolroom poetry and its relationship to white privilege.

CHAPTER THREE

A Visit from St. Nicholas: *Pedagogy, Power, and Print Culture*

When poetry was taught in the classroom, its meanings and use-values were mediated by educational agendas. But what happened to school-room poetry in more commercial contexts? In 1872 the publishers of *Scribner's* asked Mary Mapes Dodge—who was already well known as a children's poet and as the author of *Hans Brinker; or, The Silver Skates*—to edit a new juvenile periodical, *St. Nicholas Magazine.* Dodge responded with an article for *Scribner's,* published anonymously under the title "Children's Magazines," that served as both a mani-festo and a brilliant piece of advance publicity for the venture. The essay begins with an image of mixed feelings, with fear on one plac-ard and desire on the other:

> Sometimes I feel like rushing through the world with two plac-ards—one held in my right hand, BEWARE OF CHILDREN'S MAGAZINES! the other flourished in my left, CHILD'S MAGA-ZINE WANTED! A good magazine for little ones was never so much needed, and such harm is done by nearly all that are published.[1]

Dodge was a successful editor in part because she could capture the zeitgeist, and this image of two placards allegorizes an anxiety com-mon among the producers and (adult) purchasers of children's mag-azines. On the one hand, children must enjoy reading, but, on the other hand, they must avoid the corrupting influence of pleasure. The contradiction is critical, because it marks the shifting role of pedagog-ical texts in American culture in the second half of the nineteenth cen-tury, getting at some fundamental questions: what does it mean to be pedagogical, and what, exactly, should pedagogical texts teach?

Dodge's manifesto cleverly unravels the connections between pleasure, peril, and virtue, with the startling (and, as we shall see, disingenuous) charge that didacticism harms children. Most chil-dren's magazines, her essay claims, are aimed at parents. They are full of "sermonizing," the "wearisome spinning out of facts," and the "rat-tling of the dry bones of history." In short, they are educational and moralistic, and this is not just dull but deleterious. These complaints seem to be aimed at the era's most popular and profitable magazine, the *Youth's Companion*; since 1821, the editors at that magazine had ensured that its contents were suitable for the whole family to read together, that forbidden pleasures (sex, alcohol, tobacco) were invisible in its pages and its advertising, and that the (Christian) moral worth of every feature was clear. By 1872 the *Youth's Companion* was less overtly evangelical, and less prone to the descriptions of youthful death that had filled its antebellum issues, but its values remained firm: excessive pleasure was deemed harmful, and even moderate pleasure (say, ice-skating) must lead directly to virtue (learn to share, or a fall through the ice is guaranteed). Dodge argued, by contrast, that a child's magazine should be a "pleasure-ground," where children can live "a brand-new, free life of their own for a little while, accepting acquaintances as they choose and turning their backs without ceremony on what does not concern them."[2] Rather than entering a traditionally quasi-parental relationship with its readers, the ideal children's magazine would offer them space for themselves.

But what does it mean for a child to be his or her "self"? The two early-nineteenth-century models, of children as dangerously willful or transcendentally innocent, were both out of date by the 1870s; instead, Dodge embraced a kind of pedagogical idealism, assuming that subjectivity emerged from taste—that "art" and "culture" expressed universal values that all children could and should appreciate. The most harmful aspect of most children's literature, Dodge asserts in "Children's Magazines," is not that it is constricting but that its didacticism renders it awkward and ugly: the cats are so poorly drawn that "the editors must purr for them," and the jokes are so "halt and lame" that readers grimace instead of laughing. Children benefit, she concludes, not from endless lessons but from beauty, and through beauty they can be steered in the direction of "truth":

> Doubtless a great deal of instruction and good moral teaching may be inculcated in the pages of a magazine, but it must be by hints dropped incidentally here and there; by a few brisk, hearty statements of the difference between right and wrong; a sharp, clean thrust at falsehood, a sunny recognition of truth, a gracious application of politeness, an unwilling glimpse of the odious doings of the uncharitable and the base. In a word, pleasant, breezy things may linger and turn themselves this way and that.[3]

Freedom, then, would not involve exploration (though to give her credit Dodge encouraged more intellectual inquiry than most children's editors) but rather the "sunny" and "polite" recognition of truth. It is tempting to conclude, then, that "harmful" pedagogical urges underwrote *St. Nicholas* from the outset, albeit garbed in Arnoldian sweetness and light rather than in sentimental Christianity. But the project of producing and managing children's pleasure is not so simple: children are not passive receptacles, and "quality" is not easy to promote or even to define. Dodge's choices as an editor—and especially her choices as an editor of poetry—reflect her position as a major arbiter of "quality" in later-nineteenth-century America, but they also reflect her position as one of the first modern marketers to children. Dodge was not just policing pleasure; she was also selling pleasure, and the stresses (again, rooted in fear and desire) of these incompatible editorial objectives led to a proliferation of poetic forms and ultimately to a reworking of the terms under which both poetry and childhood might be profitably enjoyed.

Lawrence Levine has described late-nineteenth-century America as a "world of strangers" in which cultural elites such as Henry James and Henry Adams—and, I will add, Dodge—saw their hegemony as members of old, established families threatened by America's shifting demographics. Both James Mapes, Dodge's father, and William Dodge, her husband, were members of the St. Nicholas Society, an elite organization reserved for the descendants of eighteenth-century New Yorkers. Dodge grew up in a rarefied atmosphere of books and art; her father was a prominent artist and editor who seemed to know (or to be tangentially related to) everyone who was anyone in mid-century New York. James Mapes's cultural capital was not matched by any significant financial capital; he was "ruined" early and often, and when Mary Mapes married William Dodge, her father drew his son-in-law into ill-advised investment schemes. In 1858, when Mary was a twenty-seven-year-old mother of two, her husband William drowned in an apparent suicide, distraught over his finances. Like many prominent nineteenth-century women, she started her writing and editing career because she needed the money, and, as an editor, she was determined to make the magazine profitable as well as culturally enriching. The two goals were often compatible; as one little boy, Willie Reynolds, wrote to *St. Nicholas*, "The first piece I ever spoke at a Sabbath-School concert was selected from *St. Nicholas*, called 'A Cloud Picture.'" Willie went on to explain that his father would continue to buy him the magazine because "My papa says he will do anything in his power to improve my mind, he is so anxious to have me educated."[4]

Education in the later nineteenth century, as I have discussed elsewhere and as Willie's activities suggest, involved acquiring the trappings of "culture," especially forms of culture (such as the poem "A

Cloud Picture") that could be performed or displayed. Taking a cue from Raymond Williams, Levine traces the definition of "culture" as it evolved in the period between 1870 and 1914, showing how the term became synonymous with a Weberian "status order" that ratified certain cultural forms (opera, poetry) as "higher," "purer," and "truer" than others (vaudeville, dime novels). Cultural elites had their own status to protect, and, while they sometimes protected it by keeping "others" wholly at bay (as the St. Nicholas Society did), an evangelical wing also emerged that sought charitably to extend the virtues of culture—as defined by upper-middle-class easterners—to all.[5] Levine points out that American magazines in particular promoted the move toward order and hierarchy that created highbrow and lowbrow categories. This is certainly true of *Scribner's*, *St. Nicholas*'s "parent" magazine until 1881, and of its successor, the *Century*. As the literary historian Arthur John puts it, the editors Josiah Gilbert Holland, of *Scribner's*, and Richard Watson Gilder, of the *Century*, hoped that "the American middle class, if sufficiently exposed to the traditional culture and traditional values that supposedly embodied ideal standards, would move to a higher plane of appreciation for literature and art, would impose morality on American public life, and would create a just, ordered, and gracious society."[6]

Among examples of ideality, Gilder and Holland were united in their admiration for poets as the "custodians of noble thought" who, "in the midst of a sordid world are trying to keep alive the harshly blown-upon and flickering flame of the ideal."[7] As an editor, Dodge used poetry to promote "the ideal," to invent American traditions that could be learned and defended by children (traditions that reflected the magazine's middle-class values), and to create a hierarchy of values. Between 1873 and 1904, the period when Dodge served as editor, *St. Nicholas* published a significant amount of original poetry by most of the major poets of the later nineteenth and earlier twentieth centuries except Whitman: Henry Wadsworth Longfellow, John Greenleaf Whittier, William Cullen Bryant, Oliver Wendell Holmes, Harriet Spofford, Emily Dickinson, Oliver Hereford, Lucy Larcom, Sarah Orne Jewett, Thomas Wentworth Higginson, Ella Wheeler Wilcox, Palmer Cox, Edith Thompson, Laura Richards, Gelett Burgess, Rose Terry Cooke, Celia Thaxter, and many others. Dodge's correspondence reveals a combination of charm and aggression as she cultivates her connections, but recruiting poets for the magazine was made easier by its competitive pay rates (on par with *Scribner's*, and much better than the *Youth's Companion*) and by its quickly established reputation as the "best" American children's magazine ever published—a reputation that it has largely sustained

[71]

among critics and historians. Whittier declared it "the best children's periodical in the world," and Charles Dudley Warner wrote (in a comment that reveals the magazine's ideological slant), "It has been made level with the comprehension of children, and yet it is a continual educator of their taste, and of their honor and courage. I do not see how it can be made any better, and if the children don't like it, I think it is time to begin to change the kind of children in this country."[8]

The very idea of "quality," of being "the best," relied on standards that the magazine not only met but also helped to invent. As with so many institutions in the later nineteenth century, *St. Nicholas* relied on compartmentalization and hierarchy to educate children's tastes. The table of contents developed a three-tier system for poetry, in which pieces were classed as either "poems" (important, valuable, virtuous), "verses" (less important, less valuable, less virtuous), or "jingles" (not important, not valuable, not virtuous). This enabled lofty ideals (as expressed by, say, Bryant) to coexist with silly animal rhymes or mild ethnic humor—while giving readers clues about how to "read" different kinds of poetry, not just for its contents but also for its varying value as symbolic capital.

To understand how this poetic hierarchy worked (and I will argue that it worked in unexpected ways), it is useful first to picture the disciplinary space of the magazine as a whole, and how it registered the late-nineteenth-century experience of childhood as a compartmentalized phase of life. By way of illustration, we might consider the place of *St. Nicholas* at the Children's Building, at the 1893 World Columbian Exposition in Chicago. As Clara Doty Bates describes it to *St. Nicholas* readers, the Children's Building was conceived by a woman who thought "if men were to have stately and magnificent structures, and women were to have a white palace devoted to their work and to their comfort, then children might have their own building, too." Like Dodge's imagined readers, who just want "a brand-new, free life of their own," these children are given a place apart from adults, a utopia divided into departments that are in turn divided by both function and age of children. The lowest floor has a "crèche," a day-care facility for small children, and an "assembly room" for older children, in which "there will also be dramatic, literary, and musical entertainment carefully adapted to suit the intelligence of varying ages." On the second floor are demonstration schools, featuring Indians (in one room) and deaf-mutes (in another), and also a library, featuring reading materials including *St. Nicholas*. Finally, on the roof, there is a playground: "This is a lovely garden, all inclosed with a wire screen for safety. It is full of flowers and plants, and live birds are flying about in perfect freedom. Toys of all nations are on exhibit here, from the crude child-trinket of the savage to the talking, walking, working playthings of France. And they are not for show, merely, but for the children to play with."[9]

It is appropriate that *St. Nicholas* should have been featured in the Children's Building, because the building, with its birds "flying about in perfect freedom," yet "all inclosed with a wire screen for safety," can be seen as a structural allegory of the magazine, replete with the energy that is so often generated by cultural contradictions. From the first, *St. Nicholas* was divided into departments and sections, often spatialized, such as the Letter Box or the Treasure-Box of Literature. Different sections were targeted at different age groups, so that the section For Very Little Folks featured, for instance, "Three Little Kittens" in large type, while older children (we would call them teenagers) could read, say, serialized chapters of Twain's *Tom Sawyer Abroad*. These divisions echo both the subdivided realm of the world's fair and also the demographically targeted areas of that close cousin to world's-fair pavilions, the department store. If we follow the line of thought made famous by Foucault, we might conclude that compartmentalization in *St. Nicholas* was a hyperarticulation of control technologies: even children's play must be discussed, described, and regulated. An analysis of its prose features has caused R. Gordon Kelly to conclude that the magazine was essentially conservative. He argues that its plots champion tradition over commercial novelty, sincerity over artifice, and parental authority over youthful impetuousness: "The apparent changes taking place with such rapidity in American society during the 1870s and 1880s did not imply the obsolescence of the parental definition of things. Their world remained subjectively plausible within the formulas of children's fiction."[10] But if the "parental definition of things" remained strong in the magazine's fiction, its destabilization was evident in the poetry.

Even if we agree that the magazine's social message was mostly conservative, the multiple departments and categories of poetry in *St. Nicholas* set a number of competing discourses in motion, not all of which supported "the parental definition of things," or even the definition of things advanced by the magazine's own editor. In his study of recreation and play in the 1890s, Bill Brown has developed the idea of a "material unconscious" that "names literature's repository of disparate and fragmentary, unevenly developed, even contradictory images" that are not part of a text's "master narrative." Brown asserts that leaving such contradictory images unexplored "amounts to recirculating the dominant cultural memory."[11] While poetry is not precisely material culture (although, as we shall see with the Brownies, it can shade into material culture), its multiform presence in *St.*

Nicholas can perhaps be understood as performing unconscious functions alongside the conscious "master narratives" of the prose pieces. That is, poems, verses, and jingles worked as a repository of disparate images and aims that did indeed register and contribute to the "changes taking place with such rapidity" in the Gilded Age.

NOBLE POEMS, NOBLE READERS

Prestigious names legitimated *St. Nicholas* from its very first issue, which opened with a new William Cullen Bryant translation of "The Woodman and the Sandal-Tree," "from the Spanish." In a conventional, didactic form recognizable from "To a Waterfowl" (a poem written a half century earlier that would have been familiar to child readers and their parents), the poem expresses both tremendous ambition and spiritual (but not precisely religious) yearning:

> Beside a sandal-tree a woodman stood
> > And swung the axe, and, as the strokes were laid
> Upon the fragrant trunk, the generous wood,
> > With its own sweets, perfumed the cruel blade.
> Go, then, and do the like; a soul endued
> > With light from heaven, a nature pure and great,
> Will place its highest bliss in doing good,
> > And good for evil give, and love for hate.[12]

The Arnoldian principles of "sweetness" and "light" are explicit in the poem. Unlike Bryant's "To a Waterfowl," in this poem however, in this poem the soul, rather than the "Power" behind the soul, is the most potent force. The waterfowl is guided by an unseen hand, but the tree in this poem has its "own sweets" and is energized by the frontier spirit, however "cruel," of the woodsman. Despite the poem's reference to heaven, the message is secular: "Go, then," and do good in *this world*. The poem ends with an image of moral exchange; it is as much about social responsibility as about the individual soul.

Bryant's placement at the beginning of the first issue authorized the magazine in several important ways. He was the most culturally conservative of the schoolroom poets, dedicated to what he saw as the "purity" of the American language against the "vulgarity" of slang and colloquialism. As an editor in antebellum New York City, he had adamantly connected language use with virtue, drawing on the eighteenth century's esteem for gentlemanly rhetoric but also anticipating the postbellum "sacralization of culture." He was a moral, but not a religious, leader; as Brander Matthews put it in a later profile for

St. Nicholas, "He did nothing mean in literature or in life, nothing small, nothing unworthy; his poems, free of shams and gaudy conceits . . . are sustained nearly always at the same highest level."[13] He was thus the perfect vehicle to express the magazine's ambitions, to achieve "a nature pure and great" that took its mandate of constructing children's subjectivities—building their character, as Dodge would put it—seriously.

St. Nicholas relentlessly promoted "classic" American authors, helping to invent them as a tradition in the latter part of the century. Articles appeared regularly lionizing Bryant, describing Whittier's boyhood home from *Snow-Bound,* and even soliciting donations from American schoolchildren for the founding of a memorial garden for Longfellow.[14] While they were alive (all were elderly by 1873), these poets were lobbied (and handsomely paid) for new work or translations. A self-perpetuating cycle developed, in which the magazine promoted the moral and literary excellence of the schoolroom poets, while the presence of the poets' names promoted the moral and literary excellence of *St. Nicholas.* The tradition represented by the schoolroom poets was literary, not folk; it was on the "highest level," not vulgar or commonplace; and it was theoretically open to all children, through reading and recitation, just like the Longfellow memorial garden that they (the children of America, as addressed by *St. Nicholas*) helped to fund. I have discussed the troubling limitations of the schoolroom poets' hegemony elsewhere: obviously, their white, male, eastern, literary selves were models of impossibility, rather than possibility, to many children whose lives and selves could not mirror this narrow vision of the democratic ideal. But this hegemony was itself limited in magazines as it was not in actual schoolrooms, because magazines were driven by the forces of the marketplace.

Although her advocacy for American authors never wavered, Dodge's editorial tone and choices do register the difficulty of getting children excited about poets who were closely associated with schoolrooms. In 1880 she launched the Treasure-Box of Literature section, in which established gems of British and American literature, such as Longfellow's "Skeleton in Armor," were reprinted in appealing and sometimes condensed form. Dodge gingerly justified the Treasure-Box to her young readers before its first appearance:

> Gifted men and women are the spokespeople of all the rest. They write, they paint, they act, or they live the best and truest things that are in us all, but which they alone can express fitly . . . A human soul, however generous or poetic it may be,

[75]

must recognize a thought before it welcomes it; and this is one great reason why we all required education: so that we may recognize the things, deeds, and thoughts that are to delight and elevate us, and lead us in brotherhood to the highest. Any little boy or girl may be one with the world in this upward march.[15]

This passage perhaps could have been predicted, rehearsing as it does the magazine's ideology of moral elevation through aesthetic appreciation. But Dodge's further justification is more surprising:

But, beyond all this, we want to make you better acquainted with us grown folk. Children and their elders, in spite of near relationships and happy home-ties, are too apt to be ignorant in regard to each other. Though familiar enough in some ways, they are, in others, too far apart. The children need to know how their elders really feel, just as the grown folk need to understand better the secret workings of the eager, long-wandering spirits that animate their troublesome and dearly loved boys and girls.[16]

If a Treasure-Box poet such as Longfellow was a children's poet, he was a specific kind of children's poet who could draw young and old together through a common body of familiar texts. This, as I have argued elsewhere, was part of Longfellow's appeal: his accessible verses created an imagined community of readers. He was not the private property of adults or children but rather the public common ground of all middle-class Americans.

In the context of *St. Nicholas,* the emphasis must be on "middle-class" rather than "Americans": the Treasure-Box as a whole is cosmopolitan, not nationalistic; it assumes that true quality can transcend national borders. And yet the border that remains significant and subject defining is the border between youth and age. What is remarkable in Dodge's defense of literature (apart from its slightly defensive tone) is her anxiety about the distance between adults and children—a distance that registers a change in reading practices, from family-centered sentimental reading aloud to the private reading of age-targeted texts by individual family members. As a "children's pleasure-ground" consisting mainly of explicitly children's literature, *St. Nicholas* was, by and large, contributing to this split between elders and children, and the Treasure-Box was offered as an antidote to this compartmentalization—albeit, a neatly spatialized and compartmentalized antidote that children were instructed to "open" only if it pleased them.

Although Dodge introduced the Treasure-Box as a free offering, her editorial voice anxiously frames each selection, emphasizing its value, its status as a "treasure," so that, by way of introduction to Bryant's "The Planting of the Apple-Tree," Dodge asserts, "Life is not all conflict and excitement, young friends;—indeed, to many of us it seems often commonplace and dull." But, she counters, to be bored by something is often to misinterpret its importance:

> Many a deed that seems trivial may be followed by great results; and no one can teach us this lesson better, or in sweeter words, that the great American poet, Bryant, whose songs, written out of a calm, thoughtful life, have wrought vast and far-reaching good in the world. You will admire more and more, as you grow older, the noble poems of this great and good man.[17]

Surely the "schoolroom poets" had no stronger advocate than Dodge. And yet the Treasure-Box was figured as a box with a lid, and its contents were elevated above, and metaphorically closed off from, the other selections in the magazine; the treasures were marked as "noble" and therefore, as Dodge seems to have recognized, potentially boring. Despite or because of its extreme veneration, its "sacralization" of classic texts, the Treasure-Box was unpopular with child readers and was allowed to lapse after 1882: it had lasted less than two years.

Why did the Treasure-Box fail, if it represented the magazine's aspirations so well? Above all, Dodge had to keep her readers entertained. As Patricia Meyer Spacks has argued, boredom is not a transhistorical experience but one that is socially constructed, rooted in social expectations, so that in the mid-nineteenth century it was assumed that bored readers (even children) needed to adjust their level of disciplined engagement, whereas by the early twentieth century a bored reader was expected simply to find something less boring to read.[18] In other words, the obligation to be "interesting" had transferred from the reader to the text. The anxieties generated by this shift are present in Dodge's advocacy of Bryant's "Planting of the Apple Tree": Dodge places the burden of generating interest onto the reader but comes close to admitting the poem's dullness while pressing for its worthiness. Moreover, as a commercial venture, *St. Nicholas* could not afford to advocate the earlier view that virtuous readers cannot be bored by virtuous texts; the magazine, from its earliest conception in "Children's Magazines," was dedicated to the more modern, emerging proposition that boredom is generated not by readers but by texts; an editor "must give just what the child demands."[19]

As I have argued throughout this study, poetry was an integral part of many middle-class people's daily lives in the later nineteenth century. It is thus paradoxical that, compared with schoolroom poetry, which sparked performances, or newspaper poetry, which was often funny or topical, much of the upper-middlebrow adult magazine verse of the period was boring, even to readers and editors at the time. While this is a sweeping generalization that might be partially challenged by the richness of recent anthologies such as John Hollander's *American Poetry: The Nineteenth Century*, it remains true that readers at the time complained that American poetry lacked dynamism: "Every singer takes his net and chases and butterfly . . . There are none climbing up to the eagle's eyrie."[20] Issues of the *Century* from the 1880s and 1890s are filled with vague poems about birds and monuments; a poem by Richard Watson Gilder, the *Century*'s editor, a *St. Nicholas* cofounder, and a sometime *St. Nicholas* contributor, can serve to illustrate the aspirations and the limits of poetry as most adult magazine poets (with some notable exceptions) conceived it in the later nineteenth century:

> The poet's day is different from another,
> Though he doth count each man his own heart's brother.
> So crystal-clear the air that he looks through
> It gives each color an intenser hue;
> Each bush doth burn, and every flower flame,
> The stars are sighing; silence breathes a name;
> The world wherein he wanders, dreams and sings
> Thrills with the beating of invisible wings,
> And all day long he hears from hidden birds
> The multitudinous pour of musicked words.[21]

As an *ars poetica* Gilder's verse offers its readers an ideal portrait of an ideal poet, necessarily remote from the grubby specifics of daily life (and from the grubby realist fiction that the *Century* was beginning to publish).

The specifically juvenile audience of *St. Nicholas*, though, put pressure on Dodge to think more imaginatively about how poetry might work and what it might do for readers besides offering them lofty sentiments. Ultimately, the schoolroom poets operated as figureheads in *St. Nicholas*, representing an "ideal," a "master narrative" of authority and value. But this narrative was not necessarily reinforced by Dodge's other verse selections, which aimed to please as much as to instruct. Indeed, the effect of demarcating different types of rhymes (poems, verses, jingles) was to set up a dialectic, whereby the value of elite poems was supported but also sometimes undermined by less-serious verses and jingles. The magazine's focus on child readers and its editorial compartmentalizing implicitly floated a set of questions that magazines for adults did not necessarily have to confront. Must poetry celebrate "the ideal" in order to be "good"? What if different kinds of poems are "good" for different people, at different stages in their development or at different historical moments? What is the relationship between a poem and its illustrations? What is the relationship between a poem and its readers? What are children's desires, and how can poetry satisfy them?

Attempts to negotiate these questions emerge in the light verses and jingles that appeared in the metaphorical (and sometimes the literal) margins of the magazine. From 1873 to 1905, when Dodge died, famous poets such as Whittier were given pride of place, and their upcoming poems were heavily promoted. But the most prolific and popular contributors to *St. Nicholas* were Dodge herself, who wrote a majority of the unsigned verses, sometimes under the pseudonym Joel Stacy; Laura E. Richards (especially in the 1870s and 1880s); Palmer Cox (1880s); Carolyn Wells (1890s); and Gellet Burgess (1890s). These poets worked in three genres that emerged as especially important between 1872 and 1905: nursery rhymes, nonsense, and illustrated verses. As the century waned, more space was given to light verse and less to serious poetry, and the light verse itself became more carefully crafted. In these pieces, we can find something rare among new works in the later nineteenth century: we can find poetry that addresses (while constructing) the immediate anxieties and desires of its readers, drawing on older traditions not to parrot them but to make them new. We can also find strains of a commercial aesthetic that offers a patchy but persistent counterdiscourse to the assumption that poetry must be universally "true" to be "good." We even get a hint of a much more radical idea: that among children, a poem need not be "good" to be "good," if by "good" we mean "loved" or "useful" or "memorable." Instead, to be "good," a poem must be simply amusing—and must, at all costs, avoid being boring. This registers a changing horizon of expectations that undercut the Treasure-Box of Literature.

PLUCKING MOTHER GOOSE

Starting with the earliest issues of *St. Nicholas* and continuing through the turn of the century, nursery rhymes appeared, both in their traditional forms (but with new illustrations) and in new permutations. Nursery rhymes have, of course, a long history as children's literature, and they have a history of straddling the line between oral ("folk") and written ("commercial") culture. Indeed, the first secular children's publisher, John Newbery, was circulating a collection of "the most Celebrated Songs and Lullabies of the good old Nurses," titled *Mother Goose's Melody,* as early as 1765. This British book depicts an old nurse spinning by a fireside as she recounts rhymes. The commercial circulation of nursery rhymes, then, is as old as children's publishing itself, although before the Civil War the vast majority of children's rhymes printed in America (as opposed to Britain, where, curiously, rhymes were less preachy) were didactic along the lines of "Mary's Lamb." What was new and remarkable, however, was the irreverent way in which *St. Nicholas* authors "played" with familiar texts, rewriting and reframing them to do more immediate cultural work.

In the anonymous Miss Muffet that appeared in successive issues from 1875 to 1876, ethnic children (an Eskimo, an Irish lass) are scared away from their food; for instance, in "Miss Muffet No. IV," a Chinese girl is depicted:

> Little Peeky-Wang-Fu, with her chopsticks so new,
>   Sat eating her luncheon of rice,
> When a rat running by
> On the rice cast his eye,
>   And Peeky ran off in a trice.[22]

By reframing "Miss Muffet" in terms of ethnicity, the poem takes on the immediacy of what Dodge called "Our Country To-Day." Dodge, who published (and probably wrote) the Miss Muffet series, had already had a rousing success with her dialectal sketch "Mrs. Maloney on the Chinese Question," which the actress Charlotte Cushman made famous as a comedic performance piece. Peeky-Wang-Fu, then, is not just a revised Mother Goose character; she is part of a national debate about immigration and foreign workers that led to legislation such as the Chinese Exclusion Act of 1880. But "Miss Muffet IV" is not just about exclusion. Like much mass-cultural ethnic humor, the lessons that it teaches are more ambivalent than that. The poem (like all of the poems in the Miss Muffet series) relies on its readers' common knowledge of nursery rhymes to instill "common knowledge" about other children, implying that children of all national origins can be subjects bound by the laws of the nursery-rhyme genre.

It assumes, in other words, that the cultural materials of childhood—as epitomized by the image of St. Nicholas (or *St. Nicholas*) traveling all over the world—are exportable and potentially universal. This is, of course, a fantasy generated from the dominant position of the English-speaking, middle-class American child. Indeed, the familiarity of the original Miss Muffet underscores the foreignness of Peeky-Wang-Fu. Nevertheless, it is a fantasy of inclusion, and a common one in *St. Nicholas,* relying on the crucial assumption that *age marks the body even more definitively than nationality.* Every seven-year-old in the world, from Peeky-Wang-Fu to Little Biddy O'Toole, is a potential Miss Muffet and a potential peer. Although Dodge did not live to experience the phenomenon of Walt Disney's "It's a Small World," she was one of the first to introduce its underlying ideology, that children are the same the world over, and that this sameness is to be promoted and celebrated—especially through the distribution of shared commodities. It is no accident that this idea emerged during America's first age of international imperial expansion, but it is also true that this ideology resulted in a focus on other children and other cultures that was unmatched by earlier children's magazines.

By the 1880s, as the historian Howard Chudacoff has argued, graded public schools and the field of pediatric medicine were convincing middle-class Americans that intellectual and physiological traits were less a matter of class, character, or ethnicity and more a matter of mental and physical age.[23] This intensification of age norms was also, of course, a boon to commercial writer-editors like Dodge, who could tailor their verses to age-graded peer groups while also helping to form and maintain such groups. The notion of a universal peer culture (often based quite explicitly on a "universal" desire of children for toys) was reinforced by nonfiction articles on children of other cultures, such as Alice Donlevy's "East Indian Toys," which stresses how much East Indian girls love their dolls.[24] Nursery rhymes in *St. Nicholas,* then, functioned ambivalently. On the one hand, their generic familiarity offered a supposed point of commonality to all children (of all cultures and generations). And yet, on the other hand, these same nursery rhymes addressed the specific consuming desires and anxieties of late-nineteenth-century American middle-class children, giving them something to laugh about together.

But the emergence of age-graded peer culture required more than just topical nursery rhymes; it was also very important that these rhymes retain some of their traditional play-based functions in the daily lives of children. This led to peculiar hybridizations of tradition and commercial materials. The February 1876 *St. Nicholas* featured a "Mother Goose Pantomime" that showed children how to organize a performance of "The Rats and the Mice," complete with suggested costumes, props, and stage directions. In this traditional nursery rhyme, a bachelor is overrun with rats and mice, so he goes to London to "fetch a wife." In the *St. Nicholas* version, however, the whole rhyme is to be sung by a "concealed singer" to the tune of "Zip Coon," a popular minstrel tune. This grafting of minstrelsy onto a nursery rhyme is not surprising; minstrel shows were already being performed in the nursery by a bevy of mechanical toys, such as the miniature steamboat, recommended in the January 1874 issue of *St. Nicholas,* which featured a "colored gentleman" on top: "Fire up the engine and he has to dance, whether he wants to or not."[25]

Bill Brown has argued that both toys (such as the steam-engine dancer) and literary forms (such as the fairy tale or the nursery rhyme) could stage versions of a conflict that was already developing in the 1870s between premodern forms of life (nursery rhymes, country dancing) and modern mass culture ("pop" music, magazine verses, mechanized toys). The stakes, Brown suggests, pitted ruralist traditions against the worldly, urbane materiality of the consumer marketplace.[26] The "Zip Coon" version of "The Rats and the Mice" manages the gap between the premodern and the modern, between tradition and novelty, by hybridizing old and new cultural forms. Children performing this piece could stage an apparently independent and localized production of a traditional rhyme that was nonetheless underwritten by the text of a national magazine and by the tune of a popular song. And, in the process, up-to-date manifestations of national discourses, such as the particular racism of the Jim Crow era, could seep into traditional forms and seem as old and inevitable as a nursery rhyme.

As Dodge implicitly understood, her "troops" were not willing simply to identify with timeless images of childhood; they wanted not just their "own magazine" but their own childhood, rooted not just in timeless nature and age-old rhymes but also in the popular and material culture of the postbellum American middle classes. When Dodge asserted that children wanted their own magazine, she did not mean that children wanted to produce it themselves, like the March sisters' "Pickwick Portfolio" in *Little Women,* but rather that they wanted to buy it, or at least to consume it, themselves. This desire for what we might call purchasable "peer historicity" was new, and it was generated in part by the mass-educational and mass-marketing systems that created an obsolescent children's public sphere, a place where "Miss Muffet," "Zip Coon," St. Nicholas, and *St. Nicholas* could circulate and interpenetrate.

To call this emerging mass-cultural pleasure ground a "public sphere" is to stretch the meaning of the term almost to the breaking point; certainly, this sphere was too heavily commercialized to be a disinterested part of "civil society." In an essay titled "The Public Sphere of Children," Oskar Negt and Alexander Kluge have distinguished between what they see as a genuine children's public sphere, which would be self-organized, self-regulated, and truly autonomous, and the fragmentary, ghettoized "enclaves" of middle-class childhood that, in their view, "faithfully mirror the bourgeois public sphere."[27] From a utopian point of view, *St. Nicholas* was never and could never be a "genuine" children's public sphere. But to assume, therefore, that it simply "mirror[ed] the bourgeois public sphere" is to assume that later-nineteenth-century America (even the white, middle-class, *St. Nicholas*–reading part of it) comprised one unified, visible culture that *could* be mirrored; instead, as I have been arguing, children's culture was a hybrid response to tensions within the culture—tensions that pitted modernity against nostalgic antimodernism, propriety against pleasure, and (increasingly) children against their parents. In other words, the middle class was not coherent: it was both family-oriented and peer-oriented, tradition inventing and innovative, nostalgic and topical.

St. Nicholas enabled children to become visible to themselves as individuals and as a distinct group, linked by both the oral residue of nursery rhymes and the material detritus of contemporary advertising. But children did not function simply as faithful reflections of the adult world. Often, they wrote in to the Letter Box to share, with other readers, their playful responses to emergent mass-cultural forms. For example, one young "Helen M." wrote in 1889 to explain how she made a paper-muslin book out of advertising cards (including numbers of "darky cards"), with the pictures cut out and repasted to illustrate rhymes like "One, Two, Buckle My Shoe." Helen concludes:

> I named it "Pluckings from Mother Goose, by One of her Goslings," and I dedicated it to my sister Nan, and her large darky doll, Topsy. . . . I would like to know whether any one else has tried a Mother Goose scrapbook, and with what success.[28]

While this little girl has clearly metabolized the casual racism that pervaded the American culture of the period (as evidenced also by the cast-iron steam engine discussed above), she disregards the commercial function of these "darky" images, transforming them from instrumental sales ploys into idiosyncratic illustrations. Moreover, she takes personal credit and pride in herself as the "author" of this transformation.

Helen's creative work with advertising cards and Mother Goose mimics (without precisely mirroring) the kind of work that was beginning to dominate the days of many middle-class women—namely, shopping. As William Leach has pointed out, the new consumer culture (department stores, catalogues) of the Gilded Age gave women a sense of power, as their choices multiplied and as these choices were seen to represent the women themselves: their individual tastes, their resourcefulness, and their public "authority."[29] But if selecting, cutting, and pasting advertising cards gave children like Helen a sense of personal power, this power was also explicitly social and explicitly public: in her letter, Helen expresses the urge to find other children engaged in the same activity and to connect with these newfound peers (peers who share a knowledge of both traditional rhymes and contemporary advertising cards) via the spatialized *St. Nicholas* Letter Box. We might recognize, here, a "peer culture" forming not on the village level but on the national level— a culture that depends on the signifying systems of nursery rhyming and of commercial advertising but that does not always play by the rules of either system.

The peer culture that was developing through *St. Nicholas* had, like women's department- store culture, an ambivalent (if ultimately financially dependent) relationship to patriarchal authority figures (Bryant) and the ideality that they represented. Antebellum magazines such as the *Youth's Companion* had been aimed at parents as well as children; since 1823, the magazine had billed itself as "a family paper, devoted to piety, morality, brotherly love—no sectarianism, no controversy."[30]

By contrast, the postbellum figure of St. Nicholas himself (as revised by the illustrator Thomas Nast, Dodge, and Wanamaker's Department Store) is not precisely a "youth's companion": he delivers the goods, and then he gets out of the way. The magazine's choice of name brilliantly reinforced the ambiguous authority-figure status of its editor. By 1873, the interpenetration of tradition and commerce had resulted in the emergence of St. Nicholas, or Santa Claus, as a rallying-point for nineteenth-century children. In Clement Moore's seminal 1823 poem, "A Visit From St. Nicholas" (which was reprinted, perhaps inevitably, in *St Nicholas)*, St. Nicholas is divorced from his earlier role as a religious disciplinarian. He carries no switch or lump of coal; instead, he "looks like a peddler just opening his pack," preparing to instigate the secularization and commercialization of Christmas.[31] By the later 1860s, when Nast transformed him from a folkloric and faintly sinister imp into a benevolent patriarch, St. Nicholas was becoming the chief symbolic underwriter of children's material culture. Although he was sometimes called "Father Christmas," St. Nicholas was not precisely a father figure. External to the family, he was part of an emerging mass-cultural public sphere, generating a "public" composed of middle-class children that he supposedly visited in an uncannily inclusive journey through the sky each Christmas. And, like St. Nicholas, Dodge related to child readers through an editorial voice that, while structurally authoritative, spoke to children's desires as much as to adults' fears.

By calling the new magazine *St. Nicholas*, Dodge was able to use the common currency of Santa Claus to draw an explicit analogy. In her opening letter to child readers of the magazine's first issue, she points out that both St. Nicholas and *St. Nicholas* are "fair and square," visiting children regularly and bringing not disciplinary measures but material treasures. Reinforced by children's preexisting, extrafamilial relationship to the iconic figure of St. Nicholas, Dodge was also able to address her readers as a cohesive public, making them visible to themselves: "DEAR GIRL AND BOY—No, there are more! Here they come! Near by, far off, everywhere, we can see them—coming by dozens, hundreds, thousands, troops upon troops, and all pressing closer and closer."[32] The presumably solitary act of reading a new periodical was transformed into a spatialized event (like a visit from St. Nicholas) taking place at a specific moment and involving a specific cohort of children who press "closer and closer" as they troop to their brand-new magazine. They are drawn to the magazine, but this also draws them close to one another.

In her many letters to her readers, Dodge's voice recalls Richard Brodhead's notion of "disciplinary intimacy," the new approach to education, through love and "gentle bonds," that had emerged concurrently with antebellum sentimental culture. But Dodge's disciplinary measures vary slightly from the sentimental model because they are not domestic. Her voice, rather, might be seen as practicing a new form of "disciplinary publicity," in which both desire and fear are routed, not through family bonds of affection, but through national, generational bonds of consumption. The "troops" of children "pressing closer and closer" are linked through the act of buying and reading the magazine. The shift from disciplinary intimacy to disciplinary publicity is not merely a shift in emphasis or audience; with it comes, I think, a shift in aims. While earlier children's editors sought to discipline children by speaking as surrogate parents, teaching them (albeit lovingly) to pray and obey, Dodge's voice is a public voice, teaching children to be public citizens, members of a middle class defined less by individual family values than by the "ideal" values of the magazine.

And yet, in *St. Nicholas*, although the prose is full of covert lessons (more frequently about propriety and sportsmanship than about morals per se), Dodge as editor also allows for a certain conspiratorial "naughtiness." An example can be drawn from a nearly sacred children's text. Already by the 1880s, Sarah Josepha Hale's "Mary's Lamb" was one of the best-known rhymes in English. In 1830, when Hale wrote it, animal poems in American children's magazines fell into two categories: either they were allegorical morality tales or they preached kindness to animals. "Mary's Lamb" falls into the latter category, ending with a teacher's voice informing "eager children" (in four lines that have generally dropped from the oral version):

> And you each gentle animal
> In confidence may bind,
> And make it follow at your call,
> If you are always kind.[33]

In 1884 a Letter Box contributor—relying on the widespread familiarity of the poem—sent illustrations of three lines from "Mary's Lamb." In the first sketch, Mary is dragging a large, reluctant ram by a chain; in the second sketch, meant to illustrate "And so the teacher put him out," the ram is butting into the teacher, who is airborne, with his spectacles flying off as he sails out the door.

The extraordinary thing is not that a child drew such sketches but that *St. Nicholas* published them, thus parodying not just pedagogical poetry but also the pedagogue himself. As reimagined in the sketch, "Mary's Lamb" silences the lecturing voice of the teacher (who is not quoted) and becomes more closely aligned with the children, who cluster as peers in the background watching their teacher being ousted. And this peer clustering does not rely just on the immediate solidarity produced when a teacher is charged by a lamb, or when a funny drawing is surreptitiously passed around a schoolroom. Through its appearance in *St. Nicholas*, the joke generated a larger public, composed of schoolchildren from New York to California who dreamed the same anarchical dream of undermining school authorities.[34] If the public schools were functioning, by 1884, as part of an ideological state apparatus, a way to produce obedient citizens, then images like that of the rampaging lamb put pressure on this apparatus, signaling an emerging tension: on the one hand, the "free market" depended on authoritative institutions such as the school and the family to support it, but, on the other hand, the products of that market—*St. Nicholas* for example—catered to children's desire to lead "a brand-new, free life of their own for a little while," beyond the reach of all disciplinary measures. The fantasy of rebellion was built into *St. Nicholas*, and this surely contributed to its popularity with children.

St. Nicholas: *Pedagogy, Power, and Print Culture*

LAURA RICHARDS'S NONSENSE

If the tensions between the constraints of middle-class childhood (manners, morals, school, parents) and the laissez-faire dictates of mass culture could not be resolved, they were nonetheless repeatedly replayed, and provisionally managed, in the light verse of the period. Nonsense did not commonly appear in American children's magazines until the 1870s. But its emergence in the pages of *St. Nicholas* makes perfect sense, because the basic conventions of the nonsense tradition—animate objects, amoral activity, and humor—were well suited to the postbellum task of making space for children's pleasure while also managing that space.[35] It is not surprising, then, that the poetry in *St. Nicholas* could evolve or devolve into nonsense in its drive for novelty.

One of the most frequently published poets in the early issues of *St. Nicholas*, besides Dodge herself, was the "nonsense" writer Laura Richards. Richards was the daughter of Julia Ward Howe, author of "The Battle Hymn of the Republic"—a biographical tidbit that is worth mentioning because it marks, almost too neatly, how the market for poetry had changed in the decades following the Civil War. Howe's lyric rests on the assumption of a divinely inspired, mystical "union" of American subjects. Like the older and more traditional American magazine *Youth's Companion*, "The Battle Hymn of the Republic" spoke to young and old in a tone of high moral seriousness. Richards's lyrics, by contrast, catered to a public that had been demographically split: children read Richards's "The King of the Hobbledy-Goblins" in *St. Nicholas*, while their parents read poems such as Dodge's "The Two Mysteries" in *Scribner's*, and instead of identifying with the moral values of their elders, children were encouraged to "play" with, and even to question, those values.

This new America, composed of multiple publics, required new lyrics, but Richards did not experiment with formal modernity as Emily Dickinson did; instead, she reworked the nursery-rhyme form, producing poems such as "The Owl, the Eel, and the Warming-Pan," which appeared in the August 1876 *St. Nicholas*:

> The owl and the eel and the warming-pan,
> They went to call on the soap-fat man.
> The soap-fat man he was not within;
> He'd gone for a ride on his rolling-pin;
> So they all came back by way of the town,
> And turned the meeting-house upside down.[36]

The reenchanted world of "The Owl, the Eel, and the Warming-Pan" is a distinctly premodern place, where soap is still handmade and the disruptions caused by the three animated creatures culminate in a neat inversion of the "established order" of the meetinghouse. As Susan Stewart has pointed out, nonsense relies upon, and thereby upholds, its flip side—common sense—even as it turns public space (in this case, a meetinghouse) upside down.

The "public sphere of children" implicitly imagined in "The Owl, the Eel, and the Warming-Pan" is not chaotic or disorienting, because it relies on the ahistorical, magical, reversible conditions of the non-sense rhyme: the violence is contained in a predictable formula, offer-ing children the experience of subverting a public space (the meetinghouse) that is not so much public as it is located in what Stew-art calls an "impossible context," a context that can never actually "take place" in—and thus can never contaminate—the "real world."[37] Children's anarchic impulses (so graphically expressed in the "Mary's Lamb" sketches) are given free rein here, but they are also contained by the laws of the genre.

"The Owl, the Eel, and the Warming-Pan" appeared as the lead poem in a special section of work by Richards called "Some Funny Summer Verses." The next "funny verse" depends on coined non-sense words to depict another chaotic public space; it asks how vari-ous men "take their tea," including an emperor, a cardinal, and an admiral. The last stanza reads:

> Oh, Pillykin Willykin Winky Wee!
> How does the President take his tea?
> He takes it in bed, he takes it in school,
> He takes it in Congress against the rule,
> He takes it with brandy, and thinks it no sin,
> Oh, Punkydoodle and Jollapin![38]

This picture of the scandalous Grant administration (a long way, indeed, from Howe's providential union) is framed by explicit lines of nonsense that are nonetheless ineffective barriers, in the sense that the nursery-rhyme formula is everywhere contaminated by the "real world" of national politics.

But, tempting as it is to see "Punkydoodle and Jollapin" as politi-cally subversive, this is hardly the case: even as the "real world" intrudes, it is rendered not just ridiculous but nonsensical. Indeed, the remarkable thing about Richards's verse is not its political satire but its depoliticization of the President himself, who is just one in a series of absurd but ultimately generic authority figures. In the accompanying illustration, they are all gathered pompously around a tiny table, tak-ing their tea in a context that is almost as "impossible" as that of the meetinghouse in "The Owl, the Eel, and the Warming-Pan." If the poem is at all subversive, it is subversive only because it empties the President of his life's work, turning him into just another playfellow.

Or perhaps, given its "impossible contexts," it is inaccurate to call Richards's work "subversive" at all, although its irreverent tone was certainly new, at least in the context of the American juvenile magazine. Clearly, poems like "The Owl, the Eel, and the Warming-Pan" or "Punkydoodle and Jollapin" are not aimed at dismantling the existing order so much as simply disengaging from order to make space for *play*. And yet this play space is not an Edenic or natural or domestic space; instead, it teems with artifice, chaos, and novelty and with creatures who embody not virtue but excess. For instance, in another Richards poem, a dandified shark sits on a rooftop, "smoking cheroots" and caroling until he makes "everyone ill / And I'll wager a crown that unless he's come down / He is probably caroling still."[39] The shark is a form of entertainment run amok: his pointless singing drives the poem to its amoral, open-ended, and pointless (if humorous) conclusion, while the impossibility of the context again contains the fantasy, keeping its playfulness under control.

The delicate balance between playfulness and control was not confined to Richards' poetry, or to children's poetry in general; it was also becoming a central function, as Jackson Lears has pointed out, of the nascent advertising industry—an industry that also relied on magical thinking, impossible contexts, and the controlled release of desires.[40] A turn-of-the-century advertisement for Nestlé's formula, bound into *St. Nicholas*, shows a stork in a pince-nez counseling a baby on a lily pad. In the ad, as in the act of feeding a baby commercial formula, the mother is excluded and the child relates directly to a commercial entity, who takes the form, here, of an impossible animal—nature modified and improved by culture.[41] While Richards's poems do not attempt to sell anything beyond the sheer pleasure of the text, they nevertheless taught children to read differently: not for the moral but for the punch line; not for a sense of connection to the adult world but for a sense that their "own" world might be found among the magical objects and creatures (walking warming-pans, absurd cardinals, singing sharks) that populated the new mass cultural children's public sphere.

INVASION OF THE BROWNIES

The first children's poetry to inspire a major consumer craze and to generate national advertising campaigns was Palmer Cox's Brownies series. The Brownies made their debut in *St. Nicholas* in 1883, and, as the *New York Times* put it in Cox's 1927 obituary, "It is doubtful whether any fashion in children's literature has ever swept the country so completely as Palmer Cox's Brownies took possession of American childhood in the early eighties."[42] The Brownies, whose escapades were related in illustrated couplets, spawned a vast commercial enterprise, with spin-off dolls, rubber stamps, card games, wallpaper, spoons, candy molds, Christmas ornaments, and even a Noah's Ark with pairs of Brownies taking the place of animals.

The Brownies, a group of "cunning" little men loosely based on the Scottish folklore that Cox had heard as a child in Canada, sneak out at night to play and make mischief.[43] But mysteriously, by morning, they manage to put everything back in its place, so that adults never realize (though children suspect) that Brownies have been afoot:

> When people lock their doors at night,
> And double-lock them left and right,
> And think through patents, new and old,
> To leave the burglars in the cold,
> The cunning Brownies smile to see
> The springing bolt and turning key;
> For well they know if fancy leads
> Their band to venture daring deeds,
> The miser's gold, the merchant's ware
> To them is open as the air.[44]

Despite their origins as Scottish folklore, the Brownies' tastes are up-to-date; their favorite places to invade are stores, where they "borrow" newfangled gadgets including bicycles, ice skates, roller skates, baseball equipment, and hot-air balloons. The Brownies' attraction to "merchants' wares" is not really surprising, since by the 1880s merchants were beginning to peddle the promise of magical transformation through material goods. The Brownies embody this promise, gaining instant power over commodities while evading (as advertisements themselves tend to evade) the specter of money changing hands. At any rate, the Brownies' power is not purchasing power; indeed, like children, they are not even properly *consumers,* since they do not earn or spend money but only avail themselves of a material world produced, marketed, and paid for by others.

And yet, if the Brownies concretize children's marginal relationship to the marketplace, they also paradoxically represent both their desire to participate in this marketplace and their urge to be independent of it. Cox's poems and drawings press the new mass culture of the child to its logical conclusion, envisioning a world populated exclusively by peers: among the Brownies there are no families, no compulsory schools, no moral trajectories, and no demands beyond the demands of pleasure. As the Brownies "took possession of childhood in the early eighties," they not only modeled age-graded relationships but also offered peers a mass-cultural marker: children swept up by the Brownies craze were marked as members of a historically specific peer group, or what we might call a *generation*.

The sociologist Karl Mannheim has defined a *generation* as "a particular kind of identity of social location, embracing related age-groups embedded in a historical-social process."[45] Before the Civil War, if "generations" formed at all (and the modern conception seems to date from late- eighteenth-century romanticism), they formed not in childhood but in the transition to adulthood, as the result of large-scale cataclysms such as war or revolution.[46] The experience of childhood was by and large a subset of family experience: if children were affected by large-scale conflicts (as Little Eva was, for instance), this knitted them closer to adults as they shouldered adult concerns. But the cataclysmic cultural changes of the Gilded Age (mass manufacturing, the playground movement, the child-study movement, public schools) pushed middle-class children into each others' actual and imagined company, drawing energy and interest from outside the family circle and giving children what Mannheim calls a "distinct social location" that marked them not just by class but by age.

This location was not always an actual place; often, it might be described as a kind of "Toy-land" produced by the popular culture of the postbellum era. Significantly, this "land" was not a natural, rural, or timeless zone; the Brownies inserted children—albeit by proxy— into historical-social processes; in one adventure, for instance, they attend the World Columbian Exposition in Chicago. Modernity and novelty were central; in one of its first issues, *St. Nicholas* assured readers that they could rely on the magazine "to always be on the lookout for new games and playthings," so that children might know of "the latest inventions from Toy-land."[47] If Toy-land was a place—even a pretend place, a phantom public sphere—it also functioned as a social location where children might encounter each other, not as part of the family circle, but as independent entities like the Brownies.

The children of the eighties could thus use their knowledge of mass culture to revise and adjust older rhymes, reflecting the tastes of their specific milieu, as some children in Carrington, Dakota Territories, did in 1886 as part of a (strikingly secular) Christmas entertainment. A nine-year-old, Theodora C., described the scene to *St. Nicholas*:

We called it "An Evening with Mother Goose and the Brownies." Yes—we had all the cute little boys in Carrington dress up like Brownies. They did mischief very nicely, all quietly in their stocking feet. While Mother Goose was singing her melodies, they came and stole away her goose, and they pelted Mother Hubbard with paper balls . . . they tripped up Jack and Jill, upset Blue-Beard, stole Jack Horner's plum, overturned the bachelor's wheelbarrow, little wife and all, let the spider down from the tree onto little Miss Muffet, and tied Bo Peep's sheep-tails to a tree, and woke her up with their baas . . .[48]

Theodora's Brownies are much more aggressive than Cox's, taking the basic principles of "mischief" and pushing them (albeit in a performative context) to violent extremes. Uncontained by the magical reordering that makes Cox's Brownies invisible and unthreatening, "Mother Goose and the Brownies" ends in unplanned chaos, as the "maiden all forlorn" (from "The House That Jack Built") throws a cat across the stage, causing the house to collapse on several Brownies.

The America that the Brownies (and the children of Carrington) confronted—a world created by the merchants, inventors, and entrepreneurs that Alan Trachtenberg identifies as agents of incorporation—could be overwhelming in scale.[49] As Michel de Certeau has argued, such a world threatens the survival of individual agency: "Increasingly constrained, and yet less and less concerned with these vast frameworks, the individual . . . can henceforth only try to outwit them, to pull tricks on them, to rediscover . . . the 'art' of the hunters and rural folk of earlier days."[50] Children, whose agency was "increasingly constrained" by the "vast frameworks" of the Gilded Age, found in Cox's fragmentary "folk" images a way to recall an independent, self-contained world—a world where "play" was an unincorporated (undisciplined, unproductive, or perhaps even violent) activity. The irony, of course, is that the Brownies were themselves a corporate entity, selling within the context of the vast frameworks that they were depicted as invading.

If we take the Brownies seriously, then, a certain pathos emerges. With their tiny, fat bodies, they are halfway between children and toys; if they appropriate material objects for their own pleasure, they are also objects themselves, easily appropriated for the pleasure of others. As ancestors of the Goops and later the Kewpie doll, the Brownies as illustrated by Cox are among the earliest children's illustrations that twenty-first-century observers might recognize as "cute."[51] Like children, the Brownies have the power to subvert the system (by stealing a bicycle, for instance) but not to change it: by morning, everything is always back where it was, and little people remain marginal, their very "cuteness" a sign of their potential objectification by adults. From this perspective, it is not surprising that the most successful Brownies tie-in product was America's first inexpensive portable camera, Eastman Kodak's "Brownie": finally, children could be captured on film by their parents. And indeed, a verse in the September 1898 *St. Nicholas* describes how cameras, then as now, were used; although the vacationers meant to take pictures of waterfalls and farms, "Yet folks will laugh to see, I fear, / Twelve dozen views of Baby dear!"[52]

"Cuteness" as a category is predicated on the distance between childhood and adulthood, a distance that Dodge, from her first days as editor, both promoted and feared. The cultural critic Daniel Harris argues that cuteness "is not something we find in our children but something we do to them," and that to find or make something cute is to render it helpless, underlining the "vast discrepancies of power" between the adult and the child.[53] Insofar as the Brownies are fantasy stand-ins for children, their cuteness and ultimate ineffectuality (everything is returned to normal by daybreak) reflects what Vivian Zelizer has called the new "pricelessness" of childhood in the later nineteenth century. Zelizer suggests that, prior to this period, children were seen as an economic asset to their families, whereas, beginning around the 1870s and continuing through the turn of the century, childhood was "sacralized," so that productivity was no longer expected of children. Instead, their "jobs" became to take pleasure and to give pleasure—not to *do* but to *be*—and to *be*, specifically, cute.

The technology of the portable camera also resonates strongly with the surveillance technologies of "child-study." In the last decades of the nineteenth century, social scientists, educators, and parents began to document the minutiae of children's leisure activities; the anthropologist Fanny Bergen, for instance, published popular essays in the *Atlantic Monthly* on children's uses of wild plants.[54] Child-rearing practices were becoming less punishing (the ideas of both infant depravity and infant perfection seem to have been on the wane) but more hyperarticulated, as elaborated, for example, in the 1897 *Proceedings* of the First Annual Conference of the National Congress of Mothers. The rising interest in sensitive and productive discipline sparked a new interest in the concept of play; at the grassroots level, this resulted in the organization of sandlots, recreation centers, municipal theaters, pageants, and other forms of supervised recreation. This new interest in what I have called disciplinary publicity resulted in the control not of individual children but of masses of children. And the bonds of affection thus generated were also massified—imagined to flow through institutional, corporate, and commercial systems, rather than just from parent to child.

The rhymes and jingles in *St. Nicholas,* especially those such as "The Rats and the Mice" that came with performance instructions, might seem like part of the same tendency to practice disciplinary publicity. *St. Nicholas* (despite the persistent personifications of the magazine as "dear old *St. Nicholas*") was of course not a teacher or a parent but an object: a beautiful red and gold package full of spatialized "departments" such as the Letter Box and the Treasure-Box of Literature. This object arrived every month, as the *Literary World* put it in a laudatory review of *St. Nicholas,* "with the brilliancy and beauty of new coins of gold dropping from the mint, and with something of the regularity and precision of their appearance."[55] Although Dodge became famous as the "conductor" (she refused to be merely an editor) of *St. Nicholas,* she never developed what we might call a "controlling interest" in children's play. Unlike child-study experts, she was not finally primarily concerned with making play socially or developmentally productive; she was also concerned with making play profitable in a literal sense, which meant catering to children's desires. This does not mean that children's desires were given free rein; the "rebellions" staged by, say, Cox's Brownies were contained by verse forms and impossible contexts; they disturbed without destroying the social order. Indeed, the *St. Nicholas* rhymes, for all their archaic and carnivalesque qualities, are perhaps mostly "about" learning to be middle class and to take pleasure (but not excessive pleasure) in commodities, in "new coins dropping from the mint." Children had to learn a specific kind of freedom—the freedom to be consumers.

To market pleasure and play, then, involved challenging (without entirely dismantling) the older sentimental version of "childhood" as a family affair determined by the family's social position and ethnicity. The "social locations" of middle-class children's play expanded to include both real and imagined age-mates, who might together escape surveillance on bicycles, on roller skates, or through their "very own magazine." Transgressive behaviors were tolerated or even encouraged in *St. Nicholas* as the values of the marketplace clashed with the values of home and family life. Sometimes these transgressions took partial cover under folk and nursery-rhyme conventions (as in "My Uncle Jehosephat" or the Brownies), but sometimes they were quite unapologetically realistic and contemporary, as in an extraordinary 1874 Dodge poem that begins: "One rainy morning / Just for a lark / I jumped and stamped / On my new Noah's Ark."[56]

If children didn't really have their "own" magazine or their own truly autonomous public sphere, incidental poetry nonetheless helped them to make time and space for themselves. *St. Nicholas* offered its rhymes and jingles to children as objects that could be played with; it gave them the chance to pursue their own agendas and to meet their own needs—especially their need (itself a product of later-nineteenth-century middle-class culture) to escape their parents. If children, like Brownies, could seldom be truly subversive in the sense of questioning the fundamental assumptions of later-nineteenth-century society, they could nonetheless tactically resist incorporation into the institutions that increasingly defined and contained childhood. Rhymes and jingles gave children a lyrical time and place where they could "jump and stamp" *just for a lark*—and in a culture obsessed with productivity, progress, and development (including "child development") this incidental social location must have been precious indeed.

Of course, the "escape" from production and productivity into consumption and play is hardly a leap out of the commercial marketplace. Rather, the dynamics of the Brownies represents the transformation of the commercial marketplace into a complex landscape (like the landscapes drawn by Cox) with "hidden" nooks and crannies that are only obliquely part of that marketplace. Authors such as Richards and Cox cannot be seen as resistant to the commercialization of childhood, but they can be seen as wholly transformational on the level of genre, steering poetry as a practice away from the midcentury sentimentalism that located children mainly in the family unit. This is especially striking in the case of Richards, whose prose writings were sentimental in the extreme. *Captain January*, her most popular novel (later a movie starring Shirley Temple) venerates archaic language and imagines an intergenerational bond between a crusty lighthouse keeper and a little girl. But, as I have shown, *St. Nicholas* as a spatialized social location did not consistently encourage intergenerational bonds. While sentimental family-centered work did appear in *St. Nicholas*, and while such work seems to have been popular with adults and children alike, in the magazine's light verse, up-to-date language and peer culture ruled. And Richards's verses, as opposed to her prose writings, reflect the demands of this new, unsentimental strain within the popular culture of childhood.

What does this mean for the history of poetry and its practical uses? It means that, by the end of the long nineteenth century, American poetry had reached what might be called a crisis in rhyme and meter, a crisis in popular poetic forms. On the one hand, the older American authors such as Longfellow and Whittier were still venerated, and half-lovingly, half-parodically imitated by popularizers-of-the-already-popular such as James Whitcomb Riley. These authors were also seen as admirable role models for the young, and as worthy namesakes for elementary schools. They were part of the "Treasure-Box" of American literature, valued because they were traditional, and as traditions they served as a common bond between generations of readers. In addition, the most often-repeated poems in the popular canon were ubiquitous because they delivered specific overt and covert ideological content, especially about racial and class identity, as well as about the relationship between childhood and adulthood. In this way, the work of popular poets such as Longfellow, Whittier, and Riley remained in circulation, functioning not just as rote recitations but as social performances of an invented tradition of middle-class American poetry. Such poetry gave the middle classes a literary genealogy in addition to, or (more likely) in place of, the more exclusive family genealogies offered by organizations such as the Daughters of the American Revolution. Through "schoolroom poets," and institutions like the Treasure-Box, middle-class people were offered a way not just to remember but also to hand down to their children "the very best" of America's past.

When Matthew Arnold sacralized "sweetness and light," however, he was pitting these qualities against materialism—a dichotomy that was problematic to a commercial magazine that had to sell itself. Joan Rubin makes this point in her study *The Making of Middlebrow Culture*. She quotes John Kasson, who notes that the editors of popular periodicals "participated in the commercialization of American culture; but in their public postures they resolutely directed their gazes above the coarse and vulgar realities of everyday life to the lofty realm of the ideal."[57] The contradiction was impossible, and in the pages of *St. Nicholas*, established family-oriented poets (whose work touched both adult and juvenile audiences) comprised a small and ever-shrinking portion of the authors published. By 1905 the most popular poetry in the magazine was Gelett Burgess's Goops series, aimed exclusively at children. While ostentatiously preachy, the Goops series is more a parody of didacticism than a deployment of it. Dodge's editorial voice was a delicate balance between the familial disciplinarian and the playground peer; Burgess's rhymes tip that balance, speaking to children as part of an inside joke, as part of an "us" aligned against the grown-ups:

> I think that it would help you much
> If you'd remember not to touch!
> For there are many stupid folks
> Who do not fancy children's jokes.
> They think that children shouldn't touch
> What isn't theirs. Beware of such![58]

The Goops are even cuter (more stylized, more neotenous) than the Brownies, and unlike the Brownies they are not little men but—recognizably—children. And not only are they cute because they are children—they are cute because they are naughty. On the literary-historical level, the most profound shift that the magazine registered was this "us-against-them" division between "adult" poetry and "children's" poetry, marked by the Goops' distance from anything resembling adulthood.

While the later nineteenth century is not generally seen as a pivotal era in the history of American poetry, this distance between children's and adults' poetry dealt a serious blow to the schoolroom poets even as it energized the first wave of American modernism. Two parallel aesthetics were set into motion: an adult aesthetic and a children's aesthetic. Increasingly, elite poetry was dominated by the aesthetic of modernism, which banished the conventions of schoolroom performance and repetition in favor of formal experiments and novelty. This does not mean that the thumping rhymes and meters of "Paul Revere's Ride" were banished entirely, however; it means that they were relegated to the now-compartmentalized realm of children's literature, which expanded to contain a great deal of formerly intergenerational nineteenth-century poetry and poetic conventions. Nowhere is this splitting more evident than in the work of that reluctant American and erstwhile *St. Nicholas* reader T. S. Eliot. Eliot's "Waste Land" is an "adult" poem that undoes many nineteenth-century assumptions about what poetry should look like, sound like, and accomplish. The poems in his *Old Possum's Book of Practical Cats*, however, are coded as children's literature and thus revert to rhyme and meter. Formally and thematically, the *Cats* poems could almost be nineteenth-century poems; they assume that nineteenth-century conventions are children's conventions. In Eliot, the split between adulthood and childhood (which functions, also, as a split between the twentieth and nineteenth centuries) is pronounced and periodized almost to the point of pathology.

Under Dodge's editorship, *St. Nicholas* hastened this split while periodically deploring it. The social conditions that produced and sustained nineteenth-century popular poetry as an intergenerational art form produced *St. Nicholas Magazine*, and some of the magazine's much-noted "quality" comes from its use of famous "adult" authors. At the same time, however, Dodge also playfully ushered in a new set of conditions, rooted in the niche-driven marketplace, that would make forms of poetry that had previously been intergenerational into the exclusive domain, the private property as it were, of children. Dodge was right to express both desire and anxiety in her two placards, "CHILD'S MAGAZINE WANTED" and "BEWARE OF CHILDREN'S MAGAZINES." In her thirty-four years as an editor, she helped to destabilize a literary tradition of intergenerational poetry— a tradition that she herself venerated—while presiding over the emergence of a chaotic and vital commercial aesthetic: a "children's pleasure-ground" of rhymes and jingles.

CHAPTER FOUR

Performing Class: James Whitcomb Riley Onstage

"The goodest men they is ain't good
As baddest little childs!"
—James Whitcomb Riley[1]

In 1889 the poet James Whitcomb Riley and the prose humorist Bill
Nye appeared at Tremont Temple in Boston, in a show sponsored by
the Boston Press Club and booked through the Redpath Lyceum
Bureau. They were introduced by Mark Twain, who amused the audi-
ence with an anecdote claiming that P. T. Barnum had discovered
Riley and Nye when they were "orphans" joined at the chest:

> Now at that time, before the severance of that old bond, this
> one's name (pointing to Mr. Riley) was Chang Riley and this
> one's Eng Nye. These were Siamese names—names not con-
> ferred on them—born with the names. You could tell it because
> there was a hyphen between them. (Laughter.) Those Siamese
> names I could translate into English, but it would be very diffi-
> cult and would require a great deal of machinery (applause), so
> that it is not worth while to do it.[2]

Twain pressed the joke, claiming that Chang Riley and Eng Nye
were bound together because they could not work independently;
Chang Riley had all the moral sense, but Eng Nye had all the intellectual initiative:

> And when Mr. Chang Riley enchants your spirit and touches your
> heart with the tender music of his voice . . . you will remember
> to place him where justice would put him. It's not his music, it's
> the other man's. (Laughter.) He only turns the crank.[3]

Tremont Temple was the pinnacle of Bostonian respectability, and
"Chang Riley" was funny partly because he was incongruous in that
context. But "Chang Riley" was not simply incongruous: as Twain

[99]

jokingly linked Riley to Barnum's Chang, he also linked Riley to a network of cultural anxieties about the value of "high" versus "low" art forms, the ethnic and racial content of popular entertainment, the class positions of popular audiences, and the fate of poetry in the age of mass-marketed and mass-produced ("he only turns the crank") entertainment.

As the figure of "Chang Riley" suggests, and as I will argue, Riley can be seen as a hinge figure in the history of American poetry, a poet who incorporated "high" and "low" culture into a precarious balancing act that was further destabilized by racial, ethnic, and class anxieties. Van Wyck Brooks articulated one aspect of the crisis in 1915, when he divided America into two cultural camps, "highbrow" and "lowbrow," and complained that "between university ethics and business ethics, between American culture and American humor, between Good Government and Tammany, between academic pedantry and pavement slang, there is no community, no genial middle ground."[4] By 1915 the most influential poets in America would be appearing in Harriet Monroe's *Poetry,* an elite publication with a small circulation. But Riley, who died in 1916, one year after Brooks codified this great divide, built an enormous middlebrow following between 1877 and 1915, despite the shifting and shrinking of the "genial middle ground" that had supported midcentury poets such as Longfellow and Whittier. Riley considered Longfellow's works his "poetical bible," and sent the famous poet copies of some of his early work. When Longfellow replied with mild compliments, Riley capitalized on the endorsement, publishing Longfellow's letter in the *Hancock (Ind.) Democrat.*[5] And yet the cultural work of popular poetry was changing direction by the 1890s, so that Riley framed his career in terms very different from those of the patrician Longfellow, reflecting (and producing) a changing horizon of expectations.

Riley's success was bolstered by his performances: in the 1880s and '90s, he gave hundreds of spectacular live readings in towns from Kokomo to Concord, thus providing a mass-entertainment context for poetry at the very moment when poetry—like "classical" music— was being sacralized as high culture. As a 1911 issue of the *Bookman* put it, reaching back to Riley's toddler days:

> Jim's Gab's what made him famous, for since he began to walk
> He allus wuz a feller that was gifted with slick talk.
> Jim's got a nack o' sayin' things in sich a clever way,
> Without them hifalutin words the edjicated say.[6]

"Jim's Gab" brought minstrel, medicine show, and other popular theatrical traditions into the palatably middle-class milieu of the lyceum
bureau lecture series. Instead of evoking medicine-show Indians or
blackface "Jakes," however, Riley spoke primarily through children or
infantilized (crippled, subliterate, or "raggedy") rural white adults. Riley
became a schoolroom poet, widely celebrated and performed by children, but here I will concentrate more on his role in what might be
called "adult education." People went to his shows to laugh but also to
improve themselves, and he succeeded because he told them what they
wanted to hear and taught them what they already, in some sense, knew.

To fathom Riley's tremendous appeal, and to understand the cultural work that he did, it is important to note the rigidifying and yet
unstable social conditions that divided later-nineteenth-century
America. The sociologist Stuart Blumin has put it succinctly:

> The most clearly defined social structure in American history,
> and the deepest awareness among Americans of the classes that
> divided them, emerged in the years following the Civil War. Yet,
> continuing industrialization, institutionalization, and other such
> phenomena would eventually confuse and erode class bound-
> aries and alter the meanings of class.[7]

This new awareness of both class and class insecurity had many
effects, from the rise of organized labor to the rise of opulent "cot-
tages" at Newport. But one major effect that this awareness and insecurity had on middle-class people was that they came to value
cultivation, or "culture," as a form of symbolic capital. "Culture," as
famously objectified and sacralized by Matthew Arnold (who did lecture tours of the United States in the 1880s), became a way to achieve
distinction without wealth, a way to take advantage of eroding class
boundaries while also affirming them.[8] Thus, by the turn of the century, a reader could write to the *Ladies' Home Journal* and "venture to
ask if you would be so kind as to give some idea how to start right to
obtain culture. I have plenty of time and a good library at my disposal,
but no money to employ teachers."[9]

Riley's relationship to "culture"—to the ideals of refinement and
education, Arnoldian sweetness and light—was ambivalent, and yet
this very ambivalence was a source of social mobility and power for
him. An anonymous essayist, writing in the *Minneapolis Journal* in
1893, interarticulated her own ambivalence with Riley's to create a
striking description of "culture" at its most oppressive. The essayist
explains how she recently dined at a friend's boardinghouse:

> At the next table sat a number of schoolteachers, one a teacher
> of Greek and Latin, another a drawing teacher . . . and so on; not
> common, ordinary teachers, you see. I remarked to my friend
> that it must be a source of great pleasure to live in a house where
> so many cultivated minds are brought together . . ."They are all
> right once in awhile, but for a steady diet they are awful . . . fancy
> people who always spend their evenings reading Browning, dis-
> cussing social problems and going out to lectures . . . After two
> or three hours of their dusty, musty conversation I long, with the
> little girl of James Whitcomb Riley's family, to 'mock them, and
> shock them, and kick my heels and hide.'"[10] I laughed indis-
> creetly and one of the dignified women scanned me with her eye-
> glasses. "She is fixing you in her mind," said my friend, "and
> deciding what grade of life you belong to . . ." "Oh, Jean," said I
> as we left the dining room, "let's go out and catch on bobsleds."[11]

I quote this essayist at length, not only because she uses Riley as a
counterweight for social pretension, but also because, in identifying
specifically with Little Orphant Annie and by deciding to go catch on
bobsleds, she makes a significant leap, imagining an escape from the
"dusty, musty" confines of Browning societies and social reform by
reverting to childhood.

The leap away from cultivation and edification into fun and games,
which might be seen as a change in registers from high to low culture,
is thus figured as a temporary regression to childhood: reversible,
safe, and refreshing. Riley often made this very leap, onstage and in
print. Childhood, for him, was not a memory but a spectacle: it provided the opportunity for a theatrical reversion to a state of popular,
unrefined humor within the respectable generic confines of poetry.
And, through this infantilized and infantilizing poetic discourse,
Riley helped his mostly white, middle-class audiences to occupy a
structural position—the position of the young at heart—that gave
them both access to, and distance from, "the popular": medicine
shows, ethnic humor, minstrelsy, and other nonedifying forms of
entertainment. If, as I argued in my chapter on *St. Nicholas*, the functions of pedagogical poetry were changing for children, becoming
less baldly didactic and more closely linked to commerce (and to
play), then the same changes were occurring among adult audiences,
who wanted to be both cultured and entertained.

In other words, by ventriloquizing children and naive "Hoosiers,"
Riley could appear to dismiss the increasingly "hifalutin," Arnoldian
aspects of American culture while still keeping those values in play.[12]
Like Mary Mapes Dodge, he struck a precarious balance between

edification and entertainment as he catered to people who wanted to feel worthy while they had fun. Thus, for instance, he responded "To the J. W. R. Literary Club" with deadpan innocence:

> Well, it's enough to turn his head to have a feller's name
> Swiped with a *literary* Club! But *you're* the ones to blame!
> I call the World to witness that I never *agged* ye to it
> By ever writin' *Classic-like—because I couldn't do it.*[13]

Although Riley claimed that he couldn't write "Classic-like," his work nonetheless articulates the middle-class struggle for what Pierre Bourdieu has called "distinction."

This struggle was intensified in the last decades of the twentieth century as the cultivators of Arnoldian culture confronted and were perhaps occasionally seduced by the burgeoning commercial "culture industry." Even as edifying institutions—chautauquas, lyceums, and lecture series (such as those that sponsored Riley)—were cultivating their audiences, less worthy diversions such as arcades, kinetoscope shows, and department-store extravaganzas were broadening the appeal of popular culture; mass entertainment gained borderline acceptability (if not respectability) among middle-class audiences as, for instance, risqué concert-saloon acts gave way to tamer vaudeville shows.[14]

But this corrosion of boundaries also required that they be redrawn to admit the middle classes to popular pleasures while still allowing them to mark their own social distance from such pleasures.[15] As Bourdieu has put it, more broadly, "It is in the indeterminate positions of social space, especially in the United States, that the indeterminacy and objective uncertainty of relations between practices and positions is at a maximum, and also, consequently, the intensity of symbolic strategies."[16] Riley's successful symbolic strategy involved performing innocence but not innocently: it involved invoking desire (for play, for innocence, for easy laughs) but also mockery, and it involved "playing" on the ambivalences of an Arnoldian cultural milieu that both craved and feared the lure of Chang and Eng, which was the lure of popular culture.

SHAKESPEARE AT THE SIDESHOW

Riley's career can be framed in terms of the direct (if submerged) tensions and connections between Barnum-style sideshows and the high-toned Tremont Temple. Riley's first public tour, in 1872, was run not by a lyceum bureau but rather by one "Doc" McCrillus, "wholesale dealer and proprietor of McCrillus's Tonic Blood Purifier, Oriental Liniment, and Hoarhound expectorant."[17] By 1876 Riley had advanced to the much-larger Wizard Oil Company, canvassing Indiana and Ohio in a blue and gold wagon, interspersing songs, recitations, and sideshow presentations with sales pitches for Townsend's Magic Oil and Worm Candy. Medicine shows relied heavily on racial and ethnic humor; as Brooks McNamara reports in his study *Step Right Up*, the action was usually mediated by a "Jake" in blackface, and punctuated by routines in German, Irish, and black dialect.[18] Riley's biographer, Marcus Dickey, describes Riley's role in an early McCrillus show:

> Riley strapped an empty soap-box to his shoulders, turned a crank in imitation of an organ-grinder and played the French harp while his chum called attention to the Wild Girl from the Congo (a local merry-maker), who, in torn garments and long-disheveled hair, at the opportune moment, rose like a phantom from the deep box on the wagon.[19]

A medicine-show act was by definition a crowd-pleaser: if it did not draw immediate approval from the audience, it was dropped. And audiences at McCrillus and Townsend shows wanted to see freaks and stereotypes: strange enough to be thrilling but boxed-up enough to be safe, and to safely reinforce boundaries between white and black, normal and deviant, controlled and wild.

If medicine shows—like minstrel shows—reinforced the boundaries between white midwesterners and "others" like the Wild Girl from the Congo, they also forged bonds among the spectators themselves. While McCrillus and Townsend were not entirely respectable, their audiences were drawn from a wide spectrum of society. Lawrence Levine has used the erstwhile mass popularity of Shakespeare to argue that mid-nineteenth-century Americans, despite their divisions, shared a public culture that was "less hierarchically organized" and "less fragmented into relatively rigid adjectival boxes" than the public culture of their twentieth-century counterparts.[20] At one point, Riley attracted crowds to the Wizard Oil wagon by drawing pictures and poems on a chalkboard; as he wrote to his friend John Skinner,

> Last night at Winchester I made a decided sensation by making
> a rebus of the well-known lines from Shakespeare—
> > Why let pain your pleasure spoil,
> > For want of Townsend's Magic Oil?
> ... Oh! I'm stared at like the fat woman on the side-show banner.[21]

As Levine has argued, casual mixings of Shakespeare and sideshows were growing less common by the 1870s, but such admixtures remained a feature of Riley's broadly appealing work through the turn of the century, as in his *Rubaiyat of Doc Sifers,* a piece that both parodies Fitzgerald's *Rubaiyat of Omar Khayyam* as "hifalutin" and yet assumes a knowledge of the *Rubaiyat's* literary conventions.

Bliss Carman, writing in an 1898 issue of the *Atlantic Monthly,* praised Riley's allegiance to an older tradition of "rich public culture":

> The whole tatterdemalion company of his Tugg Martins, Jap Millers, Armazindys, Bee Fesslers, and their comrades, as rollicking and magnetic as Shakespeare's own wonderful populace, he finds "right here at home"; nothing human is alien to him; indeed, there is something truly Elizabethan, something spacious and robust, in his humanity.[22]

In some ways, Riley's very popularity can be seen as a holdover from— or a public expression of longing for—a more broad-based, more "spacious and robust" moment in American literary history. And yet this longing was also a form of social and cultural distancing: a spectacularized child heroine like Armazindy was clearly part of a "populace," a form of "the popular," that could be invoked to entertain—*but that did not include*—Bliss Carman and the readers of the *Atlantic Monthly.* Authenticity was produced by watching, reading, or imagining a "spacious and robust" public that, while it may have been "right here at home," was also distant enough to be seen as "Elizabethan."

THE LANGUAGE OF PUBLIC DESIRE

Riley began his public life with "Doc" McCrillus, but he became a household name through small-town newspapers and, to an even greater extent, on the public lecture circuit. To a remarkable degree, Riley's poetic language and performative style were developed in collusion with his readers and audiences, even as he consciously sought to manipulate them. With an apparent disregard for the standards of objective reportage, Riley told the *Milwaukee Journal:* "My journalistic work taught me to give the public what it wants." Truth, for Riley, was not dependent on accuracy but rather on popularity, and particularly on the popular responses of his live audiences: "An audience knows what life is. It knows when you tell a true thing, strike a true chord, paint a true picture . . . I trust my audiences absolutely to shape what I say. I am made by my audiences."[23] Riley thus presented himself as a performer who was truthful precisely because he told people what they wanted to hear; his performances were putatively both moral and democratic because they were shaped by consumer desire.

From the very beginning of his newspaper career through his last days on the lecture circuit, Riley produced a stream of clever advertisements: in the early years, he used his poetry to advertise products; later, he simply used his poetry as a self-reflexive advertisement for James Whitcomb Riley. For example, when he was working at the *Anderson (Ind.) Democrat,* he inserted promotional jingles among the other poems in his column. This one draws on a poem, Charles Eastman's "Grandfather," which would have been familiar to many readers from its inclusion in *McGuffey's Fifth*:

> The farmer sat in his easy chair
> Smoking his pipe of clay
> While his hale old wife with sprightly air
> Was clearing her voice to say:
> "Read aloud" to the child that sat
> On Grandfather's knee with the *Democrat*.[24]

This intersplicing of a homey scene with a sales pitch is an explicit example of the implicit tension that runs through all of Riley's work, the tension between, on the one hand, a responsiveness to the particularity of everyday, middle-class desires (for intergenerational bonding, for instance) and, on the other hand, a deliberate manipulation of those desires. As Stuart Hall has pointed out in his analysis of British tabloids, the popular media tend to be the site not simply of "cultural implantation" but also of cultural struggle, because "alongside the false appeals, the foreshortenings, the trivialisation and shortcircuits, there are also elements of recognition and identification, something approaching a recreation of recognisable experiences and attitudes, to which people are responding."[25]

This dialectical opposition—a responsiveness to the public versus the manipulation of public response—is particularly complicated in light of Riley's unusually *public* "public." When Riley declared that he was "made" by his (live) audiences, he meant this in an unusually comprehensive sense. Riley's "public" was empowered and articulated through a dense network of lyceums, lodges, literary societies, and cultural clubs that flourished between the Civil War and the First World War. As one young Riley speaker announces:

> Oh! What ef little childerns all
>> Wuz big as parents is!
> Nen I'd join pa's Masonic Hall
>> An' wear gold things like his![26]

These institutions were especially powerful in the Middle and Far West, as Sinclair Lewis's Carol Kennicott discovered in her dealings with the Gopher Prairie Dramatic Association. As the only public forums available in newly established towns, they functioned as simultaneously inclusive (inexpensive, democratic, not too intellectual) and exclusive (socially ambitious, morally unimpeachable) sources of "culture." For example, the Rocky Mountain Lyceum, which welcomed Riley as part of its 1897 reading season, described itself as "a series of Civic associations organized for literary, moral, and political improvement. While it provides entertainment as recreation, the Lyceum also seeks to touch the springs of public opinion, strengthen the public feeling, arouse the public conscience, and ennoble the public mind."[27]

Riley toured for personal profit, of course; his public appearances between 1882 and 1903 not only made him a very wealthy man—wealthy enough to live from poetry alone—but also garnered substantial profits for his management firms, most notably the Redpath Lyceum Bureau, which had also sponsored Dickens and Twain. Nonetheless, Riley's performances cannot be seen as "purely" commercial. Individual clubs—the First Presbyterian Youth Group of Rochester, the Cincinnati Elks, the Washington Franz Abst Club—engaged Riley through the lyceum bureau at a flat fee. Any money earned above the fee went to the local organizers, so "An Evening with James Whitcomb Riley" was usually also a fund-raiser; thus, for example, in 1892 Riley appeared at the Lyceum Theater in Memphis, "under the auspices of the Vassar Student Aid Society, the object of the entertainment being to raise money to assist deserving girls of getting the benefit of Vassar College."[28]

Riley's performances did not just generate revenue for local clubs, however; they also provided a forum for amateur participation in the evening's entertainment. Most professional lecturers and performers exercised their authoritative skills in a way that de-authorized the audience. Dickens, for instance, appeared as the sole attraction in his performances, refusing to acknowledge his audiences—who were relegated to "a pleasant twilight"—while he read.[29] Riley's acts, by contrast, were almost invariably produced in collaboration with performers from the sponsoring club. For example, a typical Riley appearance, sponsored by a Chautauqua Club and held at the East Aurora (N.Y.) Baptist Church, began with a cornet solo, "Slumber On," performed by Mr. F. W. Spooner. This was followed by selections by Riley (billed as "The Robert Burns of America"), after which Mrs. F. W. Spooner sang "Spanish Serenade," and Miss Ella Gager finished the evening with a vocal solo, "Spring-Tide."[30] The Spooners and

Gager were clearly East Aurora residents; programs from Riley's tours show that while his poetry selections remained (numbingly) constant, musical acts varied from town to town. Thus, Riley's performances were not simply what Hall calls "cultural implantation"; they can be seen, in a significant sense, as financial and expressive collaborations between a professional poet and the communities that he visited.

POETS ALL

Amateur poets also responded to his invitingly nonprofessional, antiliterary language; after Riley's death Marcus Dickey compiled scrapbooks that contain dozens of poems directed at Riley and written in Riley's style. These do not appear to be parodies but rather enthusiastic additions to the "Riley" oeuvre that honor the power of his language while also usurping that power, as in this rhyme, "To J. W. Riley," from the *Indianapolis Herald*:

> Your pictures! I love them so well, ah! so well;
> They tell just the things that I so long to tell,
> When Charlie and I have read all the lines through,
> We clip from the paper, with blessings on you.[31]

These lines also remind us that middle-class nineteenth-century Americans were inveterate scrapbook keepers and that, in addition to Riley's official books, his work probably appeared in hundreds of one-of-a-kind "anthologies" compiled by ordinary folks who cut his poems out of the newspaper.

Even his most humiliating moment—when his lecture tour with Bill Nye was canceled because Riley went on a weeklong drinking binge—inspired cracker-barrel verse in newspapers, such as this one by Will Allen from the *Nashville Journal,* titled "Riley on a Tear":

> We hope to see you Riley,
> Some day come creepin' back
> When the frost is on the pumpkin
> An' the fodder's in the rack.
> With that "old sweetheart" Riley
> For whom you uster care,
> An' we promise not to mention
> Jim Riley's Famous Tear.[32]

His public persona was such that his "Bohemian" traits—his alcoholism, his lack of interest in women and marriage, his prevarications—were publicly aired and publicly negotiated.[33] Allen's assurance that "we promise not to mention" Riley's drinking problem (while of course mentioning it) signals Riley's status as an accessible, appealingly flawed celebrity rather than as an exalted role model like Longfellow. In 1916, shortly before Riley's death, Elsie Russell of Montezuma, Georgia, wrote to him:

> What a consolation to know the author of "Out to Old Aunt Mary's" and "An Old Sweetheart of Mine" is living. Listen Mr. Riley do you realize how much your works are appreciated by the average Southerner? Do you realize that before long you will be unable to write such grand poems as those mentioned above if you do not leave off drinking strong liquors? Why do you drink excessively? I write to beg you, to beseech you, to leave off this terrible habit. You owe it to yourself, to your state, to your readers, to the world to live as long as you can.[34]

Russell's startling familiarity with Riley shows the extent to which his persona offered readers the sense that they could participate in his work, not just as readers, but as writers, critics, or even personal advisers.
. Riley, then, made himself "accessible" (or at least made himself appear accessible) on many levels. His poetic style, which (seemingly) anyone could adopt, invited appropriation and dialogue, particularly in newspapers. Hall has called the language of mass-marketed periodicals "a highly complex species of linguistic ventriloquism," and yet he argues that this ventriloquism "cannot get by without preserving some element of its roots in a real vernacular—in the popular."[35] In newspapers and on the platform, Riley was ostensibly struggling to ground his poetry in a "real vernacular," to give poetry a democratic accent in the broadest and most participatory sense of the word. As he wrote in "The Poems Here at Home":

> No "Ladies' Amaranth," ner "Treasury" book—
> Ner "Night Thoughts," nuther—ner no "Lally Rook"!
> We want some poetry 'at's to Our taste,
> Made out o' truck 'at's jes' a-goin' to waste
> 'Cause smart folks thinks it's altogether too
> Outrageous common—'cept fer me and you!—
> Which goes to argy, all sich poetry
> Is 'bliged to rest its hopes on You and Me.[36]

But reading Riley's verse, and the verse of imitators like Will Allen, one is indeed struck by the "accent": Riley's most popular poems are written in a Hoosier dialect that sets itself off from "smart folks," who presumably read "Night Thoughts" or the "Ladies' Amaranth." It is worth asking, however: if Riley's rhetorical "You and Me" are not "smart folks," then what kind of folks are they? Eric Lott, writing about minstrelsy, calls "plantation" dialect lyrics a form of "orthographic derision." Are Riley's Hoosier dialect and his down-home persona also a form of derision? Riley was certainly viewed as a comic performer, but who was laughing at whom? And why were "the people" so willing to collaborate with him?

PLAYING IN PEORIA

Riley played hundreds of venues on his grueling lecture tours, with Bill Nye in the later 1880s and alone (after his "Famous Tear" dissolved the Riley-Nye partnership) in the 1890s and early 1900s. Although he did perform in skating rinks, churches, and club lodges, he most frequently appeared in "opera houses." For example, on his 1892 tour he was booked into the Burtis Grand Opera House in Davenport, Iowa; the Wheeler Opera House in Toledo, Ohio; and the Grand Opera House in Peoria, Illinois. Riley's performances thus tended to be framed by, say, a proscenium arch decorated with a larger-than-life Euterpe, holding in her hand a harp illuminated by a gaslight. They were also framed by the social ambitions, and contradictions, that these small-town "opera houses" represented.

A gaslit Euterpe hovered, for instance, above the stage at the Peoria Grand Opera House, an edifice that had been built in 1882 through the efforts of the newspaper editor Eugene F. Baldwin, with donations from local businessmen. The Opera House's famous ceiling fresco, copied from "Lord Beaconsfield's Mansion in England" (as the *Peoria Journal* put it) was meant to create an atmosphere "suitable for the highest grade of talent." "[T]here is nothing tawdry about it," the *Journal* reported. "The brilliant colors do not end in the exploitation of half-naked women depicting mythological deities in sensuous positions. All that the eye sees in flowers and birds and bright colors and golden tints."[37] The Grand Opera House, with its aristocratic ceiling, was meant to be both democratic and "ennobling." Thus, it was with some disappointment that the *Peoria Daily Transcript* reported that the most-favored act in the opening season was not "serious" opera but rather a burlesque spoof of Longfellow's *Evangeline* that featured a dancing trick cow: "The Grand this year has had more packed houses than were ever known in this city before and *with the exception of the highest toned troops*, everyone made money. Probably the public tastes will change in this respect, but now it turns to a desire for spectacular effects" (italics mine).[38] Riley's lecture tours, then, coincided with a pronounced public effort to find a range of middle-class entertainment that would be as diverting as a trick cow but that would also elevate the audience to the implicitly ennobling standards of the Grand Opera House ceiling.

The Anglophilia that inspired the Grand Opera House ceiling design was no local phenomenon; a national fascination with Britain was also boosting Americans' receptivity to Matthew Arnold. Arnold's definition of "culture" emphasizes the "best that has been thought and said" in the "main stream of human life." In other words, it ranks art vertically—from best to worst, highest to lowest—creating hierarchies that helped Americans to link, say, Shakespeare with self-improvement and minstrelsy with self-degradation. The Opera House seating was also ranked vertically: the most exalted citizens sat in the boxes, followed in ascending order by those placed in the dress circle, the parquet, and the balcony. Thus, the tensions between the high culture of opera and the low culture of a trick heifer, between the elitist ideal of an ordered and orderly theatrical space and the democratic ideal of a civic auditorium, were creating definitional difficulties even as "culture" became a more fully defined term: what (and whom) was the Peoria Grand Opera House *for?*

When Riley played in Peoria, he was booked through the Western States Lyceum Bureau. Like modern-day public television, lyceum programming had to skirt the line between its educational mandate and its need to cater to the public taste. H. L. Mencken captures this ambivalence in his history of the Indian loanword *chautauqua*, in *The American Language:* "At the start [1874] *chautauqua* meant a summer-school, permanently housed and of some pedagogical pretensions. But toward 1900 it began to signify a traveling show, often performed under canvas, and including vaudeville acts as well as lectures."[39] Riley, together with Nye, and also his friends Joel Chandler Harris and Mark Twain, worked the lecture circuit during a time when these "pedagogical pretensions" were being counterbalanced (but not negated) by the nascent popular- culture industry.

In other words, the warring attractions of elite and popular cultural forms increasingly demanded that middle-class Americans perform a balancing act. This balancing act should not be read as an either / or proposition pitting, say, the tastes of Consuelo Vanderbilt against those of a shoeshine boy. Middle-class Americans were already experimenting with a fluid, market-based, multiple-choice system that allowed them access to *Othello* and—in the same season, and on the same stage—P. G. Lowery's Komical Kolored Koons.[40] My point is precisely that middle-class Americans did not represent a stable stratum of taste: they responded to the instant pleasures of popular entertainment but also to the cultural-capitalist cachet of elite culture. As these two categories—popular and elite, lowbrow and highbrow—became more stratified, conflicting desires played upon those in the middle, who were neither heiresses nor shoeshine boys. Hence, the rise of the Peoria Grand Opera House as a palace of both self-abandonment and self-aggrandizement, and hence, also, the rise of James Whitcomb Riley, the antiliterary literary man.

THE RAGGEDY MAN

Riley produced a large number of poems between 1877 and 1916, but only a few dozen ever made it onto the stage as honed performance pieces. His core repertoire included "Little Orphant Annie," "The Raggedy Man," "The Bear Story," "Out to Old Aunt Mary's," and "The Happy Little Cripple," spoken in dialect by child characters; "When the Frost Is on the Punkin," "Dot Leedle Boy," "The Old Swimmin' Hole," "Tradin' Joe," and "Annals of the Poor," spoken in dialect by adult characters; and "An Old Sweetheart of Mine," the only "blockbuster" Riley poem spoken in standard English by an adult character. Overall, although Riley produced more than a thousand poems in his lifetime, his performance pieces remained fairly constant—perhaps because, especially after 1890, he allowed audience requests to dictate much of his program. As he repeatedly insisted, "Genius is a sort of taste. It is finding out what most people want."[41]

Riley's performance style was notable for its naturalness; newspaper accounts stress that he established a rapport with his audiences by speaking colloquially, with his hands in his pockets. As the *Rochester Morning Herald* reported, after Riley appeared at the local opera house under the aegis of the First Presbyterian Church youth group:

> The entertainment was rendered more delightful by the fact that every element of formality was lacking. The stage was set with a pretty drawing room scene, and Mr. Riley was its only occupant. He recited several of his favorite poems, and interspersed them with remarks upon the romance of every-day life . . . He is a master in the speaking of all the dialects which he employs so effectively in his writings, and his voice, though very unlike that of the elocutionist, has a charm almost as subtle as that of the lines he has written.[42]

While none of Riley's poems reward scholarly close reading, they were not designed to do so; they were written to be effectively performed, and, as a performance, each piece stakes out territory on the cultural landscape and stirs up distinct tensions—or rather, tensions of social distinction—even as it seeks to resolve those tensions.

"The Raggedy Man," for instance, begins by stating what might be a troubling relationship between labor and capital: "O the Raggedy Man! He works for Pa." And yet this tension becomes a source of comic relief when we realize that the poem is being narrated by a little boy who admires the Raggedy Man: "An' he's the goodest man you ever saw!" The Raggedy Man, as it turns out, is a childish character himself:

> An' sometimes the Raggedy Man lets on
> We're little prince-children, an' old King's gone
> To git more money, an' lef' us there—
> And *Robbers* is thick ever'where;
> An' nen—ef we all won't cry, fer *shore*—
> The Raggedy Man he's come and 'splore
> The Castul-Halls, an' steal the gold—
> An' steal *us* too, an' grab an' hold
> An' pack us off to his old "Cave"!—
> An'
> Haymow's the "cave" o' the Raggedy Man!—
> Raggedy! Raggedy! Raggedy Man![43]

The poem's punch line comes in the last stanza, when the Raggedy Man asks the little boy if he plans to grow up and "keep a fine store" like his father, "An' be a rich merchunt—an' wear fine clothes?" And the little boy answers, predictably, that *no*, "I ist go' to be a nice Raggedy Man! / Raggedy! Raggedy! Raggedy Man!"

Riley's own estimation of "The Raggedy Man," as offered in an interview with the *San Francisco Examiner* in 1892, was egalitarian in sentiment if slightly condescending in tone:

> There is more human nature and more poetry with both the boy and the man than with the highly educated—those who would totally ignore such people. They wouldn't have anything to do with anyone of this class, but they are nearer to Him who sought out the poor and ignorant than many who would not give them a thought.[44]

Riley's egalitarianism nonetheless emphasizes a class gulf between the Raggedy Man and more sophisticated folks—a gulf that Riley himself reproduced in his performance style. While audiences were impressed by Riley's "impersonations," they were equally impressed by the distance that he kept from these impersonations. Bourdieu describes "strategies of condescension" as "those strategies by which agents who occupy a higher position in one of the hierarchies of objective space symbolically deny the social space between themselves and others, a distance which does not thereby cease to exist, thus reaping the profits granted to a purely symbolic denegation of distance."[45] "The Raggedy Man" could be admired, but only when the speaker was "in character" as a child speaker. In a letter sent to Riley during his 1892 tour, his friend Dan Paine advised him to "Make it clear that Riley in person is equal in dignity, poise, and breeding to any in the audience. It is Riley the artist who commands laughter, pity, tears, and jeers."[46]

Riley was evidently committed to this division, because reviews of his performances commonly stress the clear lines of demarcation between Riley-the-man and his characters. The *Kansas City Star,* for instance, reported:

> Riley is a plain-featured, boyish-looking young man with colorless hair and a voice whose ordinary nasal tone gives no preliminary intimation of its wonderful skill in expressing character and sentiment. His face, too, is a blank until it becomes the portrayer of a succession of emotion.[47]

To become a little boy, prattling about a raggedy man, and then to return to blank "neutrality"—this was Riley's consummate skill, a skill that might be identified, in Fredric Jameson's words, as "a kind of psychic compromise or horse-trading, which strategically arouses fantasy content within careful symbolic containment structures which defuse it."[48] The fantasy of Riley's performances, then, is the fantasy of controlled release, a kind of "recess" where power relationships can be playfully overturned so that the Raggedy Man gets the gold and "rich merchunts" are less respectable than hired hands. But this fantasy is also a joke—Riley was first and foremost a humorist—and as a joke it defuses (while airing) any class anxiety that the specter of a man in rags may arouse. A child can admire a "Raggedy Man," and imbue him with an aura of power and glamour, because a child has no real power to defend; likeways, an adult playing the part of a child can also play at collapsing hierarchies—not to challenge them, but ultimately to maintain them.

THE BALANCE OF POWER

In Riley's most popular performance pieces, power relationships are made fluid by the complete absence of sober, middle-class, standard-English-speaking white men and women. The single exception to this rule—"An Old Sweetheart of Mine"—nonetheless goes to great, indeed almost pedophilic, lengths to keep adulthood at bay. In this poem, a literate man sits in his study, smoking a Havana cigar as he listens to the sounds of his children getting ready for bed. He then falls into a reverie; remembering a little girl that he knew at school, during "Childhood-days enchanted!":

> I can see the pink sunbonnet and the little checkered dress
> She wore when I first kissed her and she answered the caress
> With the written declaration that, "as surely as the vine
> Grew 'round the stump," she loved me—that old sweetheart of
> mine.[49]

The speaker rhapsodizes about how he gave this little girl marbles and promised to love her forever, but then the "dream is broken" as his wife opens the study door. As a final kicker, however, it turns out that his wife *is* "that old sweetheart of mine"; the little girl and the grown-up mother are one and the same. In this way, childlike desires (for a little girl, or for lowbrow toys like marbles) are respectably maintained and managed by the adult speaker. He can partake of an omnibus of options without relinquishing his comfortable position as a man of means. He can, in other words, walk the line between the elite space of the study and the popular space of a playground.

This line—between study and playground—is precisely the line that defined Riley, enabling him to "impersonate" children and innocent adults without compromising his own dignity. Like the "Old Sweetheart" who is imaginatively transformed from adulthood to childhood and back, Riley's act depended on the boundaries that he transgressed; as the *Pittsburgh Bulletin* put it, "he has an absolute respect for children as a distinct species of the human race." In the world of nineteenth-century American theater, distinct races required distinct dialects, so his "respect" for children led to poems in exaggerated baby talk, such as the highly popular "Bear Story":

> W'y, wunst they wuz a Little Boy went out
> In the woods to shoot a Bear. So, he went out
> 'Way in the grea'-big woods—he did. An' he

> Wuz goin' along—an goin' along, you know,
> An' purty soon he heerd somepin' go "Wooh!"[50]

Audiences with a taste for adventure could enjoy "The Bear Story" with the confidence that Riley—like the "Old Sweetheart"—would eventually return from the wilds of childhood with his sense of grown-up power (over syntax, over nature, over culture) intact.

The impulse to take a fantasy trip back to childhood, and some of the ideological underpinnings of viewing childhood as a "distinct race," emerge in a letter exchange between Emilie B. Stapp, the literary editor of the *Des Moines Capital*, and Riley. In 1914 Stapp asked Riley to be the symbolic head of a loose organization of people who were pledging to be helpful model citizens:

> It seems to be the desire of the children of Indiana that you should be designated Chief of the their happy tribe. The Go-Hawks' Happy Tribe is composed of good little Indians from 7 to 77 who are discovering that the only real happiness in life lies in service. All over the country children are showing fealty to the tribe by donning the button emblem of service. So here's your button which makes you a life member. If you are caught without it some young Indian brave or squaw may rise up and scalp you.[51]

Riley replied that he was happy to be "the chief of both the little children and those with the spirit of little children, even though 'the golden hair be gray.'"[52] Stapp then wrote back, asserting, "I am so glad you have not grown up. Neither have I. You must never tell my employer, nor any of those many publishers who overwhelm me with books for criticism, but I still believe in fairies."[53] The Go-Hawks were probably inspired by similar "leagues" and "tribes" propagated by other periodicals, including *St. Nicholas*: such groups tended to inspire loyal readership by giving children a sense of belonging. But what is remarkable about this exchange is how, even in private, Stapp and Riley perform a reversion to childhood *themselves* as they plan the Go-Hawks project. In doing so, they imagine crossing not just the line between childhood and adulthood but also a racial line that is *figured* as an age marker. Riley and Stapp are not giving up their autonomy as cultural leaders (a writer and an editor respectively) by reverting to childhood; they are shoring up their power by doing so. They are establishing the fact that as powerful white middle-class adults they have many options—including the option to (claim to) believe in fairies or to imagine themselves as "braves" or "squaws" or children. Stapp jokes that Riley must never tell her employer that she believes in fairies, thus underlining that such a belief is an amusement for her—a way to maintain her privilege through strategies of condescension, but also a way to enjoy the sense of freedom and variety that imaginary border-crossing provides.

BLACKFACE / BABYFACE

As the Go-Hawks exchange suggests, the line between childhood and adulthood, and between elite and popular culture, often over-lapped—especially in the late nineteenth century—with the color line. Indeed, the very terms "highbrow" and "lowbrow" are derived from racist phrenological categories.[54] Thus, to be positioned as a popular (hence potentially "lowbrow") practitioner was to be viewed through a lens of racial anxiety. And, as I have pointed out, Riley did emerge from a medicine-show tradition that relied heavily on racist humor.

Riley did not perform poems with black characters, though they do appear in his published work. In "Uncle Remus," for instance, he speaks in the dialectal voice of a white man addressing a black man. But this white man positions himself as a child:

> We love your dear old face and voice—
> We're *all* Miss Sally's Little Boys,
>> Climbin' your knee,
>> In ecstasy,
> Rejoicin' in your Creeturs' joys
> And trickery.[55]

The prospect of "loving" a black man and acknowledging his power as a storyteller is mitigated, in this poem as in Joel Chandler Harris's Br'er Rabbit series, by the presence of the white child auditor. For the most part, however, children supplant rather than supplement stereo-typical black characters in Riley's poems—and this is particularly true of his performance numbers.

However, the ghost of a minstrel show—which was, after all, the most popular form of nineteenth-century entertainment—still hov-ered around Riley. For example, Clinton Scollard reviewed Riley's *Book of Joyous Children* (which was, incidentally, dedicated to Harris) in these terms:

> Here is sunshine, here is laughter, here is the untrammeled spirit of spring. Mr. Riley is a minstrel who is always welcome. He is slave to a magic that he sets free in song, and straightaway we are all slaves—and willing ones.[56]

[117]

Scollard's odd characterization of him as a minstrel and his readers as happy slaves provides, perhaps, a clue to Riley's effectiveness as a dialect practitioner: readers were not willing to wish themselves across races, but it was becoming increasingly acceptable for adults unabashedly to wish themselves back into childhood.[57] In other words, childhood was a locus of pleasure that offered the irresponsibility and sensuality that (some) whites associated with blacks. And yet, unlike blackness, childhood seemed to carry no price or stigma: it was the land of happy slavery, where fantasies of powerlessness could be imagined without a loss of "face." Blackface minstrelsy was about reinforcing borders that could be crossed through cross-dressing but not dissolved: white spectators were expected not to identify too closely with "Jakes," but rather to mark their difference from them even as they fantasized about inverting that difference.

Riley's "babyface" minstrelsy, by contrast, was about dissolving the borders between putatively hardworking adults and playful, powerless children, giving all his audience members equal and seemingly unproblematic access to children as objects of pleasurable identification and desire. Miles Orvell historicizes the nostalgia of the period:

> It was as if the middle-class American were trying to hold on to his "real" self amidst the rapid changes of society. The pervasiveness of nostalgia . . . was a way of habituating men to the present, of retaining a sense of proportion and scale, of human stature, during a period when the individual's capacity to assimilate change was being pushed to the limit.[58]

Riley's specific power was to channel this nostalgia into speakers and images that let people picture children as figures for his readers' "real" selves that could be taken out—and put away—at will. Through Uncle Remus, white audiences had shown their willingness to appropriate African-American culture as a commodity (an impulse that would accelerate throughout the twentieth century), but Riley offered something even "better," or at least easier: access to authenticity through "others" whose charm was related to their infantilization.

THE GOBBLE-UNS 'AT GITS YOU
EF YOU—DON'T—WATCH—OUT

Even children, however, could not eliminate the uncertainty and even fear that accompanied the mixing and sorting out of highbrow and lowbrow, black and white, and rich and poor during the 1880s and

'90s. In "Little Orphant Annie," which was probably Riley's all-time greatest hit, an outsider invades the young narrator's home:

> Little Orphant Annie's come to our house to stay,
>   An' wash the cups an' saucers up, an' brush the crumbs away,
> An' shoo the chickens off the porch, an' dust the hearth, an' sweep,
> An' make the fire, an' bake the bread, an' earn her board an' keep;
> An' all us other children, when supper things is done,
> We set around the kitchen fire an' has the mostest fun
> A-list'nin to the witches-tales 'at Annie tells about,
> An' the Gobble-uns 'at gits you
>   Ef you
>   Don't
>   Watch
>   Out!⁵⁹

When the Gobble-uns finally appear in the poem, they come as "two great big Black Things a-standin' by her side." While it might be stretching the point to identify the two black goblins as the repressed ghosts of the minstrel show, Orphant Annie herself is clearly serving the function of a mediator between worlds, between the pulp-fictional world of sensational body snatching and the respectable domestic sphere of the child whose house she invades. And clearly, Orphant Annie's status—she is neither old enough to be sexual nor dark enough to be threatening like the goblins—makes her a perfect ambassador to the middle-class sensibility.

Riley wrote a short essay about the "real" Orphant Annie, Mary Alice Smith, after his poem became famous; the essay was first published in the *Indianapolis Star* and later reprinted in his *Complete Works* with the title "Where Is Mary Alice Smith?" The essay describes a malnourished and neglected child, rejected by her living relatives, who repeatedly announced that she was "going home": "The spindle ankles that she so airily flourished from the sparse concealment of a worn and shadowy calico skirt seemed scarce a fraction more in girth than the slim blue-veined wrists she tossed among the loose and ragged tresses of her yellow hair, as she danced around the room." And yet Riley's piece is awash in nostalgia for her as a "pixy" or "elf-child," as he puts it, bringing dramatic entertainment to himself and his siblings. He ends the essay with an ambivalent plea:

"Oh, where is Mary Alice Smith?" She taught us how to call her thus—and now she will not answer us! Have we no voice to reach her with? How sweet and pure and glad they were in those old days, as we recall the accents ringing through the hall—the same we vainly cry to her. Her fancies were so quaint—her ways so full of prankish mysteries! We laughed then; now, upon our knees, we wring our lifted hands and gaze, through streaming tears, high up the stairs she used to climb in childish glee, to call and answer eerily. And now, no answer anywhere! How deft the little finger-tips in every task! The hands, how smooth and delicate to lull and soothe! And the strange music of her lips! The very crudeness of their speech made chaster yet the childish thought her guileless utterance had caught from spirit-depths beyond our reach. And so her homely name grew fair and sweet and beautiful to hear, blent with the echoes pealing clear and vibrant up the winding stair: "Where—where is Mary Alice Smith?" She taught us how to call her thus—but oh, she will not answer us! We have no voice to reach her with.[60]

For Riley to announce that he has "no voice" is a rare event, but he seems to be acknowledging here that his voice is not directed at the Mary Alice Smiths—the common folk, the poor people—of Indiana. Riley's middle-class "voice" cannot actually communicate with his subject, or with her real-life counterparts, even as he is celebrated for ventriloquizing them. Indeed, Mary Alice Smith's distance from Riley is necessary to his social position. In his essay he longs for her "prankish mysteries," for the frisson of his family's brush with her goblins, but he also tacitly admits that he is representing her, not reaching her. And indeed, unsurprisingly, when the *Ladies' Home Journal* tracked down the "real Orphant Annie" in 1915, Mrs. Smith told Edmund Eitel that for most of her adulthood she had not heard that Riley was a poet nor that she was his most famous subject—despite the fact that she lived on a farm in Indiana, where (at least among middle-class people) Riley was the state's most famous citizen.[61] She learned of Riley's success, and of her own role in it, only after Riley's secretary contacted her in 1888. Her polite, but terse, responses in the *Ladies' Home Journal* article evoke the memories of a painfully sad childhood; she tells the interviewers that she made sure, as a mother, to protect her own daughter from such suffering.

Orphant Annie, then, was not "really" Mary Alice Smith; she was a "pixy" that Riley invented to manage the borders that kept his own class position, and the class positions of his readers, in place. Little Orphant Annie, the Raggedy Man, and the "Old Sweetheart" can all be seen as guards patrolling the boundaries of the middle class: they are figures of power shake-ups, jokes, inversions, and surprises, but they are also instantly recognizable as part of an act, reinforcing the very social boundaries that they transgress. Orphant Annie brought "gobble-uns" of poverty and class and perhaps even racial anxiety to the surface, but she was popular because—as a child addressing other children—she contained them as well. One Riley imitator—a Mormon folk poet, Peter McBride—makes the "border patrol" motif explicit in his version of "Little Orphant Annie":

> You can't pick up a paper or magazine today,
> But it's full of current events that's passed so they say;
> The world is in commotion, on the land and on the sea,
> And everybody's planning what they'll do and plotting;
> The profiteers have planned for years to turn the world around,
> But the Bolsheviks will get them if they
>
> >>> don't
> >>>> look
> >>>>> out![62]

In the speaker's position—between the profiteers on the one hand and the Bolsheviks on the other—we find a plainspoken, ordinary man negotiating class tensions in terms of his own fears of powerlessness. In real Riley poems, similarly real threats lurk, but they do not materialize as such extreme forces as profiteers and Bolsheviks. Instead, these threats are displaced into figures such as Orphant Annie, who embodies the tensions between "highbrow" and "lowbrow" (rich and poor, white and black) while also marking this tension as child's play.

PLEASURES OF REPETITION

When Twain asserted that Riley was not original—that "he only turn[ed] the crank"—he was in fact describing the pleasures afforded by Riley's verse, which depend not on novelty but rather on repetition and recognition. As the *Kansas City Star* put it, in a review of an 1897 performance,

> Mr. Riley, happily, has not changed since he was here last. There is the same droll, humorous expression that we laughed at some years ago . . . and those who laughed heartiest were those who heard him before—who knew exactly what was coming. The Hoosier poet has reached that point which is the pinnacle of

entertaining. He has arrived at that stage when the public say to him, "We do not ask anything new of you. Give us the old favorites."[63]

Like present-day pop singles, the best-loved Riley poems were written to be instantly familiar—even to the point of reiterating familiar poems by other authors. Thus one poem, "The Schoolboy's Favorite," repeats the *entire text* of Lydia Maria Child's "New England Boy's Song" ("Over the River and through the Woods . . .") as it rhapsodizes about the "boyhood pleasures" that the poem can continue to invoke, even among adult readers. And of course, Riley poems became themselves almost instant schoolroom classics, included in school readers and inscribed in the memories of children who were educated at the turn of the century.

Riley aimed to please: if he could find a marketable formula—his own or someone else's—he used it. Ambrose Bierce, for one, dismissed him as a shameless huckster when Riley passed through San Francisco in 1892:

> His pathos is bathos, his sentiment sediment, his "homely philosophy" brute platitudes—beasts of the field of thought. He preaches with an impediment in his preach. His humor does not amuse. His characters are stupid and forbidding to the last supportable degree; he has just enough of creative power to find them ignoble and leave them offensive. His dictum is without felicity, his vocabulary is not English, his—in short, Mr. Riley writes through his nose.[64]

Bierce is refreshingly frank, but it is worth noting that he could also be trenchantly elitist, and his article is contemptuous not just of Riley's "dreary literature" but also of his audiences, "whom it serves royally right."

As Riley himself admitted, his verse was written to sell, to "play in Peoria," as it were. When he was headed west on his 1892 tour—the same tour that elicited Bierce's scorn—he wrote to his friend George Smith:

> Am worryin' on West slow as old molasses; but none the less my interminable "show" seems to bore nobody but myself. Even my fragile manager, Mr. Glass, is not wholly shattered yet, though my program is as monotonous as the menu on a two-kinds-of-meat restaurant.[65]

The extent to which Riley cynically "wrote through his nose" is impossible to determine and to some degree irrelevant—certainly, he never failed to admit that he considered poetry a business and that he sought to make "oodles of money."[66] Nevertheless, the question of what precisely he was selling, and why people bought it, remains. I have suggested that some of his more popular performance pieces helped both to air and to manage anxieties about "high" and "low" culture, and the attendant questions of race and class that this emerging dichotomy posed. But this does not completely account for Riley's success. Bierce notwithstanding, it seems clear that Riley's audiences were neither stupid nor gullible; rather, they "bought" him because he offered something that they felt was both valuable and vanishing.

If historical forces (urbanization, class insecurities, Arnoldian cultural ideals, mechanical reproduction) were creating a split between "high" and "low" culture that left little room for a "genial middle ground," Riley's performances did seem to give (or rather sell) people the chance to experience poetry as a communal activity. Through his informal, "natural" performance style, his openness to local talent, and his accessible cast of children and "Hoosiers," he developed what appeared to be a personal relationship with his audiences. As the *Minneapolis Tribune* put it in 1892,

> Mr. Riley and his audience were . . . on the most intimate terms. There was no formality, no uneasiness, nothing artificial and stilted. The relationship between the poet and his audience was one of easy and matter-of-fact hospitality and jovial familiarity. The mutual understanding was perfect.[67]

Riley's poetry made people feel at home—not just as national subjects or individual consumers, but also as members of a comfortable (not "stilted") and seemingly authentic (not "artificial") community. The peculiar intimacy that his performances could spark can be seen in an anonymous letter, written by a woman who first saw Riley in 1878, when he was just beginning his career, and never forgot the experience; over thirty years later she wrote to Riley that her early encounter with him made her feel close to him:

> I've been a steadfast friend to you—the unknown friend and well-wisher—I hope my friendship has unconsciously strengthened you . . . Now the best wishes of my heart follow you where'ere you be—now I am no unbalanced crank—no autograph seeker—just a normal, thoughtful friend.[68]

This letter writer seems to struggle against the conditions of celebrity that distance her from Riley. She insists, with a degree of self-consciousness that half-acknowledges her impossible position, that she can be his friend, and even a support to him, without any contact beyond a single public performance in 1878 followed by years of reading and re-reading his poems.

The advance publicity for his 1888 lecture tour announced that—in every town from Hornsville, New York, to La Crosse, Wisconsin—he would address "Not a mere public audience, but a host of personal friends."[69] This advertising slogan—manipulative though it may be—promises an aesthetic milieu that Fredric Jameson has specifically linked to precapitalist forms of life: "[T]he old precapitalist genres were signs of something like an aesthetic 'contract' between a cultural producer and a certain homogeneous class or group public; they drew their vitality from the social and collective status . . . of the situation of aesthetic production and consumption."[70] In other words, "precapitalist" generic repetition (for example, folktale conventions) reinforces not market values but collective social values. Jameson argues that capitalism invariably destroys this contractual relationship between artist and audience, and that twentieth-century American mass-cultural repetition should be understood as "the historical reappropriation and displacement of older structures in the service of the qualitatively very different situation of repetition."[71] From this perspective, Riley's work marks a moment of uneven development, balancing "folk" and commercial forms, or at least representing "folk" forms commercially. And a few of his poems did pass back into something like a folk tradition. In the 1970s the folklorist Keith Cunningham interviewed Alice Tripp, whose maternal grandmother had been born in the 1880s. Tripp reports,

> I have lived the biggest part of my life between Dallas and Fort Worth, but my recitations come from my maternal grandmother. She was from Lexington, Kentucky, and I just learned her recitations from her by repetition. Because I was the oldest of four, I heard them four times longer than the youngest child would have. They were strictly for kids. She would sit and knit and tell stories and do poems. One of them was "Little Orphan Annie." I like "Little Orphan Annie."[72]

Tripp then reproduces "Little Orphant Annie," although—ironically, since this is an actual folk performance—in a less "folksy" dialect than Riley's original.

In Jameson's view, capitalism eventually destroys one form of repetition (authentic, collective, like the refrain in a folk ballad) and installs another form (manufactured, alienated, like the refrain in a pop ballad). But, as I have shown, and as Jameson also implies, this is not an instantaneous transformation. Riley's career emerged at a moment when the middle-class public was in a state of insecurity about how (if at all) the genre of poetry could be enjoyed. People expected more from popular poetry than it could offer—a horizon of (high) expectations that perhaps contributed to its decline. The condition of nostalgia reflected a longing, not just for lost forms of life, but also for the art forms (popular poetry chief among them) that small-scale communities could sustain but that larger-scale institutions could only mimic or imagine. Departing from a schematic Marxian historicism—while retaining Jameson's useful view of the two different functions that repetition can serve—I want to suggest that Riley's poetic repetitions operated in both functional registers (authentic and yet manufactured, collective and yet alienated, folk and yet pop) simultaneously. His performances were of course commodities—like meat in a restaurant, as he himself put it. However, they were also expressions of nostalgia for a form of collective aesthetic experience that predated Riley himself, that did not simply serve the needs of the marketplace, and that was still imaginable—if not fully realizable—in late-nineteenth-century America.[73]

"Seein' Things at Night": Eugene Field and the Infantilization of American Culture

The Eugene Field House in St. Louis, Missouri, is marked with a plaque: "Here was born EUGENE FIELD, the Poet, 1850–1895." Field's friend Mark Twain dedicated the plaque in 1902, but just before its unveiling, he was informed by Field's brother Roswell that Field had not actually been born at the site. Twain supposedly replied, "Never mind. It is of no real consequence whether it is his birthplace or not. A rose in any other garden will bloom as sweet."[1] Fittingly, then, one of the later nineteenth century's most "boyish" pranksters, the "children's poet" Eugene Field, is remembered with a plaque that conceals as much as it reveals. Twain, like Field, was a former journalist who cared less for journalistic accuracy than for the success of the public spectacle. News cameras captured the dedication for the *St. Louis Globe-Democrat,* and a crowd of "shirt-sleeved factory hands cheered," and their approval was what mattered.[2] Fittingly, too, the inside of the Eugene Field House is a toy museum based on his own extensive collection of bisque dolls, mechanical banks, and miniature books. In the summer of 2003 the Field House was hosting a special exhibit, A Century of Teddy Bears, showcasing the popular stuffed animal inspired by Teddy Roosevelt—a politician who encouraged American men, as Michael Kammen puts it, to "recall more of their barbarous, prehistoric youthfulness."[3] Twain, Roosevelt, and Field have this in common: they were all partly constructed by, and also highly responsive to, new public perceptions of "childhood" and its enduring power in adult life. But in a crowded public arena of overaged youngsters, it is not surprising that Field—a poet, practicing an already infantilized literary genre—stood out as exceptionally, and even to some observers excessively, childlike. Through his Denver and Chicago newspaper columns, and through his popular poems such as "Little Boy Blue," "Wynken, Blynken, and Nod," and "The Sugar-Plum Tree," Field put on an act that blurred—while it also fetishized—the line between childhood and adulthood.

Field's popularity is part of his mystery, and part of why he is worth considering. He himself told Hamlin Garland, "I have never put a high estimate on my verse. That it's popular is because my sympathies and the public's just happen to run on parallel lines just now."[4] Many twenty-first-century readers are likely to concur. Unlike Longfellow, Whittier, or Riley, all of whom can be defended as fluent, competent writers, Field is often awkward and inconsistent, veering into baby talk, fake Middle English, unconvincing Hoosier dialect, and schoolboy Latin. And yet, in the 1890s, he was a "good" poet, if by good we mean "beloved": his work outsold Emily Dickinson's, and his celebrity as an eccentric sprite rivaled hers. As his contemporary Edmund Stedman put it, "Yes, Field 'caught on' to his time—a complex American, with the obstreperous *bizarrerie* of the frontier and the artistic delicacy of our oldest culture always at odds within him—but he was, above all, a child of nature, a frolic incarnate."[5] The question becomes one that demands as much cultural spadework as literary analysis: why did Field's poetry—and his persona—catch on? Why was he so compelling to so many readers?

In an affectionate portrait for the *National Magazine,* Eugene Debs called James Whitcomb Riley and Eugene Field the "poets of common life," and the "people's poets," noting that they were both "carefree souls": "Like Riley, whom he resembled strongly in many ways, he [Field] was an intense lover of children, and if there were any little ones about he was very apt to forsake the grown folks."[6] Certainly, Riley and Field drew on a common horizon of expectations: as western journalist-poets, they promoted themselves through newspapers, performed (occasionally together) on the lyceum circuit, emerged as schoolroom celebrities, and measured their "success" in numbers—and dollars—rather than by the standards of the eastern critical press. But if—as I have argued—Riley was a poet who performed and maintained social boundaries, Field was a poet who blurred boundaries, especially the boundary between childhood and adulthood. When Riley recited "The Bear Story" to his audiences, he was careful to code it as a performance and to return to his dignified poet self between recitations. But Field's entire public life (including his very public private life) was a performance: he consistently acted like a child, and in doing so he reimagined the relationship between children and adults. In his poems, he seeks not just to understand children but also to appreciate them as aesthetic objects, to make contact with them physically, and to interpret or dictate their dreams—often while positioned on the edge of their beds, or in their beds.

Early- to midcentury sentimental poetry tends to feature dead children, which has led Mary Louise Kete to argue that the dominant form of the popular sentimental poem was the apostrophe, a speech act directed at a missing person. While Field's poems use some of the language of sentimentalism, and certainly in most cases privilege feelings over thoughts, they ultimately turn children into pedagogical objects—drawing them close and engaging with them in ways that sentimental conventions do not allow. For Field, children are not absent but perennially present (except in the case of "Little Boy Blue," which will be discussed); indeed, for Field "the child" seems to function, not so much as a separate being, but as a part of the adult self—a small, archaic, and perhaps even sexual part of the self. Freud did not visit the United States until 1909, fourteen years after Field's death, and his ideas did not really enter popular culture until the 1920s. I am certainly not arguing that Field's readers read him psychoanalytically; that horizon of expectations, while nascent, was not yet in place. However, as Carolyn Steedman has argued, the idea of the "human subject" that culminated in Freud's discovery—or invention—of the unconscious, was an idea that had its most immediate roots in the intellectual and popular culture of the 1880s and 1890s. In his seminal work *No Place of Grace*, the historian Jackson Lears analyzes the central place of "antimodernism" in American culture after 1880, linking the antimodern impulse to the arts and crafts movement, to medievalism, and to the valorization or even fetishization of childhood.[7] All these impulses, Lears argues, were reactions against the anxieties of industrialization and the increasing pressures on adults—and men especially—to fit into narrow market niches that seemed to reduce their humanity and render them "weightless" and insignificant. The relationship between Field and Freud is not causal, but it is also not coincidental: both tapped into antimodern discourses that focused on childhood while also asking if—and how—adults could in some sense remain children for life. Field's poems, and his persona, fed a growing public desire for avenues back into a more primitive (and powerful) state: he presented himself as a child; he drew on archaic sources, especially the *New England Primer*; he satirized old-fashioned pedagogical methods that stressed the gulf between adults and children; and he offered his readers an alternative to this gulf, imagining an intimacy between adults and children that gave—or seemed to give—children new powers even as it rejuvenated adults.

A VERY PUBLIC CHILDHOOD

At Field's funeral in 1895, the Reverend F. M. Bristol lauded him for teaching his readers "the greatness of the child spirit." It is unclear, from Bristol's text, whether Field merely depicted the "child spirit" or whether that spirit somehow lingered in Field's adult frame. William S. Lord added to the confusion by reading these lines to the assembled mourners:

> My child, do you know that your lover is dead?
> That the friend of all children lies low?
> Last night he was living, when you went to bed,
> And now—what is choking me so?
> An angel came down from the precincts of heaven
> And finding a pure white soul,
> She folded it up in her breast snow-driven
> And hurried away to its goal.
> Up there, little child, he'll have tenderest care,
> He'll be rocked in a cradle like you,
> And when he awakes his dreams he'll share
> With his own dear Little Boy Blue.[8]

The poem addresses "my child" even though Lord faced a church full of adults; it also transforms Field from a "lover of children" into a child or even an infant rocking in a cradle. The angel coming down from heaven quotes a scene from one of Field's most famous poems, "Little Boy Blue," in which an angel steals a sleeping child; in death, then, Field was imagined to have merged with the juvenile subject of one of his own verses.

This merger occurred not just at Field's funeral but also in the wider public sphere, as Field was sanctified as a "pure white soul" and a "child spirit." As one reviewer of Field's posthumous *Collected Works* put it in *The Bookman*:

> The first rude shock of public grief caused by the death of Eugene Field a few months ago has passed, and there has arisen out of the ashes of mourning a sweet remembrance of him as he was when he was still with us; a memory, indeed, that reincarnates for us the true spirit of the man bereft of earthliness and mortality, and which is preserved as in a precious phial "to a life beyond life" in these beautiful volumes which serve as a fitting memorial of the dead poet. Death could not rob us of that; what it did was to rend the fleshly veil and flash the soul of this man upon us in all its childlike purity and playfulness. For it is because of this childlike quality in Field that all sorts and conditions of men, women, and children alike will continually rise up and call him beloved.[9]

The emphasis on the books as a memorial to the personality makes sense, because Field was a massmedia celebrity who kept himself in the public eye. His column, Sharps and Flats, was based at the *Chicago Morning News,* but he pulled stunts that gave at least some of his writing a national audience, since other papers would pick up, and reprint, his copy. Making up outrageous lies about celebrities was one way to do this; hence, when Edmund Stedman came to Chicago for the first time, Field announced in print that he would be greeted with an absurd amount of hoopla; Stedman reports that he read the story in an eastern paper:

> It was headed, "Chicago Excited! Tremendous Preparations for his Reception," and went on to give the order and route of a procession that was to be formed at the Chicago station and escort me to my quarters . . . It included the "Twentieth Century Club" in carriages, the "Browning Club" in busses, and the "Homer Club" in drays; ten millionaire publishers, and as many pork-packers, in a chariot drawn by white horses, followed by no less than two hundred Chicago poets afoot! I have no doubt that Eugene thought I would enjoy this kind of advertisement as heartily as he did. If so, he lacked the gift of putting himself in the other man's place. But his sardonic face, grinning like a school-boy's, was one with two others which shone upon me when I did reach Chicago.[10]

Field's "school-boy" grin excuses him in Stedman's eyes, as it generally—though not always—did. Edward Bok, whose (real) fiancée was seriously embarrassed when Field released, to the national press, announcements of Bok's engagement to two other women (one a fictive patent-medicine heiress and the other Mrs. Frank Leslie), uses the language of therapeutic release to excuse Field in his own memoir: "[T]he boy in him could not be repressed."[11]

And, of course, Field interspersed his columns with his own verses, especially poems that celebrated children, making the link between his own behavior and a boy's pranks seem only natural—a form of "childlike purity and playfulness." "To a Usurper," for instance, is both playful and insistent on its speaker's right to remain a child:

> Aha! a traitor in the camp,
>   A rebel strong and bold,—
> A lisping, laughing, toddling scamp,
>   Not more than four years old!
>
> To think that I, who've ruled alone
>   So proudly in the past,
> Should be ejected from my throne
>   By my own son at last!

> He trots his treason to and fro,
> As only babies can,
> And says he'll be his mama's beau
> When he's a "gweat big man"![12]

Field's colleague and biographer, Carl Dennis, writes in a chapter titled "Did Field Love Children?": "I have thought that the attitude of Field toward children was the attitude of one dispossessed of a prized inheritance toward those who were in full enjoyment of the privileges denied to him."[13] By framing the family home as an army camp, Field ups the ante: the boy is more powerful than the man because he is cuter, trotting "his treason to and fro." The father's solution is to engage in competition with him at his own level—competing to be cute, which is also the goal that Field seemed to set in his columns.

Field's early death in 1895, at the age of forty-five, only added to the fulsome public discourse about his childlike persona; as Henry Ellsworth Hadon put it in a memorial poem in the *Chicago Sunday Times*: "The world is in tears over Little Boy Blue / Its sweetest voice is still."[14] Finally, in 1901, one William Marion Reedy published a pamphlet, *The Eugene Field Myth,* declaring that "the saccharine slavering of his name and fame" had became "positively nauseating." Reedy's revisionary reading of the Field "myth" notes ruefully that "nearly every city of any importance contains a public school named after Eugene Field. That Field was, in a sense, the American poet of childhood, cannot be denied. The people have taken up his verses and they live on the popular lips everywhere. There is no disputing the people in such matters. They know what appeals to them."[15] Reedy then recounts an anecdote in which Field turned down an invitation by saying, "I've only got to go home now, and write some mother-rot," "only the word," Reedy adds, "wasn't rot, but something much worse."[16] He concludes by pleading, "Let us not be maudlin over Field for the work at which he was wont to scoff and jeer as a pose and a pretense. Let us even name schools after him, if we will, but let us not continue to fool the people by picturing him to them as a sort of Sunday School seraph with a facile trick of titillating the tear ducts and a tendency toward pulling pathos."[17] Reedy assumed that what "the people" needed was the truth about the man; what he failed to realize was that "the people" were Field's collaborators. Readers who adored *Little Lord Fauntleroy, The Prince and the Pauper,* and the Goops (and, a little later, Peter Pan) wanted Field to strike a particular pose, and he was rewarded for meeting their expectations.

As a national public figure, Field collaborated with his public by tracking his own popularity among newspaper editors and readers. In

1899 Leon Mead recalled a visit to Field's newspaper office in the early 1880s:

> One of Mr. Field's fads at the time was to clip out all of his original poems, copied in other papers, and paste them on the ceiling and boarded walls . . . These walls, and ceiling as well, were covered with poetry by Eugene Field. You would see the same poem in a dozen places, scissored from as many papers, and the effect on the eye was odd and curious.[18]

After his death, *Scribner's* noted his ubiquity in the nation's newspapers: "Perhaps no one appreciates so well the quality of his deliverances as the little army of exchange editors in newspaper offices whose duty it is to glance through piles of newspapers, scissors in hand, and clip out . . . the verses of merit enough to bear transplanting."[19] This meant that Field's persona was not lifted wholesale from his own columns; rather, those verses and quips that most conformed to the public taste were scissored out and reproduced, making his national persona into a collaborative bricolage of those qualities that a "little army" of editors thought their readers (in Laramie, Wyoming, or Aurora, Illinois) might like. Readers then used their own scissors to cut Field's poems out for scrapbooks or recitation; as one Aurora farmer wrote to the *Chicago Times-Herald* after Field's death:

> It is doubtful if he knew how many aspiring young elocutionists contributed to local parlor or church entertainments with recitations of such poems as "Little Boy Blue" and "Knee Deep." There is a larger percentage of reading people in the country than in the city and, being lovers of nature, they could not resist the laughing meadow-brooks of the sunny Field.[20]

Most Field fans never saw him in person, of course, and so their experience of him was through the newspaper and also through the mouths of "young elocutionists" who performed his work. Their youthful voices and bodies must have contributed to the public impression—so often expressed, and so carefully cultivated by the poet—that he was a child himself who was recovering (and helping his readers to recover) the "prized inheritance" of youth.

PUBLIC CHILD/PUBLIC SCHOOL

In 1881 Field's contemporary (and fellow Williams College alumnus) G. Stanley Hall published a study, "The Contents of Children's

Minds," which became the foundation of the new "child-study" move-ment. The results, tabulated in page after page of scientific tables, purport to lay "children's minds" bare: in 1880 in Boston, 9 percent of all children recognized the concept of a "bee," 11 percent recog-nized the concept of "seasons," while 69 percent recognized the con-cept of "repetition in speaking."[21] The child-study movement turned human subjects into scientific objects, suggesting that the way to edu-cate children best was to stop trying overtly to control them and start trying to understand them. Of all the social-scientific revolutions of the period, child study had the most immediate impact on everyday peoples' lives, because its premises were taught in teacher-training colleges and thus disseminated through the schools. Romantic exper-iments in progressive education, such as Bronson Alcott's Temple School, had not found widespread acceptance during the earlier nineteenth century, but by the 1880s and 1890s, as teachers across the country were professionalizing, they were also educating them-selves to redefine pedagogy. "Memory-cramming," as Hall termed the old method of learning through rote recitation, was slowly being replaced by more progressive child-centered methodologies.

By the 1890s the pantheon of New England schoolroom poets—Longfellow, Whittier, Lowell, and Holmes—was fixed, although the ways that these poets were used were changing to incorporate approaches such as Olive Dana's "Whittier Folk-Gathering." The main value of the New England schoolroom poets remained their links to "tradition" and to "the ideal," ideas that were increasingly marshaled in progressive classrooms as alternatives to materialism. Riley and Field were latecomers to the group, and necessarily admit-ted under different terms, since they were largely representing them-selves as unpretentious folks rather than as paragons of ideality. Nevertheless, Mary E. Burt, in the introduction to her school text-book, *The Eugene Field Book,* seems confident that Field belongs among the schoolroom poets:

> [A]t a brilliant poetry contest at Carnegie Hall, New York, "Seein' Things at Night" (recited by a twelve-year-old boy), receiving a tremendous encore from a crowded house of schol-arly people, I was reassured that a new poet had come to share the laurels so generously bestowed by the American public on Whittier, Longfellow, Lowell, and Holmes.[22]

The authorities she ultimately cites, however, are not "scholarly peo-ple" but rather her own students; "it is in my own schoolroom and among my own pupils that the most genuine realization of Eugene

Field's genius has come to me." The editorial selection of the text-book's content has been "made upon a basis furnished by the children themselves, after repeated experiments":

> The child, when left to his own inner leadings, his opinions not constrained, speaks out with great courage; his criticism has the delicacy of the downy bloom of his own cheek. His velvet voice lingers over the lines most exquisite in finish, like his own feelings, and "from these presents" I know that the child, the perfection of creation, has found his own interpreter. A roguish brownie of eight years, as full of play as the day is long, finds leisure in some way, to learn "Wynken, Blynken, and Nod" and begs to recite it, and all the other brownies listen with eyes sparkling. A more serious child presents "The Wanderer" or "Christmas Treasures" or "Pitty-Pat and Tippy-Toes" and every rosy face becomes thoughtful. What a world of little people was left unrepresented in the realms of poetry until Eugene Field came![23]

Burt's emphasis on the child's "inner leadings" reflects the child-study movement's widespread belief that children learn best when they are allowed to experiment instead of being commanded to obey; her indulgent description of the "roguish brownie of eight years" signals this new interest in appreciating—rather than curbing—children's playfulness.

Accordingly, none of the poems in Burt's *Eugene Field Book* set up an overt pedagogical hierarchy between teacher and student; they do not command, "Listen my children and you shall hear . . . ," and they do not offer historical narratives, moral examples, or even inspirational advice. Instead, children and adults journey together into fantasy lands; the final stanza of "The Sugar-Plum Tree" promises, for instance:

> There are marshmallows, gumdrops, and peppermint canes,
>> With stripings of scarlet or gold,
> And you carry away of the treasure that rains
>> As much as your apron can hold!
> So come little child, cuddle closer to me
>> In your dainty white nightcap and gown,
> And I'll rock you away to that Sugar-Plum Tree
>> In the garden of Shut-Eye town.[24]

In a school textbook context, a poem like "The Sugar-Plum Tree" still has the pedagogical aim of teaching young children to read and to appreciate poetry. But the gratification that the poem offers is instant, and not necessarily related to good or bad behavior; if anything, the little child is rewarded for being dainty and attractive, just as Burt praises the "velvet" voices and "downy" cheeks of her students. The "dainty white nightcap" bears a family resemblance to the marshmallow in the stanza's opening line, and, as a performance piece, "The Sugar-Plum Tree" invites children to perform a new kind of social competence: they are not citizens-to-be or moral-paragons-in-training, or even aspirants to a vaguely defined "ideal." Instead, they are spectacles and consumers.

Field could not really be elevated to the exemplary plane occupied by Longfellow and Whittier; he had to be framed in different terms. This was not necessarily problematic in the context of schools that were beginning to admire children's playfulness as a trait to be observed (and perhaps even chuckled at) instead of as a fault to be remedied. The *Eaton Fourth Reader* (1906) compares Field and Longfellow: "Side by side in the hearts of the American children is the earnest, fatherly face of Henry Wadsworth Longfellow and the tender, brotherly face of Eugene Field."[25] The *Art-Literature Reader*, a turn-of-the-century text for third graders, puts it slightly differently, framing Field as a roguish brownie in his own right:

> As Eugene Field grew older he liked fun and mischief more and more. He published a boy's paper for which he wrote clever stories and put in many jokes about the other boys in town. College days came and still he seemed only a big boy who never lost a chance to play a joke on classmates or teachers. Though his fun sometimes made people a little uncomfortable, it was always harmless.[26]

In the school textbook genre, in which every biography is a hagiography, the admission that Field "sometimes made people a little uncomfortable" marks his awkward position in the schools: he was an adult, but not an adult who "acted" like an adult. This mirrored, perhaps too closely, the uncomfortable position of many progressive educators as they tried to control their classrooms and also to follow their students' "inner leadings."

During his lifetime, Field's relationship to the New England schoolroom poets was ostentatiously competitive, pitting, as he framed it, youth against age, West against East, and populism against pretension. One of Field's most popular poems, "Little Boy Blue," was first published in 1888 in the magazine *America*; the same issue contained a new poem by James Russell Lowell titled "St. Michael the Weigher." Carl Dennis remembered the ensuing "race":

There speedily developed a curious race for popularity between Lowell's poem and "Little Boy Blue," a race that was watched with very great interest by Field and myself. Here was the product of a poet of long-established reputation pitted against that of a mere aspirant to the title of poet. Which would receive the greater degree of recognition from the newspapers of the country? We kept a close lookout, searching daily the columns of the hundreds of newspapers that came to the office. Both poems were widely copied. Wherever found, we clipped them and matched the two sets of clippings numerically against each other. To Field's immense satisfaction "Little Boy Blue" soon began to outrun its more pretentious rival.[27]

Like Mary Burt, who looked to child readers for validation, Field looked directly to his readers, bypassing scholars, critics, and established magazines, which were mostly East Coast–based, and biased, he thought, toward poets of "established reputation."

"Little Boy Blue" was, in fact, a runaway hit: set to music, recited at church fund-raisers, and printed in many broadside editions, it became one of the most frequently repeated poems of the American 1890s. Compared with Lowell's "St. Michael the Weigher," the poem is notable for what it does not attempt. Unlike most poems by the New England schoolroom poets, "Little Boy Blue" does not ground itself in American (or European) history, in a strong moral sense, or in the impulse to create a civil religion. If "Little Boy Blue" has antecedents, they are the sentimental children in Lydia Sigourney's poems. But even Sigourney's poetry draws on the cultural authority of mothers. Field's poem, by contrast, begins in the voice of a parent but sheds even this authority by the end. The poem stages a scene that was familiar to sentimental writers and readers:

> The little toy dog is covered with dust,
>> But sturdy and stanch it stands;
> And the little toy soldier is red with rust,
>> And his musket molds in his hands.
> Time was when the little toy dog was new
>> And the soldier was passing fair,
> And that was the time when our Little Boy Blue
>> Kissed them and put them there.

Intervening stanzas describe how the boy has died and been taken up to heaven by an angel. But in the last stanza the toys come alive:

Ay, faithful to Little Boy Blue they stand,
    Each in the same old place,
Awaiting the touch of a little hand,
    And the smile of a little face,
And they wonder, as waiting these long years through,
    In the dust of that little chair,
What has become of our Little Boy Blue
    Since he kissed them and put them there.

Here, the speaker's consciousness merges not with the "contents of children's minds" but with the contents of *toys'* minds, leading the poem's readers to empathize with a stuffed dog and a rusty soldier and to make the imaginative leap that children make when they ascribe, as G. Stanley Hall put its, "psychic qualities to the object, and treat it as if it were an animate or sentient thing."[28] Field is drawing, then, on the emerging cultural authority of childhood: his poem reads (and rhymes) like a nursery rhyme, his speaker thinks like a child, and his readers are asked to identify with toys. "Little Boy Blue" is certainly more closely allied with sentimental writing than most of his other poems, but it is not just sentimental; it fixes on manufactured toys, as well as on a dead child, as objects of longing, and it infantilizes not just the child and the toys but also the poem's adult speaker. It is not surprising, then, that so many of Field's posthumous admirers, like William S. Lord, pictured him entering heaven by regressing to childhood. After all, the speaker in his best-known poem undergoes the same regression.

Field became a "schoolroom poet" on the strength of what he called his "love-songs of childhood," and while his work did not become as ubiquitous as Longfellow's, it overtook Lowell's—if the surviving "Field Days" reports and recitation programs are any indication. So from Field's perspective, at least, he won the race. As a western schoolroom poet, Field rejected the authority of the New England schoolroom poets: he wrote poems from a child's subject-position, he cultivated an anarchical persona, he staged a public "competition" with Lowell, and he even, at one point, lampooned the dead and highly respected Whittier in his Sharps and Flats column, suggesting that he had been a tax dodger.[29] And yet Field was, in his own way, a New England schoolroom poet after all, in the sense that he organized much of his early work around a single school text—the *New England Primer*—and built his later career as an extended reaction against it.

MY LIFE A LOADED GUN

Field spent his childhood in the heart of New England: in Amherst, Massachusetts, on the fringes of the (Emily) Dickinson family social circle. Like Dickinson, Field wrestled with his Puritan heritage. If James Whitcomb Riley was prone to wax nostalgic—and to imitate *McGuffey's Reader*—Field drew on the older and more rigidly Calvinist *New England Primer.* The *Primer* served two contradictory but ultimately related roles in Field's public career. Most obviously, it stood for the voice of pedagogical authority, against which he rebelled. At the same time, however, this very rebellion, this refusal to accept authority (or to embody it himself) allowed him to discover and to tap childhood—as constructed through and against the *Primer*—as a source of oppositional energy. In *Love Affairs of a Bibliomaniac,* Field describes a half-autobiographical, half-fictive scene:

> I never think or speak of the "New England Primer" that I do not recall Captivity Waite, for it was Captivity who introduced me to the Primer that day in the springtime of sixty-three years ago. She was of my age, a bright, pretty girl—a very pretty, an exceptionally pretty girl, as girls go. We belonged to the same Sunday-school class. I remember upon this particular day she brought me a russet apple. It was she who discovered the Primer in the mahogany case, and what was not our joy as we turned over the tiny pages together and feasted our eyes upon the vivid pictures and perused the absorbingly interesting text! What wonder that together we wept tears of sympathy at the harrowing recital of the fate of John Rogers! . . . Through the many busy years that have elapsed since first I tasted the thrilling sweets of that miniature Primer I have not forgotten that "young Obadias, David, Josias, all were pious"; that "Zaccheus he did climb the Tree our Lord to see": and that "Vashti for Pride was set aside."[30]

In repeating the lines about Zaccheus and Vashti, Field is remembering the *Primer*'s image-alphabet, with its famous opening line, "In Adam's fall / We sinned all." Patricia Crain has called the image-alphabet of the *New England Primer* a "boundary-genre: a folk-literacy primer, whose success owes something to it function as a kind of balance wheel for unresolved contradictions."[31] Field was no longer inhabiting a world defined by the original (albeit long) cultural moment of the *Primer,* in which, as Crain notes, fifth-commandment piety was clashing with the antiauthoritarian ethic of Puritanism. But American pedagogical culture was still dealing with the broader issue of authoritarianism versus individualism in debates about the proper relationship between adults and children.

Field's reaction to the *New England Primer* was conditioned by many of the same social forces that produced Emily Dickinson, and both poets clung to the *Primer,* and to Isaac Watts, with an affection that shaded into resentment. Although Field was born in St. Louis, his mother died in 1856, when he was six years old, and he and his brother Roswell were sent to live with their cousin, Mary Field French, in Amherst. Roswell later recalled that their cousin raised her wards with "that queer mixture of nineteenth-century worldliness and almost austere Puritanism, which is yet characteristic of many New England families."[32] Field's guardian, Mary French, was a witty Amherst Academy graduate, a pillar at the First Congregational Church, and a friend to both Emily and Lavinia (Vinnie) Dickinson. Jay Leyda notes that Mary French "fell out of touch" with Emily as she withdrew from the world—and as Mary French herself grew increasingly eccentric, becoming, in Leyda's words, "a wretched and peculiar figure on Amherst's streets."[33] But Mary and Vinnie remained close, and when Mary J. Reid profiled Field for *St. Nicholas* she noted that Eugene and Roswell "loved Amherst with a peculiar affection":

> Particularly they were attached to Miss Lavinia Dickinson, the sister of the poet and writer, Emily Dickinson. She is a quaint little gentlewoman, whose house and furniture have not been changed in a single detail since the early part of the century. No one mourned Mr. Field's death more than this gentle old lady.[34]

If Amherst mourned Field, Field did not, in his lifetime, mourn Amherst; in a letter to his cousin Julia Jewett he calls it a "humdrum, foggy old hamlet," adding, "When God Almighty visited the place with fire, it's a pity he didn't complete the job."[35] In another letter Field shares his memories of the New England Sabbath for Alice Morse Earle, the colonial revivalist who was so fond of "Snow-Bound"; he describes, for Earle's antiquarian pleasure, the old meetinghouse, with its freezing pews warmed only by the foot stoves of the Elect, among whom the young Eugene was not counted. He ends his letter to Earle characteristically: "There was no melodeon in that meetinghouse and the leader of the choir pitched the tune with a tuning fork. As a boy I used to play hi-spy in the horse shed. But I am not so old— no, a man is still a boy at forty, isn't he?"[36] In other words, after pointing out his own inferior, non-Elect status in the church, Field reasserts his value by claiming to be "a boy at forty." The tension, figured as one between an irreverent Field and his pious grandmother, also reflects larger historical changes that made the country increasingly pragmatic and secular in the decades following the Civil War— changes that made the exact value of a person subject to fluctuations that would have been unthinkable to the "elect" members of an antebellum New England meetinghouse.

Field obliquely marks this destabilizing secularism (and the irreverence it inspired) in his first newspaper columns for the *Denver Tribune*, which were later collected in a book, the *Tribune Primer*. These columns from the early 1880s are always edgily satirical and laced with black humor; unlike his later work, they seem immune to the lure of the sentimental. The randomly capitalized authoritative voice echoes the *New England Primer*:

> The Cat is Asleep on the Rug. Step on her Tail and See if she will Wake up. Oh no; She will not wake. She is a heavy Sleeper. Perhaps if you Were to saw her Tail off with the Carving knife you might Attract her attention. Suppose you try.[37]

The *Tribune Primer* speaks in the voice of an unpredictable and inexplicable preceptor who bears a strong resemblance not only to the *New England Primer* but also to the Calvinist God—albeit a version of that God who has completely lost his moorings. The pieces do not so much invert the values of the *New England Primer* as exaggerate them, exposing the sadism at work in a theological system, and an educational system, that uses violent spectacles (including corporal punishment, which Field abhorred) to intimidate children into learning.

The *Tribune Primer* often veers into a spectacular cruelty reminiscent of the *New England Primer*'s famous woodcut of John Rogers burned at the stake:

> This is a gun. Is the Gun loaded? Really, I do not know. Let us Find out. Put the Gun on the table and you, Susie, blow down one barrel, while you, Charlie, blow down the other. Bang! Yes, it was loaded. Run quick, Jennie, and pick up Susie's head and Charlie's lower Jaw before the Nasty Blood gets all over the new Carpet.[38]

The voice, here, is not parental—it is specifically institutional, woodenly reiterating established assumptions and platitudes. The power of authority in Field's *Tribune* pieces (like the capital-P Power in so many Dickinson poems) is absurd but inescapable; capitalization links the Gun to the process of learning to read—G is for Gun—so that the *Tribune Primer*'s commands seem as elemental and inevitable as the letters of the alphabet. And yet, of course, this language is so heavily ironized that the *Primer*'s authority (the *Tribune Primer*'s authority and also, by extension, the *New England Primer*'s authority) collapses. Authority in the *Tribune Primer* is contingent, not ordained: there is no good justification for the *Primer*'s voice and there is no reason to follow its absurd edicts.

Field also invokes—and deflates—Isaac Watts. One whole 1886 Sharps and Flats column is devoted to poems that, Field reports, have been circulating since the eighteenth century as the work of Isaac Watts, although Field expresses doubts about their authenticity (not mentioning that he has recently written all of them). One fake Watts poem, "The Merciful Lad," concludes with the following stanzas:

> The dumb shall never call on me
> In vain for kindly aid
> And in my hands the blind shall see
> A bounteous alms displayed.

> In all their walks the lame shall know
> And feel my goodness near,
> And on the deaf will I bestow
> My gentlest words of cheer.

> 'T is by such pious works as these—
> Which I delight to do—
> That men their fellow-creatures please,
> And please their Maker too.[39]

The lad who speaks this poem, however merciful, is clearly engaged in fruitless enterprises, which make a mockery of the final moral. The speaker has learned his lesson by rote and repeats it, nonsensical though it may be, very much like the speaker in Emily Dickinson's early poem "Sic Transit Gloria Mundi." In Dickinson's poem, the speaker repeats a line by Dr. Watts verbatim, but in a context that drains it of pedagogical meaning: "'Sic transit gloria mundi,' / 'How doth the busy bee,' / 'Dum vivimus vivamus,' / I stay mine enemy!" Watts's form and content, decontextualized, is rendered absurd and divested of its authority. To some degree, however, that authority passes from the teacher to the student, as the words are ironized by the speaker's dutiful and yet subversive delivery. The ultimate target, here, is not merciful lads or dutiful reciters but rather teachers (including Watts, whom Field calls a "tutor") who teach by dictation and whose words are as law.

I have not seen any evidence that Dickinson read Field's work (he was just rising to national prominence when she died in 1886), and Field, on reading Dickinson's *First Series* volume, noted in Sharps and Flats, "She was regarded by those who knew her as a strange, if not a weird, creature. This opinion has doubtless been confirmed by the posthumous poetry of hers which has been published, after having been very badly edited by Mr. T. W. Higginson."[40] Nevertheless, Field and Dickinson share aspects of a sensibility: both use pedagogical forms (Watts, the *Primer*) while maintaining the sense that these forms are also forms of bankrupt authority. And both, in aligning speakers against this authority, resort to the subject-position of the child, while continually negotiating what it means to be a child. The figure of the child is generally defined in relation to adults: the Calvinist child is fallen, subject to adult instruction; the romantic child is innocent, subject to adult nostalgia. But, from Field's perspective as from Dickinson's, neither model is safe or stable. Institutional powers, represented by adults, are threatening even to innocents ("This is a gun. Is the Gun loaded?"), and the hierarchies that maintain them are dangerous.

And yet, what is the alternative? Here is where the two poets diverge. Dickinson uses the tensions inherent in adult-child relationships (and in changing pedagogical practices) to stage power struggles that often remain unresolved. Field, by contrast, creates two extreme modes: satirical poems and sketches, such as those in the *Tribune Primer*, in which children are crushed by adults; and saccharine poems and sketches, including most of his later, most popular, work, in which adults (imagine that they) cede their authority to children. And yet, while the later, sweeter Field oeuvre seems to transfer adult power to children, a closer look at the dynamic in these poems reveals an ongoing anxiety, not so much about what it means to be a child, but rather about what it means to be an adult.

BEDROOM POEMS

The Eugene Field memorial in Lincoln Park in Chicago, near the entrance to the zoo, shows The Rock-a-By Lady from Hushaby Street hovering over two sleeping children; carved relief panels depicting scenes from "Wynken, Blynken, and Nod" and "The Sugar-Plum Tree" support the figures, and jutting out from this base are two long stone benches. At the end of each bench is a child-height drinking fountain; a vignette on one fountain shows the Fly-Away Horse, while the other depicts a scene from "Seein' Things at Night." Taken together, these images represent a pared-down version of Field's popular canon, and—as the sleeping children suggest—the poems have something in common: they all take place in a kind of Fieldian dreamtime, in which the everyday rules governing children's and adults' roles are suspended. And more concretely, they are located in the increasingly demarcated, "decorated," and privatized space of the bourgeois child's bedroom.

Why did Field move, so decisively, into the bedroom? In the mid-1880s Field built a much wider audience for himself by moving from satires of adult-child relationships into celebrations of those relationships; none of the poems depicted in the Lincoln Park memorial is a satire and all were written after 1885. But as he celebrated the adult-child dyad, he also worked through the problems of hierarchy and power as posed by his *Tribune Primer* pieces. Alphabet primers, as Crain argues, essentialize the social order by taking a random system of signs—A, B, C—and assigning concrete images and narratives to them: "In Adam's fall / We sinned all." Even in later-nineteenth-century schoolbooks, such as *McGuffey's*, literalism reigns as the world is revealed to be orderly and hierarchical—and non-negotiable. In many ways, American culture was becoming more orderly and compartmentalized in the turn of the century, as Alan Trachtenberg has famously argued. The rudimentary "separate spheres" notion that separated women and children from men was being replaced by finer gradations: by the turn of the century children had their own rooms, their "very own magazines" (as Mary Mapes Dodge put it), and even their own (shorter) drinking fountains. The result of all of this was not one firm line dividing childhood from adulthood but rather a series of spatial and cultural boundaries. Such a proliferation of boundaries made childhood more distant from adulthood—but at the same time, since the boundaries were constantly multiplying and shifting, the firmness of these boundaries was less and less clear. Clear hierarchies (such as those represented in many schoolbooks) were becoming harder to visualize: Were women always less powerful than men, even as they acted as the primary consumers in a consumer-driven society? Were children always less powerful than their parents, even as they were more systematically educated, formed networks of like-minded peers, participated in the consumer economy, and generated their own subcultures?

One example of a boundary that emerged in the wake of anthropology and folklore studies was predicated on the notion that children somehow have their "own" separate folk culture with its own endemic rituals. In 1883 William Wells Newell's *Games and Songs of American Children* systematized children's rhymes, collecting and categorizing them by type. Newell's text stresses that children have their own practices, entirely apart from adults, but at the same time he suggests that children's culture is older and more conservative than adult culture, repeating the same games and songs that were played in Shakespeare's time. One of the rhymes that Newell reports begins "Intry-mintry, cutrey-corn, apple-seed and apple-thorn . . ."[41] Field repeats a version of this rhyme verbatim in his poem "Intry-Mintry." But while in Newell's collection the adult observer is invisible (and hence powerful, collecting and interpreting what the children only repeat), in Field's poem the adult becomes both visible and impotent:

> Willie and Bess, Georgie and May—
> Once, as these children were hard at play,
> An old man, hoary and tottering came
> And watched them playing their pretty game.
> He seemed to wonder, while standing there,
> What the meaning thereof could be—
> Aha, but the old man yearned to share
>   Of the little children's innocent glee
> As they circled around with laugh and shout
> And told their rime at counting-out:
>   "Intry-mintry, cutrey-corn . . ."[42]

The point of the poem is that the children's peer culture creates a firm boundary line; the old man cannot share the game—he cannot even interpret it. Unlike the powerful (but corrupt) speaker of the *Tribune Primer,* this adult has no voice: he can only listen mutely. Cut free from the authority structure of schoolrooms and primers, the children inhabit a world that excludes adults. Thus the schoolroom and the playground seem to be polar opposites, but they have one thing in common: both produce boundaries between children and adults, creating extreme power disequilibriums. In the schoolroom, the adults rule; on the playground, children rule; but in neither situation is there a chance for the intimacy that the old man (if not the children) craves.

    By setting his poems in bedrooms and beds, Field is able to engineer a temporary escape from an increasingly compartmentalized social order. Dreams disrupt that order: they are by definition not subject to the laws of nature or society. As the certainties of schoolroom pedagogy are replaced by the raw materials of dreams, the authoritative speakers found in the poetry of Longfellow, Whittier, and even Riley are replaced by children's voices—and by the exploratory voices of adults who want to "feel their way" back to childhood. Although

many of Field's "bedroom" poems became schoolroom recitation-
pieces, the space of the bedroom invites different interactions
between adults and children than the space of the classroom or the
playground. In the classroom, or at least in the "traditional" nineteenth-century classroom (as opposed to the progressive kinder-
gartens that were coming into vogue), the roles of teacher and student
are clear: the teacher offers written and oral texts, and the students
absorb, remember, and repeat them. On the playground, by contrast,
adults are completely sidelined. But in the bedroom, the proper roles
of the adult and child are less clear and more open to negotiation.

One of Field's most famous poems, "Wynken, Blynken, and Nod"
(originally called "A Dutch Lullaby"), begins midfantasy; it is not
clear who is talking or where the speaker is getting the story:

> Wynken, Blynken, and Nod one night
>> Sailed off in a wooden shoe—
> Sailed on a river of crystal light,
>> Into a sea of dew.
> "Where are you going, and what do you wish?"
>> The old moon asked the three.
> "We've come to fish for the herring fish
>> That live in this beautiful sea;
> Nets of silver and gold have we!"
>> Said Wynken,
>> Blynken,
>> And Nod.[43]

It is not until the last stanza that the speaker is revealed to be a
mother. Suddenly, she is present in the poem, playfully naming her
child's body parts as she promises to populate his dreams:

> Wynken and Blynken are two little eyes,
>> And Nod is a little head,
> And the wooden shoe that sailed the skies
>> Is a wee one's trundle-bed.
> So shut your eyes while mother sings
>> Of wonderful sights that be,
> And you shall see the beautiful things
>> As you rock in the misty sea,
> Where the old shoe rocked the fishermen three:
>> Wynken,
>> Blynken,
>> And Nod.

The speaker, in the final stanza, is ambiguously situated both inside and outside the child's consciousness. While the ultimate goal is physical control (putting the child to sleep), the strategy involves not an overt assertion of power but rather a deployment of what Richard Brodhead calls disciplinary intimacy, in which the child's mind is reorganized as the body is soothed.[44]

Field's bedroom poems, then, might be read as another form of pedagogy, just as controlling as a classroom situation but more intimate and stealthier. However, blurring the lines between children and adults does not necessarily reinscribe conventional authority structures. Adults, as well as children, are changed by their exchanges, and new possibilities are revealed, as in "Child and Mother":

> O Mother-my-love, if you'll give me your hand,
> And go where I ask you to wander,
> I will lead you away to a beautiful land,—
> The Dreamland that's waiting out yonder . . .
>
> .   .   .   .
>
> There'll be no little tired-out boy to undress,
> No questions or cares to perplex you,
> There'll be no little bruises or bumps to caress,
> Nor patching of stockings to vex you;
> For I'll rock you away on a silver-dew stream
> And sing you asleep when you're weary,
> And no one shall know of our beautiful dream
> But you and your own little dearie.[45]

The mother's experimental renunciation of power leads to her regression into an intimate and infantile helplessness—a secret state of bliss that many of Field's "childhood" poems posit even when they do not narrativize it so explicitly. This bliss is characterized not so much by innocence as by unconsciousness: the mother enters a dreamworld in which she loses her self-awareness. Childhood is not so much Edenic as intoxicating; the dream is almost druggy, and it should be no surprise that at least one Fieldian dream-figure, the "Rock-a-By Lady from Hushaby Street," delivers to sleepy children poppies that "hang from her hands and her feet."[46]

Field's bedroom poems do sometimes sheer into nightmares, and in these, the issue of boundaries becomes paramount. Slason Thompson suggests that one of Field's most popular nightmare poems, "Seein' Things at Night" (1894), was actually developed from an earlier poem, "The Awful Bugaboo" (1882). The differences—and contiguities—between the two are notable. Like the *Tribune Primer* passages, "The Awful Bugaboo" uses a moralistic form to tell a horrifying parable about the abuse of power. A little girl begs her mother not to take away the lamp, because she is afraid of the dark:

> But Mamma took the lamp
> And oh, the Room was Dark and Damp.
> The Little Girl was Scared to Death—
> She did not Dare to Draw her Breath.
>
> And all at once the Bugaboo
> Came Rattling down the Chimney Flue;
> He perched upon the little Bed
> And scratched the Girl until she bled.
>
> He drank the Blood and scratched again.
> The Little Girl cried out in Vain,
> He picked her up and Off he Flew,
> This Naughty, Naughty Bugaboo![47]

The Bugaboo not only invades the sanctity of the child's bedroom and body but also invades the poem on the level of genre, taking a traditional "moral" form and infusing it with anarchic amorality. The voice of the omniscient (but again, not benign or predictable) speaker chimes in at the end with a threat in place of a moral:

> So children, when in Bed tonight,
> Don't let them Take away the Light,
> Or else the awful Bugaboo
> May come and Fly away with you.

Like the benign adult in "The Sugar-Plum Tree," the Bugaboo enters a child's room, finding her with "a pretty Nightcap on her head." But he cannot restrain himself from violating her physically: the Bugaboo has lost control, spurred by prosody that reproduces the hierarchies of a Watts poem, and also by a family structure that allows the parents to "take away the light," ignoring the child's needs.

"Seein' Things at Night," by contrast, is a poem that returns narrative and somatic control to the child. Written in Hoosier dialect and modeled very closely on Riley's "Nine Little Goblins," the poem allows a child to tell his own story, in which monsters are "a-standin' in a row / A-lookin' at me crossed-eyed an' pintin' at me so!" It turns out that the monsters—unlike the Bugaboo—are just dreams that appear because the boy has eaten too much pie at dinner. The poem ends with the boy vowing never to accept seconds at dessert time. The boy can control his own body by restricting his diet. And yet this poem objectifies the boy-speaker: he is "cute" because we know, from the beginning of the poem, that his fears are not real. As a children's recitation-piece, "Seein' Things at Night" was widely performed (including, as Burt describes it, by a twelve-year-old at Carnegie Hall) in situations that put children's voices and bodies on display in ways that subjected them to adult observation and evaluation. But such performances are also exchanges: the adults pay attention to the child speakers, listen to them, and applaud them.

At the same time, however, it is true that children in Field's poems are on display as objects of desire: they wear pretty nightcaps, they sing cute songs, they dream dreams that adults find adorable. So whose desires are finally being expressed? Whose dreamland is being described in "Child and Mother"? Moreover, the specifics in these poems—dewy streams, bloodshed—make them discomfitingly erotic. But to what extent is this an anachronistic reading? Was Field's eroticism visible to late-nineteenth-century readers? James Kincaid, in his book-length study of Anglo-American ideas about children's sexuality, notes that during this period there was a firm line between adult and child bodies, defined by sexuality: adults were sexual, children were not. He points out, however, that because this line was sexual, it had the effect of eroticizing children's innocence, making it part of a discourse that was essentially about sex.

The test case for problematic nineteenth-century depictions of childhood innocence has become Lewis Carroll's photographs of nude little girls—and although the cultural situation in Victorian England was different from that in Field's Chicago, the parallels are close enough to be useful. Carroll's "Portrait of Evelyn Hatch" (1878) is a photograph of a completely nude child lying in what appears, to twenty-first-century eyes, to be a highly suggestive pose. Morton Cohen argues that Carroll did not and could not imagine little girls as sexual beings, precisely because of the imaginary "line" between childhood innocence and adult corruption.[48] Nina Auerbach makes the opposite case, suggesting that Carroll accepted childhood sexuality without exploiting it: "The eroticism, along with the passionate and seditious powers this had to imply, belongs to the child; the artist merely understands it."[49] Carol Mavor takes a more measured approach: "As both sexual and nonsexual, the body of the little girl marked her as simultaneously different from the male viewer and (according to cultural conventions) lacking the marks of true womanhood."[50] But what does it mean to be "both sexual and nonsexual"? Ultimately, Mavor argues, such images express, without resolving, contradictory understandings of what childhood entails.

Such contradictions certainly multiplied in Field's America as well as in Carroll's England; children were savage (and what could be more sexual than a savage) but also innocent; they were seen as physically beautiful objects of desire, and yet this desire could be articulated (or even imagined) only in certain clearly prescribed ways. Insofar as a horizon of expectations can have latent as well as explicit parameters, Field's poems had an erotic dimension in the nineteenth century. In other words, it makes sense to assume that, for newspaper-poetry fans in Aurora, Illinois, or for Missouri schoolteachers orchestrating "Eugene Field Day," there was something attractive—but nothing overtly erotic—about a poem such as "Child and Mother." But it also makes sense to assume that the covert eroticism of these poems was part of their charm—and this assumption is helped along by Field's own sub rosa writings.

If the public discourse in schools, churches, and parlors framed Field's bedroom poems as nonerotic, a minor counterdiscourse did emerge in the public-private space of men's clubs, where poems were often recited that glossed or parodied—and thus more clearly articulated—the contradictory desires that circulated through the wider culture. One such poem, Field's *Little Willie*, appeared in at least twenty-seven private editions, although it was never anthologized with his other "love-songs of childhood." The poem recalls, "When Willie was a little boy, / No more than five or six . . ." and then lapses into reveries about sleeping with him:

> Closely he cuddled up to me,
>   And put his hands in mine,
> Till all at once I seemed to be
>   Afloat in seas of brine.
> Sabean odors clogged the air,
>   And filled my soul with dread,
> Yet I could only grin and bear
>   When Willie wet the bed.

After several rhapsodic stanzas the poem concludes:

> Had I my choice, no shapely dame
>   Should share my couch with me,
> No amorous jade of tarnished fame,
>   Nor wench of high degree;
> But I would choose and choose again
>   The little curly head,
> Who cuddled close beside me when
>   He used to wet the bed.[51]

This poem does not undermine or reverse any of the assumptions that organize "Wynken, Blynken, and Nod" or "Child and Mother." In both of those poems the adult and the child also share a dream with a liquid center—a "sea of dew" or a "silver-dew stream." Loss of control is a good experience because it is mutual; mother and child share the sensation of dissolving the boundaries between them. *Little Willie* simply makes these subtexts explicit: children are more attractive, more desirable, indeed sexier, than women. And yet this is not a rape fantasy like "The Awful Bugaboo," but rather a fantasy about unlimited access. Willie is not subject to control; instead, he initiates a shared loss of control, a relaxation of the boundaries between bodies, metaphorized by the "Sabean odors" that the child and the adult breathe together. Willie is both an independent entity and a blurry figure for the speaker's own remembered pleasures. What, exactly, does the speaker desire here? He desires Willie's innocence—his distance from the "tarnished" sexuality of womanhood—but this desire is eroticized precisely because, confirming Kincaid's account, it crosses that sexual-and-yet-nonsexual line between childhood and adulthood.

Field's impulse to cross this boundary was not (or not just) an individual peculiarity; it represents a broad cultural discourse. As Jackson Lears points out:

> [T]oward the end of a century of capitalist expansion the image of the sickly-sweet child pervaded popular novels, plays, and poems. Its appeal was intensified during the 1880s and 1890s by the crisis of cultural authority. As social conventions stiffened, their religious basis weakened, and the psychic demands of adulthood grew more onerous. As familiar definitions of selfhood and maturity became less trustworthy, childlike traits became more alluring.[52]

Willie is alluring because he is not yet conventionally socialized, and while he is not a woman, he is also not a man. This is important because Field is escaping, quite specifically, the psychic demands of *manhood*—and performing his escape within the homosocial confines of men's leisure clubs. By refusing a "wench of high degree," or prostitute, Field is refusing to act out his masculine role as capitalist (engaging in sex as economic exchange) and conqueror (defining manhood through penetration). He is using Willie to map out an alternative space for himself, a space that absolves him of those boundaries that not only make children childlike but also (on the other side of the line) make men manly. This powerlessness is pleasurable because it relieves him of the financial, moral, and sexual responsibilities of manhood—and, of course, because it is temporary.

Little Willie was meant to be a joke-poem, and this very fact points to a contradiction that limits ways that Field's childhood poems can be read as serious social critiques—of men's roles or of anything else. His poems "Wynken, Blynken, and Nod" and "Child and Mother" appeared in the *Chicago Morning News,* wedged between crime statistics and political analysis; *Little Willie* was recited in men's clubs. Both of these social spaces—the city newspaper and the men's club—reinforce the urban, professional, masculine culture that Field's regressions to childhood attempt to escape. Like the park systems that Theodore Roosevelt would work so hard to establish, Field's poems are thus figured as leisure-time respites from the pressures of getting and spending, rather than as serious social critiques of urban masculinity. There is no contradiction in working hard all week and then regressing into childhood over the weekend.

Still, what makes Field notable is the extremes to which he went. An even more explicitly eroticized version of childhood appears in Field's one surviving work of prose pornography, *Only a Boy,* in which a twelve-year-old boy is seduced by a thirty-year-old woman. This text was never publicly released, but it circulated widely enough that Anthony Comstock a New York morals crusader, had copies of it suppressed.[53] And unlike Comstock's other targets, *Only a Boy* remains graphic even by twenty-first-century standards. So while it is true that relatively few readers saw *Little Willie* and even fewer probably saw *Only a Boy,* it can at least be concluded from them that—contra Morton Cohen—the following questions were not inconceivable in the later nineteenth century: What if adults *can* cross back into the "beautiful dream" of childhood? What if childhood never really goes away? What if, as Field put it to Alice Earle, "a man is still a boy at forty" because childhood—far from being the lost Eden that the romantics imagined—is an inescapable part of the self? What if childhood is scary? And (even scarier) what if it is sexual? Crossing boundaries generates these questions, questions that contributed to Field's appeal even though—or precisely because—few of his readers would have articulated them so explicitly.

LIVING DOLLS

In the last year of his life, Field renovated a house in suburban Buena Park, Illinois, documenting the slow transformation of its interior in Sharps and Flats columns that were later collected into a book, *The House.* But the centerpiece of Field's public private house was his bedroom, the room that he died in. More so than Longfellow, Whittier, or even Riley (who was quite private, although a showman onstage), Field managed his private life as a public spectacle, aided by his own daily column and by the journalists who found his pranks and poses irresistible. Field's bedroom was a stage on which he performed the role of "Eugene Field," and it makes sense that, soon after his death, Mary J. Reid and Henrietta Field wrote a memoir for *St. Nicholas* readers that focuses on this space:

> Before we go upstairs to Eugene Field's room, the one which holds his choicest treasures, it is necessary to remind you again that he had a child's love of grotesque toys and of barbaric colors and effects. He was especially fond of red. The room in which he died is papered with a fantastic, swirly pattern on a red ground, which is absolutely exasperating to those people who prefer soft browns and full reds . . . In Henry B. Fuller's "With the Procession" that author tells about a Chicago woman named Susan Bates, who furnished her whole house magnificently except for one little room. Upon this room she spent a great deal of money, and visited many old-fashioned stores, in order to furnish it like the primitive one she had occupied when a girl in her father's house. Now this was partly Eugene Field's idea in furnishing his own room.[54]

Reid and Field's description contains its own interpretation: in furnishing his room, Field was creating a spectacular manifestation of an inner self that is also a primitive self—the survival of the archaic child within the adult frame. This idea—archaic child, adult frame—also organized much of Field's poetry as he struggled to express the dreamworld of "childhood" (both actual childhood and the adult's perceived inner self) within the conventional lyric frames that were available.

Conventional lyric forms are social; they adhere to established conventions and encourage recitation as a form of acculturation into a real or imagined community. Longfellow and Whittier assume a national community; Dodge's *St. Nicholas* posits a peer community, and Riley imagines a tight-knit local community. But in Field's work the community has shrunk to two—or possibly even to one—while his forms continue to reflect the sociability of the other schoolroom poets. Field's strange isolation within a social framework partly reflects his chosen medium, the urban newspaper, which offered a sense of community but no personal contact; thousands of people read his columns, but in the privacy of their homes or at least in the privacy that an opened newspaper provides even in a public place. Indeed, the content of many of Field's poems can be construed as despairingly antisocial, withdrawing into the opiated world of dreams. And yet, formally, his poems are social, in the sense that they rhyme and are metrical; it did not occur to him, as it did to Dickinson (who can also be despairingly antisocial) to break the rules of prosody. Field often figured himself as a wayward, unconventional child trapped in a buttoned-up, conventional adult's body, and this figuration can also be applied to his poems, which construct alternative fantasy worlds, but within the confines of late-Victorian rhymes and meters.

Among the more mysterious objects in Field's house, and in his poems, were little figures:

> As you enter the room, you are confronted with two hideous figures. An outlandish Japanese figure is suspended from the wall by one arm. In the other it holds three Japanese gongs fastened together so as to make a loud sound when struck with the red stick. The other is the face of a hobgoblin attached to the headboard of his bedstead. Field pretended that he bought it to frighten away his babies when they insisted upon interrupting him while he was writing; but, like their father, they were so fond of the ludicrous that the strange faces the monster would make when certain strings were pulled only made them laugh; so the intended bugaboo but added to the attractions of the room.[55]

In addition to the Japanese puppet and the hobgoblin, Field collected dolls—bisque dolls, wooden dolls, and mechanical dolls—that inspired the toy museum established in St. Louis in his honor. Living-doll poems and stories were ubiquitous subgenres during this period; a whole *St. Nicholas* anthology was eventually produced, composed exclusively of doll texts. When toys come alive in Field poems, they sometimes follow the standard plots of other fin de siècle doll narratives by falling in love; female dolls, especially French ones, are prone to coquettishness: "The little French doll was a dear little doll / Tricked out in the sweetest of dresses."[56] But dolls can also be slightly sinister figures—small selves who work their magic independent of the conscious will:

> Where the moonbeams hover o'er
> Playthings sleeping on the floor—
> Where my weary wee one lies
> Cometh Lady Button-Eyes.

Cometh like a fleeting ghost
From some distant eerie coast;
Never footfall can you hear
As that spirit fareth near—
Never whisper, never word
From that shadow-queen is heard.
In ethereal raiment dight,
From the realm of fay and sprite
In the depth of yonder skies
Cometh Lady Button-Eyes.[57]

The uncanny Lady Button-Eyes might be a rag doll, but she emerges from the child's own consciousness and then, in the final stanzas, re-merges with the child's body: "Layeth she her hands upon / My dear weary little one / And those white hands overspread / Like a veil the curly head . . ." Field's archaic language underscores Lady Button-Eyes's primitivism: she is not a modern doll but the representative of an older folkloric or handcraft tradition, just as children were assumed to represent earlier stages of civilization. In 1896, in "A Study of Dolls," G. Stanley Hall argued against the prevailing assumption that dolls are mainly a child's way of imagining parenthood, with the doll as baby. Instead, Hall suggested, dolls are mirrors of another self: "Perhaps nothing so fully opens up the juvenile soul to the student of childhood as well-developed doll play. Here we see fully revealed things which the childhood instinct often tends to keep secret. It shows out the real nature which Plato thought so important that he advised drunkenness as a revealer of character."[58] Hall, a promoter and popularizer of social-scientific methods, sees in dolls not artifice but authenticity: when adults look at children playing with dolls, Hall believes that they gain access to an authenticity, a "real nature," that is not otherwise available to them, precisely because they are adults.

"Lady Button-Eyes" concretizes Carolyn Steedman's understanding of the child, and specifically the later-nineteenth-century child, as a personification of the interior self—a personification that prefigures the twentieth-century psychological ideas that readers were so quick to embrace after the First World War, and that have since become part of many Americans' commonsense understanding of what a "person" is. Unlike romantic children, who as projections of the lost self trail "clouds of glory" and a display a fundamental innocence, this new trope of the child is a figure for an adult's still-present personal history—some of which is understood and some of which is retained but not remembered or understood. Reid and

Field, commenting on Field's knickknacks, note that he is good at recovering "quaint things" that other people can't see: "Where he found that gorgeous red paper, or the old-fashioned calico for the red curtain, it would be difficult to tell, but he had a knack for discovering quaint things which other people pass by without notice."[59] Again, it must be stressed that this version of the self was not a discovery but a construction: an increasingly socially sanctioned way of understanding the relationship between childhood and adulthood that not only crossed the child-adult line but actually placed the child *inside* the adult as *part* of the adult, like an old-fashioned little room in a big modern house. Field's fantasies often close the gulf between childhood and adulthood, making childhood accessible to adults as an enduring, lifelong interior condition. Lady Button-Eyes, despite her button eyes, is not a baby (she's a lady) and not cute; rather, she is a serious figure for the American self as it was emerging in the later nineteenth century.

CHAPTER SIX

Emily Dickinson and the Form of Childhood

The infantilization of American poetry reaches both a peak and an endgame in the work of Emily Dickinson. She was, in many ways, a perfect "schoolroom poet," and (with nudges from Mabel Loomis Todd) her work appeared in *St. Nicholas* and the *Youth's Companion,* courting both child readers and adults who appreciated "childlike" poems.[1] Eventually, by the turn of the century, it was also featured in many elementary-school textbooks, so that children learning to appreciate "standard authors" were likely to encounter "Helpfulness" ("If I can stop one heart from breaking") or "Out of the Morning" ("Will there really be a morning?") as well as Field's "Dutch Lullaby," Whittier's "Barefoot Boy," and Longfellow's "Psalm of Life." Dickinson's incorporation into educational contexts makes sense, because in her 1890s incarnation she struggles—as both a letter writer and a poet—with pedagogical questions. Like Field, she asks (implicitly and sometimes explicitly) whether adults can in some sense remain children. But unlike Field, she also develops an experimental educational practice that uses—but also ultimately undermines—the social and generic conventions of the schoolroom poets. For Dickinson, acts of pedagogical transmission are imperative to attempt but impossible to complete. This impossibility is registered in the bodies of her poems, which display rough and seemingly "incomplete" surfaces. As I will argue, Dickinson's strong sense of play modifies a fundamental clause in the generic contract governing popular poetry: she forecloses on the possibility of repetition.

Dickinson can thus be understood as a participant-observer, working as a minor schoolroom poet while also questioning the premises governing schoolrooms, poetry, and poets. Of course, the Emily Dickinson of the 1890s is not only a "supposed person" (as she once called her "Representative" voice in a letter to T. W. Higginson) but also a *posthumous* supposed person—and a highly fragmented one at that. And yet Dickinson's circulation through the fin de siècle world of popular publishing is part of her because it is part of her literary history, and part of the larger literary history of the infantilization of American poetry. In this chapter, then, I will sidestep recent debates (as articulated, for example, by Domhnall Mitchell) about what Dickinson *meant to write,* in order to concentrate exclusively on what her *writings meant.*[2] More precisely, I am interested not in what her writings meant to her but rather what they meant to her early readers—to the puzzled and intrigued reviewers, textbook editors, schoolteachers, and students who encountered her work in print before the First World War. The version of Dickinson that I will discuss is composed of texts published before 1914, when Martha Dickinson Bianchi's *A Single Hound* prompted a slow resurgence of academic and critical interest in Dickinson. In this context, her handwritten manuscripts are immaterial, since they were not available to the public at the time. In advancing arguments about what this Dickinson "meant," then, I am not making assertions about authorial intent; rather, I am reading her work in light of the popular discourses (particularly the obsession with childhood) that set the terms of her first popular reception, and that effectively "socialized" her in the 1890s and early 1900s.

Willis Buckingham, in his essential work on Dickinson's reception, has focused on Higginson's link to Emerson's "Poetry of the Portfolio," arguing that when readers read her poems they felt drawn into a private communion with the author.[3] It is certainly the case that Dickinson's collections (*Poems by Emily Dickinson, Second Series* and *Third Series*) can generate this "private" effect. But it is also true that, for many readers, Dickinson's work was mediated by more heterogenous, more explicitly public, anthologies and periodicals that had the effect of socializing her, exposing the idea of a private portfolio as a polite fiction. This pre-1914 archive is an awkward assemblage, composed of poems that were sometimes renamed, repunctuated, and made to do work (in *The Lover's Mother Goose* or the *Cyr Fourth Reader*) that their author never intended. And yet, this is to some extent the case with all poems that are published and that circulate in the social world, especially when they are recontextualized in anthologies and periodicals. Moreover, the incompleteness of this "Emily Dickinson" is not just a critical problem; it is also part of the story: the Dickinson that emerges from this archive was indeed seen as incomplete by many of her readers. She was understood as more childlike and less "finished" than her later incarnations—and this, far from being a weakness, helped her to operate successfully in the 1890s, the era of "child-study," the Brownies, and Eugene Field.

I have suggested that Dickinson, despite (or because of) her childlike persona, forecloses on the possibility of repetition. But to understand the ways in which she challenges the assumptions of the schoolroom poets, it is first necessary to see she how engages with their social world, the world of late-nineteenth-century discourses about childhood and education. Dickinson "went public" in the

1890s, when the authority of the schoolroom poets and everything they stood for (patriarchal power, white hegemony, middlebrow culture, nostalgia) was at its height. At the same time, the institutions that supported these poets were changing: women were gaining ground, immigrants were altering the demographics of cities, popular magazines (*Ladies' Home Journal*) were competing with the established monthlies (*Atlantic Monthly*), and "child-study" was complicating people's ideas about themselves, their children, and themselves *as* children. Dickinson could not have anticipated these social upheavals, but her poems were well suited to register them, not because they were openly unconventional, but precisely because they verged on the conventional, as Barton Levi St. Armand and Elizabeth Petrino have pointed out.[4] They sometimes met—and often *almost met*—readers' generic expectations. This meant that Dickinson could successfully circulate as a perfectly respectable pedagogical poet in young people's textbooks and periodicals. But it also meant that, when she broke with convention, that breakage was a visible and audible (and discomfiting) part of her work: she came *so* close to writing perfect poems, her critics complained. But why couldn't she finish them?

DICKINSON IN SCHOOL

Emily Dickinson did "finish" a few conventionally executed poems, including the first one she ever published, "Sic Transit Gloria Mundi," which appeared as an 1852 valentine in the *Springfield (Mass.) Republican* and was reprinted in the 1894 volume of her *Letters*. This poem can be seen as the foundation for all of her later pedagogical struggles—and her formal innovations, which are related to those struggles—precisely because it works as a "perfect" schoolroom poem. The nineteenth century was a century of almost continuous (though unevenly implemented) educational reform, much of which attacked the rigid disciplinary structure of classrooms and the heavy reliance on rote recitations. In his *Seventh Annual Report to the Board*, Horace Mann (a Whig from Massachusetts who dominated the field of education in the mid-nineteenth century) described a typical antebellum classroom:

> The teacher holds a book with a card before him, and with a pointer in his hand, says a, and he [the student] echoes a; then b, and he echoes b, and so on until the vertical row of lifeless and ill-favored characters is completed. Not a single faculty of the mind is occupied except that of imitating sounds, and even the

number of these imitations amount to only twenty-six. A parrot or idiot could do the same thing.[5]

"Sic Transit Gloria Mundi" takes such a classroom as its premise. In seventeen lockstep stanzas, Dickinson's speaker (like a parrot or idiot, albeit a highly amusing one) replicates the conventions of a recitation piece:

> "Sic transit gloria mundi,"
>   "How doth the busy bee,"
> "Dum vivimus vivamus,"
>   I stay mine enemy![6]

The "busy bee" (like the prosody) comes from Isaac Watts's "Against Idleness and Mischief," which was taught to children on both sides of the Atlantic and which also inspired the deadpan humor of Lewis Carroll. Here Dickinson recruits catchphrases and rhythms to spark specifically "educational" memories in her readers. This makes sense because the poem was originally addressed to William Howland, a former tutor and schoolteacher. But it makes a deeper kind of sense in the context of Dickinson's subsequent career, which involved producing poems that work very differently from this one, undoing almost all the assumptions that this poem makes about education and childhood.

As in Field's parodies of Watts (in which the "Merciful Lad" announces all sorts of ridiculous "good deeds"), "Sic Transit Gloria Mundi" is full of reiterated (but only half-processed) announcements:

> During my education
>   It was announced to me
> That gravitation, stumbling,
>   Fell from an apple tree.

The poem's speaker seems to accept without question or digestion everything that is "announced" to her, and she renders the stance of the good student—and the act of verbatim recitation—absurd. The speaker in this poem is utterly obedient and socialized : "Good bye, Sir, I am going / My country calleth me," she says blithely, accepting a cliché as an order. By the end, she has pictured her own complete disintegration into ashes, which makes sense because she is nothing but a series of rhetorical flourishes. The speaker's "form" is also utterly obedient, and ends with a closure that forecloses the possibility of further growth:

> The memory of my ashes
> Will consolation be;
> Then farewell, Tuscarora,
> And farewell, Sir, to thee!

Dickinson's own education was a rich mix of scientific precision and theological doctrine, but while "Sic Transit Gloria Mundi" superficially reflects this dynamic, it is fundamentally agnostic in its deconstruction of the sources of pedagogical authority, from Latin textbooks to Watts to the "Hill of Science." Moreover, it parodies the more fundamental process of learning what to expect from poetry, suggesting that the laws of the genre are not so much a social contract as a form of social coercion, a way for the "country" to "call" children and to make them good citizens who know how to internalize and perform specific rules. This poem is accessible, complete, and written in the familiar form of Watts's prosody. And the student reciting the poem is also accessible and complete: obedient, well-educated, unskeptical, and "finished."

As Field understood, such students are "in Danger," not because (as Dickinson put it in a famous letter to Higginson) their gait is "spasmodic," but because it is not spasmodic enough: the individual speaking subject vanishes behind her de-individuated, fully socialized voice, a voice that is produced by the demands of the genre. "Sic Transit Gloria Mundi" is a perpetual-motion machine that will absorb any nonsense while making it sound sensible because it rhymes so well, as if rhyme and reason were synonymous. In addition to being a "perfect" poem, it is also a "perfect" anthology or textbook, in the sense that it turns blithely from topic to topic and text to text, emptying each of its contents and history, so that Bunker Hill and transcendentalism and the Garden of Eden are all basically part of the same big lesson. And this lesson, ultimately, is not about American history or Emerson or Genesis but rather about "fitting in" to the rhyme scheme and to the social world that the poem represents. Every lesson fits equally well into the poem's metrical scheme, just as every poem in Dickinson's copy of Ebenezer Porter's *Rhetorical Reader* was governed by the same laws of articulation, modulation, and emphasis.[7]

Dickinson's appearances in textbooks and young people's periodicals exert pressure on her individual poems much like the pressure that "Sic Transit Gloria Mundi" exerts on its (many) topics: overly rigid pedagogical structures suppress the individuality of the poet's voice. However, between 1890 and 1914, pedagogical power structures were also in flux, so that the lessons that her poems taught were not the lockstep elocutionary rules of the mid-nineteenth-century classroom.

Had these standards held, Dickinson would not have been included in textbooks, since, even at her "best" (by nineteenth-century standards), her later work does not read as smoothly as Longfellow's or Field's. But Dickinson's cultural work in turn-of-the-century textbooks is worth considering, precisely because her poems register anxieties—about authority, control, socialization and childhood—that were also present in the textbooks and in the culture at large.

   Dickinson's distribution in early primary-school textbooks was relatively widespread, although critics have not discussed it and her bibliographers do not list these publications. By the turn of the century her work was reprinted in primary-school textbooks, including *Nature in Verse: A Poetry Reader for Children* (1896), the *Cyr Reader, Book Four* (1896), *Stepping-Stones to Literature* (1897), *Lights to Literature, Third Reader* (1898), *Graded Poetry: Fourth Year* (1906), *Buckwater's Third Reader* (1907), *Wide Awake, Third Reader* and *Fourth Reader* (1908), and the *Character-Building Reader, Third Year* (1910).[8] Most reader series went from first grade ("First Reader") through either sixth or eighth grade, but Dickinson, for some reason, is clustered in third- and fourth-year readers aimed at eight- to ten-year-olds. Dickinson, then, functioned during her brief critical fallow period (after the mediocre reception of the *Third Series* in 1896 and before her rediscovery by the modernists) as a bona fide schoolroom poet, although a minor one. To put things in perspective, the readers listed above represent only a small percentage of the textbooks published between 1896 and 1914. A vastly larger number of those I have examined make no mention of Dickinson. Virtually all lean heavily on work by Longfellow, Whittier, and Field; Riley is also well represented, although slightly less than the others because of debates about the appropriateness of dialect. And, among women writers, Helen Hunt Jackson and Celia Thaxter appear much more frequently than Dickinson.

   Still, Dickinson's poems in textbooks reached many thousands of readers. Each series asks children to seek slightly different lessons from the texts, thereby making Dickinson's poems work in ways that have more to do with the editor's agenda than with the poems as written (although I would argue that poems as written are always and only made meaningful by their contexts). To explore competing ways of reading her poetry pedagogically, I will rely on three examples: the *Cyr Reader,* which comes closest to replicating the midcentury (socializing) expectations of "Sic Transit Gloria Mundi"; the *Character-Building Reader,* which works through tensions between individualism and socialization; and *Nature in Verse,* which advocates an individualized, "child-centered" learning process.

Ellen M. Cyr's series of graded readers was meant to teach students good taste; like Mary Mapes Dodge, Cyr assumes that with good taste will come good (American, middle-class) citizenship. The preface to Cyr's *Fourth Reader* asserts:

> The primary aim of this reader is education by means of good literature. The mere teaching of the art of reading is of minor importance compared to the awakening of interest and formation and education of literary taste. . . Great care has been taken in selecting this matter; only such authors as have written standard literature have been chosen.[9]

Like the environment of "Sic Transit Gloria Mundi," Cyr is committed to socialization, to making students meet certain preordained "standards."

Cyr thus organized her readers around monumental American figures; the *Third Reader* focuses on Whittier and Lowell, while the *Fourth Reader* takes up Holmes and Bryant. Biographical sketches describe these authors' (respectable, New England) backgrounds, their "homes and haunts," and their public services to humanity. But in the *Fourth Reader,* wedged between accounts of "Bryant's Birthplace" and "Bryant's Early Home Life," is Dickinson's poem "A Day." It begins:

> I'll tell you how the sun rose,—
> A ribbon at a time.
> The steeples swam in amethyst,
> The news like squirrels ran.
>
> The hills untied their bonnets,
> The bobolinks begun.
> Then I said softly to myself,
> "That must have been the sun!"[10]

This poem is an impeccable complement to Bryant, using a "standard" (i.e., East Coast) American landscape to describe a sublime experience. Dickinson's imagery is more fanciful and domestic than Bryant's, but this makes sense since she is a female and a minor presence, without her own biographical sketch. The second half of Dickinson's poem, describing the sunset, is more theologically and epistemologically skeptical, but it is also, as if to balance its serious themes, cuter:

> But how he set, I know not.
> There seemed a purple stile

Which little yellow boys and girls
Were climbing all the while

Till when they reached the other side,
A dominie in gray
Put gently up the evening bars,
And led the flock away.

The dominie is so gentle and the children are so obedient that it is hard to see that Dickinson is meditating on the nature of death. The dominie's authority is reassuring but illusory: the speaker actually knows nothing about how the sun sets, and a cleric is the last person who can help her learn. The most important part of the day's lesson cannot be learned, because no one knows how it ends.

This skepticism, however, is balanced by the poem's prosody, which achieves the alphabetical certainty of ABCB in every quatrain, so that at least we know how it will end: with a word that rhymes with *gray*. Although the speaker of the poem is hesitant about her ability to know, and to communicate, her experience, *Cyr's Fourth Reader* reduces this hesitancy by turning "A Day" into an oral recitation piece. At the end of the poem, a pronunciation guide ensures that students will pronounce "amethyst" and "dominie" correctly when they read. Any perceptual or epistemological questions that the speaker may have (how does the sun set? where does childhood go when it disappears? what happens when we die?) are contained by the poem's prosody and by the *Fourth Reader*'s format, which turns "A Day" into an intersubjective, public, socialized poem, much like Bryant's poetry. Ironically, the "literary taste" that this textbook promotes involves setting standards that many of Dickinson's other poems fail to meet. Poetry, for Cyr, is a socializing force that teaches children to develop a specific horizon of expectations and to perform work that meets their expectations. Such work must lend itself to oral repetition, with strong rhymes and the sense of an ending— so that the uncertainties of its message (uncertainties that were endemic to much of society by the secular 1890s) are balanced by the reassuring presence of a child's voice and body repeating the words on the page.

The *Cyr's Reader* assumes that readers should be presented with specific role models, in the form of biographies and standard poems, that they should emulate through repetition. The *Character-Building Reader* series, edited by Ellen E. Kenyon-Warner, Ph.D., takes a more nuanced and cautiously modern approach, emphasizing a balance between socialization and individualism and revealing some contradictions in the process. The *Fourth Year* from Kenyon-Warner's series takes "personal responsibility" as its theme, stating its goals in a preface:

> It is intended that the child who studies this number of the char-acter-building series shall have greatly impressed upon him as he proceeds through the book that we in a great measure are respon-sible for our conduct and its results, good and bad . . . In cases where several morals may be drawn from the same piece, teach-ers may in their questioning gently lead to the conclusion desired and so strengthen the particular growth belonging to this period. A danger exists, here, however. The moral should not be made too obvious. It should not be reiterated in the same form; in many cases it should not be reduced to form at all. What lies vaguely in the mind for some time while coming slowly to definition, weaves itself more strongly into the mental tissue than that which is sub-jected too prematurely to definition and drill.[11]

Kenyon-Warner includes Dickinson's "Out of the Morning," a poem composed of questions ("Will there really be a morning? / Is there such a thing as day?") that are never answered, although the poem's prosody again offers an uncharacteristically predictable "finish." Indeed, part of the poem's governing tension is between the youthful speaker's voice, which seems eager to learn the definitions of "morn-ing" ("Has it feet like water-lilies?" / "Has it feathers like a bird?"), and the silent authorities that can tell her nothing even though she follows all the rules.[12]

The poem's message is ambivalent at best: certainly, the speaker is taking "personal responsibility" in the search for meaning. But to what end? In the context of the *Second Series* (1891), where "Out of the Morning" appeared with many other Dickinson poems, the speaker's questions are anxiety provoking indeed. The speaker's questions are even unnerving in *St. Nicholas,* a context that I will dis-cuss shortly. But in the environment of the *Character-Building Reader's* relentless progressivism, the rest of the textbook answers the question that Dickinson leaves hanging: there will indeed be a morning, if we choose cheerfulness and optimism over despair. "Out of the Morn-ing" is paired with another "questioning" poem:

> There is a little maiden—
> Who is she? do you know?
> Who always has a welcome,
> Wherever she may go.

But this poem comes with an answer built in:

> You surely must have met her!
> You certainly can guess.
> What! Must I introduce her?
> Her name is Cheerfulness.[13]

If the random authorities (sailor, wise man) in "Out of the Morning" are mute, they are not mute in the *Character-Building Reader* as a whole. Their silence is more coy than unsettling, because this textbook's overall message is that certain traits (such as cheerfulness) can be subtly inculcated to construct good characters. Questioning has its place, but ultimately the right answers have already been formulated, so that if students cannot guess they will be told.

However, this textbook does differ from *Cyr's*, and from most earlier textbooks, in its willingness to tolerate a degree of ambiguity. Children must not be taught using "definition and drill" but rather by "coming slowly to definition." Kenyon-Warner admits that it is possible that a poem may generate several messages, and it is also possible that the reiteration of form can do more harm than good, if it results in rote repetition. Indeed, the overly explicit repetition of moral lessons is referred to as a "danger." It appears that some schools—struggling between the mandate to control the group and the desire "build" strong individuals—were offering poems such as Dickinson's "Out of the Morning" that modeled ambiguity as an acceptable mode, as long as the child's wavering eventually led to personal progress. The strong emphasis on repetition, the "reiteration of forms," was being replaced by more individuated, less explicitly authoritarian, pedagogical methods.

"Child-study" and the influence of Darwinism led many educators to think in terms of "stages." The same assumptions that led educators to teach young children *The Song of Hiawatha* (assuming that they had something in common with "savages") also led to an emphasis on "nature-study" (assuming young children were closer to nature) in the early grades. As Mary I. Lovejoy, editor of *Nature in Verse: A Poetry Reader for Children*, put it, "What more delightful medium than verse for transmitting the beauties of nature to the awakened perceptions of childhood? Children are natural lovers of poetry; its musical rhythm pleases the ear, its charm of expression stimulates the imagination, and they are easily led to search for the deeper beauty of meaning."[14] Hands-on gardens became an integral component of schooling; even the conservative Amherst school district had a large gardening program by the turn of the century. The idea was "experiential": children should not just be given information, but should learn to process it for themselves. Lovejoy's reader states its aims by focusing on its adaptability to different children's needs:

> The need of a nature-poetry reader for the lower school grades has long been felt, and it was to meet this obvious want that the present volume has been compiled. It is intended to cover the first four years of school work, and the selections have been carefully graded with a view to adapting them to the varying ages and needs of those who would use the book. A division has been made into Songs of Spring, Summer, Autumn, and Winter, and under each head will be found a wide range of selections, from the simple rhymes suited to the younger readers, to more elaborate poems such as older pupils can easily read and comprehend.[15]

The two Dickinson poems that Lovejoy includes (along with selections from Longfellow, Whittier, Bryant, Field, Dodge, Laura Richards, Helen Hunt Jackson, and even Isaac Watts) are "The Grass" ("The grass has so little to do") and "Summer Shower" ("A drop fell on the apple-tree / Another on the roof"). Everything about the collection invites teachers and students to build individual lesson plans and to cultivate independent taste. There is no biographical information about the authors, so that the students can have a direct encounter without the text, free of any mediating (and generally "improving") authority. There is no "teaching apparatus" provided, no pronunciation guides or study questions. Moreover, the preface assumes that children will come naturally to poetry and read it because it stimulates their imagination. The notion that "reading" means "performing" is replaced with a sense that reading involves an individual (and variable) encounter with the text, and that this variability is a good thing.

The two Dickinson poems in the *Nature in Verse* reader are notable because they do not rhyme perfectly; this sets them apart from every other selection in the book except a few passages from the Bible. The first two stanzas of "The Grass" read:

> The grass has so little to do,—
>   A spear of simple green,
> With only butterflies to brood,
> And bees to entertain,
>
> And stir all day to pretty tunes
> The breezes fetch along,

And hold the sunshine in its lap,
And bow to everything.[16]

Such half-rhymes (green / entertain, along / everything) were controversial among critics reviewing Dickinson's volumes, but in the context of this reader they are offered agnostically, as one optional form among many. The point is that children are "naturally" able to find the music that they are ready to hear; to meet every child's needs, a vast array must be presented. Of course, on a practical level, teachers (especially in crowded public schools) had to balance individualism with crowd control, but the ideal community that Lovejoy's anthology imagines is not coercive; it is based not on performances or declamations but on individual reading, and Lovejoy understands reading (like childhood, and like gardening) not as a teleological narrative of "building" and ultimately "finishing" a project but rather as an ongoing process. This orientation lends itself to a higher tolerance for play, not as a form of disobedience, but as a way to learn. It also lends itself to the acceptance of more experimental forms of poetry, since a poem's music is meant to "stimulate the imagination" rather than to set rhetorical standards.

DICKINSON IN CHILDREN'S PERIODICALS

During the 1890s Dickinson's work also appeared in two periodicals aimed at young people: the *Youth's Companion* and *St. Nicholas*. These publications, like the textbook appearances, "socialized" her, bringing her into contact with pedagogical discourses, but with the added pressures of commercialization. Dickinson had to represent "poetry of the first class" (as the *Companion* put it), but she also had to sell, if not herself, then the values of the periodical. The *Companion,* which featured Dickinson in eight issues from 1891 to 1898, was not exclusively a children's weekly; it had a specific children's page and filled the rest of its pages with chatty, entertaining, mildly inspirational stories, nonfiction articles, and a few newspaper-type verses, aimed at "youths," very broadly conceived. Dickinson's poem "Ready" (published in 1897) appears facing a page that advertises the *Companion*'s ambitions: "The *Companion* addresses and influences what in all probability is the most important portion of the world, the shapers of the next thirty years of its advance." By the 1890s the *Companion* was selling optimism, uplift, and ambition, and when Dickinson's poems were published in that paper they espoused its values.

The other poem to appear with Dickinson's "Ready," on 11 November 1897, celebrates a little boy's healthy development; it ends:

He has heard his parents sigh, and has greatly wondered why
They are sorry when he has such bliss in store;
For he's now their darling boy,
And will be their pride and joy
Though he cannot be their baby any more.[17]

Poems such as this one, on the theme of children's rapid growth (a stark contrast to the "dead child" elegies of the antebellum period) proliferate in the *Companion* of the 1890s, advancing the values of hope and speculation. Other prose articles on the page celebrate the social worth of teachers (who never know how far their influence might reach), the bravery of railway engineers (who stop a runaway engine), and the gallantry of the French playwright "Scribe" (who shares his royalties with a poor governess). Dickinson's tiny poem "Ready" appears in the middle of the page:

They might not need me—
　　Yet they might—
I'll let my heart be
　　Just in sight—

A smile so small
　　As mine might be
Precisely their
　　Necessity.[18]

Of course, Dickinson herself did not title the poem "Ready," but this works well in the *Youth's Companion,* whose readers are readying themselves to shape "the next thirty years of [the world's] advance." To read Dickinson's poems in serial is to get a sense that "they," the social world beyond the poem, are the objects of deep distrust. But here, read against a backdrop of brave railway conductors and inspirational teachers, "they" become unambiguously worthy of the speaker's smile, and the speaker herself seems sure of her own social value by the second stanza: she is likely to be "precisely" what the world needs as it advances, like a little cog in a big train. This poem also neatly illustrates, in its form and contents, what the *Companion* valued in poems: they should be short, sweet, and not too intellectually ambitious. Moreover, they should have some use-value: "Ready" is perfect, because it sets an example for young people, carrying the message that no one is too little to make a contribution. What Dickinson begins, the *Companion* finishes: the uncertainty of the first stanza (am I needed? why are "their" needs so hard to anticipate?) is stabilized by the overall *Companion* ideology, in which everyone who works hard is eventually needed. Even a poem—that least instrumental of all gen-res—can be recruited to the cause.

I hesitate to say that the *Youth's Companion* distorts Dickinson's poem, since part of her power is protean: no one reading can be definitive, and I do not want to claim that any reading or version is inauthentic. But her protean qualities are a function of her ambigu-ity and playfulness, and the *Companion* tolerates no ambiguity: every-thing has its worth, and everything has its price. Moreover, the magazine was committed to meeting, but not necessarily changing or expanding, its readers' expectations. The editors published only those Dickinson poems which they believed could be, as they put it, "widely appreciated." In a rejection letter to Mabel Todd, the editors wrote, "In returning these ten poems we are exceedingly sorry to lose so much that is characteristic and delightful. . . . It is a pity that we cannot think the majority of readers—ignorant of Miss Dickinson's work and unique charm—fully prepared and fit to enjoy the poems we reluctantly return."[19] The reasoning is circular: readers cannot appreciate Dickinson if they have not been exposed to much of her work; thus they cannot be offered much of it. But it also makes a cer-tain sense from a marketing standpoint and underscores my point that, when Dickinson did appear in textbooks and periodicals, she functioned socially and generated social meanings, registering the practical needs of editors and readers. The *Youth's Companion* had no room for Emersonian (or modernist) isolates.

St. Nicholas Magazine, by contrast, had "higher" literary ambitions—and this is exactly the word Dodge frequently used, placing her mag-azine at the top of the cultural hierarchy. "Out of the Morning," the poem used to teach personal responsibility in the *Character-Building Reader,* first found a youthful readership in the May 1891 issue of *St. Nicholas,* under the title "Morning." I have argued elsewhere that *St. Nicholas* was in a curious cultural position, promoting "standard" authors on the one hand but, at the same time, encouraging popular peer culture even though peer culture can be (relatively) anarchic and antiauthoritarian. The magazine's table of contents, which organized poetry into a hierarchy of "poems" (serious work), "verses" (lighter lyrics), and "jingles" (silly stuff) calls "Morning" a verse but honors it with lead status and with a full-page illustration of a curly-haired girl standing in a field of blossoms. Like the little girl called "Cheerfulness," this girl seems to reassure readers that there is, indeed, such a thing as "Day."

But while the overall tone of *St. Nicholas* is hearty and wholesome, its eclecticism and modernity avoid the one-note optimism of the

Youth's Companion, producing a more ludic and agnostic reading environment. Dickinson's poem engages directly with the popular culture of nineteenth- (and eighteenth- and seventeenth-) century American childhood by using a trope from Bunyan's *Pilgrim's Progress.* This strategy was also used by the *St. Nicholas* author Louisa May Alcott in *Little Women,* and to similar effect: even as it uses an old Calvinist story, it empties it of its theology, registering the triumph of secular over Christian values, of St. Nicholas over Jesus, and of uncertainty over faith:

> Oh some scholar! Oh, some sailor!
> Oh, some wise man from the skies!
> Please to tell a little pilgrim
> Where the place called morning lies![20]

In *Little Women,* however, the allegorical structure of *Pilgrim's Progress* remains intact, as does the traditional Calvinist move of thinking in terms of "correspondences": when Meg goes to the ball, she is replaying the scene when Christian goes to Vanity Fair. And even though her "morals" are secularized (don't be vain, and dress sensibly) they are still morals. Dickinson's pilgrim, however, is morally and even epistemologically skeptical: how can "morning" enter a system of correspondences—how can it stand for hope or paradise or anything at all—if it might not even exist? In place of clear correspondences, Dickinson depicts the ever-present threat that perhaps words do not contain, and then reveal, one transcendental meaning.

All this is present in the poem, of course. But it was also present in the magazine and in the children' culture of the period. Ingrid Satelmajar has described Dickinson's publications in the *Youth's Companion* and *St. Nicholas* as misguided and "unsettling" attempts, by Todd, to "market Dickinson posthumously as a 'children's friend.'"[21] But although every publishing context limits the meanings that a poem can produce by creating a specific horizon of expectations, it seems clear that children's textbooks and magazines did not necessarily "misrepresent" Dickinson as a simple or didactic poet. Indeed, by the 1890s *St. Nicholas* was publishing very little explicitly didactic material; the volumes from this period do not consistently link poems with "lessons," presenting instead an array of choices each month, on the assumption that children will build their own characters and their own tastes. The law of the (monological, transcendentally correct) father or preceptor is replaced by the (multiple, pragmatic) laws of marketplace—a marketplace that offers both goods and ideas. A clear moral code and a reliable authority structure are broken down by

Dickinson's questions in "Morning." But these questions appear in a magazine that was also breaking down old moral codes and authority structures, and that was comfortable figuring childhood as a series of questions: as a process of searching and discovery—a process of *play*—rather than just a site of disciplinary socialization.

DICKINSON'S EXPERIMENTAL EDUCATION

The "Emily Dickinson" of the 1890s was herself a playful, childlike figure whose first published autobiographical narrative, namely her letters to Higginson, turns on a pedagogical relationship. The very first Dickinson letters to be published appeared in an 1891 issue of the *Atlantic Monthly*, framed by Higginson's slightly embarrassed and slightly condescending commentary. These letters have puzzled critics for many reasons, not least because of their "little girl" pose. In Gilbert and Gubar's classic formulation, Dickinson's childlike stance is a mask; she is using girlhood both to express her sense of helplessness and to conceal her rage and madness about the conventions that confine her.[22] Joanne Dobson, by contrast, suggests that childhood represents a trap: "The most striking fact about Dickinson's good / bad little girl is that she lacks one essential feature of each aspect of the conventional child: she is neither redemptive nor is she redeemed."[23] Marietta Messmer has recently escaped the "compliant-or-subversive" impasse by pointing out how the dialogic voices in Dickinson's letters to Higginson compete: "Dickinson speaks alternately as a woman / pupil and as a poet, in this way juxtaposing self-denigration (submissiveness) and self-affirmation (confidence in her work)." The Higginson correspondence thus becomes "a carefully crafted balance of power appropriation and voluntary disempowerment . . . in part motivated by Dickinson's attempts to secure Higginson's continued interest in her work and thus a continuation of their (professional) friendship."[24]

Overall, the criticism of Dickinson's childlike stance assumes that Dickinson is a mobile force while childhood is a stable convention through which, or against which, she operates. But I think that the idea of the child as a persona or a mask or even a voice creates an image of stasis and artifice that is quite at odds with what these letters (and many of her poems) accomplish. Through these 1891 *Atlantic Monthly* letters, a different conception of childhood emerges: the poet defines herself as a child who is in the process of being educated and who is thus, necessarily, in a constant state of evolution and motion like the cells under Agassiz's microscope. Indeed, it is possible to say that for Dickinson childhood *is* a process—a way of representing a consciousness that is open and unfinished and thus impossible to pin down. As Higginson frames his epistolary encounters with her: "The bee himself does not evade the schoolboy more than she evaded me, and even to this day I still stand somewhat bewildered, like the boy."[25] In the *Atlantic* article, the text on the page is a pedagogical drama, jointly constructed by Dickinson and Higginson. But what is the function of this persistently educational narrative, in which the thirtyish (and eventually fiftyish) Dickinson signs her letters "Your Scholar"?

Messmer's focus on power negotiations remains useful in the context of the *Atlantic Monthly* article as Higginson struggles—with Dickinson's words, which are only sometimes helpful—to make "Emily Dickinson" presentable in public, and to help the public read her work without rejecting it. Dickinson, of course, is doing the same for Higginson: teaching him how to read her poems. But she couches this in language that makes *him* her "preceptor," and it seems wise to accept these role assignments as having some useful function for Dickinson. Messmer sees the power negotiations between Dickinson and Higginson in terms of gender, conflating the "woman" and "pupil" voices into a single discourse of submissiveness. But Higginson does not understand his "scholar" to be submissive (quite the contrary), and Dickinson's words do not invite such a bipolar (aggressive-submissive) understanding of their epistolary exchanges. It is the case that the "preceptor" at Dickinson's Amherst Academy presided over a traditional (although excellent) school, in which students learned through memorization and demonstrated their learning through Wednesday recitations. But in naming Higginson as her preceptor, Dickinson is thinking not traditionally but experimentally about education: she is wondering how it works, how it makes words meaningful, and how it might be a process of discovery conducted jointly by the teacher and the student.

The educational theorist Paolo Freire makes a useful distinction between what he calls "banking education" and "problem-posing education." "Banking education" involves the rote transfer of information from the teacher to the student: "Instead of communicating, the teacher issues communiqués and makes deposits which the students patiently receive, memorize, and repeat."[26] Problem-posing education, by contrast, is dialogic:

> Liberating education consists in acts of cognition, not transferals
> of information. . . . Accordingly, the practice of problem-posing
> education entails at the outset that the teacher-student contra-
> diction be resolved. Dialogical relations—indispensable to the
> capacity of cognitive actors to cooperate in perceiving the same

cognizable object—are otherwise impossible. Through dialogue, the teacher-of-students and the students-of-the-teacher cease to exist and a new term emerges: teacher-student with student-teachers. The teacher is no longer merely the one-who-teaches, but one who is himself taught in dialogue with the students, who in turn while being taught also teach. They become jointly responsible for a process in which all grow. In this process, arguments based on "authority" are not longer valid; in order to function, authority must be on the side of freedom, not against it. Here, no one teaches another, nor is anyone self-taught. People teach each other, mediated by the world."[27]

The distance between Emily Dickinson and Freire, a twentieth-century Brazilian Marxist, might seem far, but Freire's points are in fact romantic, echoing educational ideas from Rousseau's *Emile* to Peabody and Alcott's midcentury Temple School documents to Dewey's turn-of-the-century writings on progressive "hands-on" education. Even Emerson, who often tilts toward autodidacticism, expresses a remarkably intersubjective and pedagogical view in "The Poet," arguing, essentially, that poets teach others how to emancipate themselves. The main idea—which is central to my reading of Dickinson as a schoolroom poet and also central to most progressive pedagogical thinkers—is that education is both the most confining and the most liberating of human activities: it is dangerous to individuals (to their integrity, to their freedom), and yet it is imperative to their growth.

In the nineteenth century it was rude to ask an adult woman her age. And yet it appears, from Dickinson's second letter to Higginson as printed in the *Atlantic Monthly*, that he did so—a lapse that is explicable only because he must have inferred, from her fey and capering prose, that she was a young girl. At any rate she evades the question: "You asked how old I was? I made no verse, but one or two, until this winter, sir."[28] By way of further evasion, she crosses completely over into childhood, and in doing so, also crosses gender lines: "I had a terror since September, I could tell to none, and so I sing, as the boy does of the burying-ground, because I am afraid."[29] From a child's subject-position, she can present herself as an unformed student. Continuing to evade the facts of her own biography, she avoids mention of Holyoke, but fixes on an important theme, the theme of her education and its failures: "I went to school, but in your manner of phrase had no education. When a little girl, I had a friend who taught me Immortality; but venturing too near, himself, he never returned. Soon after my tutor died, and for several years my lexicon was my only companion. Then I found one more, but he was not contented I be his scholar, so he left the land."[30] Since Dickinson is basically auditioning Higginson for the role of tutor, her narrative is worth considering. First, her teachers are functioning, not in an institutional context, but rather as part of a highly personal relationship based on mutual agreement. Second, her education, as she defines it, has been intense to the point of danger, killing one tutor (his subject matter, immortality, overwhelmed him) and driving the other from "the land." Having articulated the risks, she poses the first version of a question that she asks repeatedly: "I would like to learn. Could you tell me how to grow, or is it unconveyed, like melody or witchcraft?"[31] This is a difficult question, as the failures of her two tutors have just illustrated, and it carries the implicit suggestion that teaching—with language, through letters—might actually be impossible.

In Dickinson's third letter to Higginson, she finally asks him to be her "preceptor," a term she will come to use in many subsequent letters. Initially, she simply seems to be asking him if she can send him poems every now and then for comment, but by the end of the passage much more is clearly at stake:

> If I might bring you what I do—not so frequent to trouble you—
> and ask you if I told it clear, 'twould be control to me. The sailor
> cannot see the North, but knows the needle can. The "hand you
> stretch me in the dark" I put mine in, and turn away. I have no
> Saxon now:—
>
> > And if I asked a common alms,
> > And in my wondering hand
> > A stranger pressed a kingdom,
> > And I, bewildered, stand;
> > As if I asked the Orient
> > Had it for me a morn,
> > And it should lift its purple dikes
> > And shatter me with dawn!
>
> But, will you be my preceptor, Mr. Higginson?[32]

Dickinson's initial "teaching" image is not hierarchical but horizontal: she is a sailor reading a compass, and Higginson is the compass, her (indispensable) instrument. To help her with her poems would be to take her hand—an image, again, not of hierarchy but of partnership. Dickinson is neither submitting to Higginson nor asserting her power over him. She is imagining a pedagogical relationship between a student-teacher and a teacher-student: two explorers (as the image of the sailor implies) working together.

The poem that she includes begins with an image of "banking education," as she holds out her hand for "alms." But it ends with a vision of education, not as a process of socialization or acculturation, but as an individuated problem-posing exchange: she is handed, not money or even information, but a large and bewildering kingdom. Her self is shattered by the sunrise—taken apart by the revelations that she receives. While education has not been identified as one of Dickinson's "flood subjects," it floods the end of this poem and makes her innocent question—*will you be my preceptor?*—a loaded one.

As a scholar, she is neither passive nor aggressive, because she has created a system in which she can work, a way to conceive of herself as a student, working with a teacher who is open to innovation rather than repetition. This is also the definition of a teacher who is open to playfulness. Once Higginson does venture some concrete advice, in a subsequent letter, she uses it as a chance to meditate—again—on the nature of their pedagogical relationship: "You say I confess the little mistake, and omit the large. Because I can see orthography, but the ignorance out of sight is my preceptor's charge."[33] This latter sentence could mean, "you accuse me of ignorance," or it could mean, "you are charged with helping me overcome my ignorance." The charge can be directed at either Dickinson or Higginson; the charge—the electricity, the responsibility, the power—runs in both directions. This passage illustrates the dialogic education that Dickinson is providing for herself, and for Higginson, through the letters. It is not a matter of accepting or rejecting his advice. It is a matter of using his feedback as the raw materials for her own education. Higginson, in the *Atlantic* article, gives this account of their relationship:

> From this time and up to her death (May 15, 1886) we corresponded at varying intervals, she always persistently keeping up this attitude of "Scholar," and assuming on my part a preceptorship which it is almost needless to say did not exist. Always glad to hear her "recite," as she called it, I soon abandoned all attempt to guide in the slightest degree this extraordinary nature, and simply accepted her confidences, giving as much as I could of what might interest her in return.[34]

Higginson is not describing the disintegration of the pedagogical relationship that Dickinson cultivates in her letters; rather, he is confirming its success: their relationship became a mutually playful, ongoing process of discovery involving acts of cognition, to use Freire's distinction, not transferals of information. Later in the article Higginson gives an even more cogent description of their relationship: they maintained "on my side an interest that was strong and even affectionate, but not based on any thorough comprehension; and on her side a hope, always rather baffled, that I should afford some aid in solving her abstruse problem of life."[35] Higginson is very clear here: he understands that Dickinson wants to work with him, not because he can teach her everything she needs to know, but because he can never teach her enough. He can only hold her hand as they move through the dark—an image of a teacher and a student engaging with an unfinished problem, the "abstruse problem of life."

THE "CHILDREN'S FRIEND"

In textbooks and periodicals, the relationship of childhood to the "abstruse problem of life" is established less by terms internal to Dickinson's poems (or any poem) and more by the pedagogical and commercial agendas of the editors. In Dickinson's collections of poems and letters, the editors—Todd and Higginson—also had pedagogical and commercial agendas, so that the texts produced are clearly collaborations between Dickinson's words and the words and choices of her interlocutors. The notion that Dickinson might have been edited or marketed to be—even in part—a children's poet has discomfited many later critics, especially (and understandably) feminists who link Dickinson's infantilization with the devaluation or forced domestication of women writers. As recently as 2003, Claire Raymond has suggested that presenting Dickinson as a children's poet "de-claws" her.[36] However, nineteenth-century children's poetry was not necessarily declawed; indeed, it was often more barbed and transgressive than adults' poetry, as my chapter on *St. Nicholas* suggests. Moreover, to build a career aimed at a dual audience of adults and children was an expected practice for poets; in the later nineteenth century, both Riley and Field followed this strategy, as did most of the women poets of Dickinson's generation. In an advance publicity piece for the *Christian Union,* Higginson groups Dickinson with three prominent later-nineteenth-century women writers: Celia Thaxter, Jean Ingelow, and Helen Hunt Jackson. All three of these women were *solidly* established children's poets; this was not a sideline but a mainstay of their careers and a source of both revenue and authority for them. Literary publishing was still a men's club in 1890, but women had always played a dominant role in children's publishing. The two American women from Higginson's list, Thaxter and Jackson (Ingelow was British) had a strong relationship with Mary Mapes Dodge, the most powerful female editor in America. The poems that Thaxter and Jackson placed in *St. Nicholas* were sometimes "cute" toss-offs but often quite serious verses that would later appear—undifferentiated—in collections with their "adult" work.

In choosing among the hundreds of poems that were available for the 1890 *Poems of Emily Dickinson,* Todd and Higginson made choices—in the poems they picked and in the ways they edited those poems—that reflect the convention of mixing children's and adults' genres together in a single collection or even in a single poem. This explains the inclusion of some work that few modern readers would agree were among Dickinson's best, for example, "Unreturned":

> 'Twas such a little, little boat
> That toddled down the bay!
> 'Twas such a gallant, gallant sea
> That beckoned it away![37]

We encounter, in this first stanza, not just "toddling" language but also the nursery-rhyme prosody of childhood, with its emphasis on rhyme and repetition. The prosody lulls its readers with a recognizable lilt. As the *Overland Monthly* noted in a review, "Unconsciously, in many of them, Miss Dickinson has fallen into the use of meters and rhythms which have come down to us in Mother Goose—the world meters and rhythms which have in them universal melody that in itself is enduring."[38] And yet, as the shipwreck occurs, the poem's form (and with it, the reader's expectation of closure through rhyme) is also essentially wrecked:

> 'Twas such a greedy, greedy wave
> That licked it from the coast;
> Nor ever guessed the stately sails
> My little craft was lost!

"Coast" and "lost" do not quite meet the generic demands of the nursery-rhyme form that the first stanza beckons us to expect. At the exact moment that the indifference of the "stately sails" becomes evident, the poem gets harder to follow: are the "stately sails" part of the craft that is breaking up? Or are they larger boats, failing to see the "craft" in the poem? Either way, Dickinson's poetic craft dictates that the last line end on a half rhyme, so that along with the speaker's presumed drowning comes a split away from the social form of Mother Goose. Nursery rhymes are oral forms that depend on implicitly intersubjective conventions; by breaking generic conventions in the end, the speaker signals that her craft is not just lost but isolated: the message is hard to transmit. The childlike speaker entices but finally jars the reader with her infantile form. Surely Dickinson is at least engaging with a children's genre here, but engaging with it in ways that reveal the perils of assuming that children's genres (or children themselves) are necessarily sweet, uncomplicated, unproblematically accessible, or declawed.

Clearly, Todd and Higginson saw Dickinson's unruly childishness (a stance that she herself cultivated) as both a problem of socialization and an opportunity for socialization—at least in the context of the 1890s, when being an unruly child was considered charming. In his preface to the 1890 *Poems of Emily Dickinson,* the first time a full collection was offered to the public, Higginson offers a telling biographical sketch:

> Miss Dickinson was born in Amherst, Mass., Dec. 10, 1830, and died there May 15, 1886. Her father, Hon. Edward Dickinson, was the leading lawyer of Amherst, and was treasurer of the well-known college there situated. It was his custom once a year to hold a large reception at his house, attended by all the families connected with the institution and by the leading people of the town. On these occasions his daughter Emily emerged from her wonted retirement and did her part as a gracious hostess; nor would any one have known from her manner, I have been told, that this was not a daily occurrence. The annual occasion once past, she withdrew again into her seclusion, and except for a very few friends was as invisible to the world as if she had dwelt in a nunnery. For myself, although I have corresponded with her for many years, I saw her but twice face to face, and brought away the impression of something as unique and remote as Undine or Mignon or Thekla.[39]

Higginson is struggling to make Dickinson a recognizable type, and the thumbnail sketch of her retirement and erratic hostessing paints her as an eccentric spinster, a New England "character" straight out of Sarah Orne Jewett. But there is something peculiar about this character: she conforms, beautifully and graciously, to social expectations, only to withdraw. Given that the anecdote might not be, strictly speaking, true, what can it be but an allegory (unconscious or not) of Dickinson's relationship to form?

At the end of his description, Higginson tries to imagine how such a half-formed, half-socialized woman might be summed up. He finally veers away from realism into the realm of the fairy tale, naming three romantic (indeed, operatic) figures who worked as tropes for half-finished stories or persons in nineteenth-century America. Of the three tropes, Thekla makes the most sense because she fits with the "nun" imagery that Higginson evokes earlier. Although in the biblical Apocrypha she is a virgin martyr, she would have been recognizable to nineteenth-century readers from Schiller's play *Wallenstein* (later an opera by E. T. A. Hoffman), in which a courageous Thekla refuses to renounce her beloved Max even though her father disapproves. Max dies before their love can be consummated, and Thekla disappears from the play to wander the world looking for Max's grave. This disappearance is what interested nineteenth-century readers: Where did she go? What was her fate? The mystery lay in the incompleteness of her story. Still, Thekla is a fairly conventional nineteenth-century female type—what Edmund Stedman called one of the "feminine martyrs of the grand drama," and from this perspective she connects, in some oblique way, to the secluded and nunlike Dickinson that Higginson sets up in his biographical sketch.[40]

But Undine and Mignon are not nuns. Quite the contrary: they are both half-woman, half-girl figures whose elusiveness carried an erotic charge for nineteenth-century readers. Undine's story, originally written by the German romantic La Fouqué, is a version of the "little mermaid" myth. But by 1890 the name had come to signify any elusive water sprite. In his late poem "The Seeking of the Water-fall," Whittier writes:

> Somewhere it laughed and sang; somewhere
> Whirled in mad dance its misty hair;
> But who had raised its veil or seen
> The rainbow skirts of that Undine?[41]

Even though, or because, she is attractive, Undine is also associated with perpetual childhood. An extended sequence in Zadel Buddington's long poem "The Children's Night," which appeared in *Harper's* in 1875, addresses Undine directly, assuming that she will always live (and reign) underwater and never marry. The poem asks lightly, "Dear Undine, say, is it nice to be / The little Crown Princess of the sea?"[42] The problem with being a mermaid is of course a problem of form: Undine cannot cross the (sexualized) line between childhood and adulthood, and this is what makes her "rainbow skirts" so compelling. She is always in the process of becoming a woman, but she never actually grows up. As Paula Bennett has pointed out, perpetual childhood was an appealing fantasy for mid-nineteenth-century women, whose options (as Jo March, for instance, understood) contracted as they aged.[43] Jane Eberwein further suggests that remaining a child allowed Dickinson to cross genders, taking advantage of little boys' pleasures as well as little girls.'[44] I would concur with these insights, adding only that, by the 1890s, the culture's own obsession with little boys and girls had made the retreat into childhood a vexed one: more erotic, more troubling, and perhaps more attractive (for more complicated reasons) to adult readers of both genders.

Mignon, the doomed, attractive, deformed child acrobat, poses the problem of form even more dramatically. Carolyn Steedman's *Strange Dislocations* takes as its central trope the figure of Mignon as she progresses, from her origins in Goethe's *Wilhelm Meister* through numerous incarnations in the nineteenth century; as Steedman argues, Mignon "*meant* something":

> [Mignon] was an idea, an entity—to those who had not read Goethe, who had never purchased the sheet music for Schubert's most famous of all the settings of her most famous song, who had never seen a shoddy *serio-comique* version of Ambroise Thomas's opera *Mignon* (let alone a staging in its pristine form); meant something to those who did not know why child acrobats performing on the music-hall stage, and young women vaulting on horseback at the circus, were so frequently called Mignon . . . The proposition is that the complex of beliefs, feelings, and sentiments that "Mignon" frequently articulated were to do with childhood, and to do with the self, and the relationship between the two, in the period 1780–1930.[45]

Steedman argues that Mignon's body (deformed through acrobatics) made people want to save and retrieve her because she represented what nineteenth-century people had come to regard as a figure for their own damaged interior selves. Mid-nineteenth-century ideas about cells and the body led people to conceive of human subjectivity by imagining that inside the adult body a little child's body survived, in the same way that small cells comprised large organisms. This little self, Steedman argues, wais not just a romantic innocent nostalgically recalled; it was more interiorized (not just a memory but a survival, a kind of psychic fossil): complicated, unfinished, and subject to constant revisiting and revision by the adult. She does not argue for the "truth-value" of this little self but merely points out (with some recourse to Foucault) its historical emergence as an idea. Dickinson, figured as Mignon, embodies this larger process of establishing childhood, not as an externalized fixed form to be nostalgically recalled, but rather as an interiorized aspect of the adult self—an aspect of the self that is threatening and beguiling, damaged and yet attractive.

DICKINSON'S A B C

Early reviews often reacted to Dickinson's disturbing forms by expressing (and sometimes indulging) the urge to fix or finish them. Thomas Bailey Aldrich—who, not incidentally, rose to prominence as the author of one of the first nostalgic "boys' books"—wrote what Buckingham calls the most influential negative review of Dickinson, framing her as half-finished and half-grown. While dismissing her poems as *disjecta membra,* he nevertheless could not resist rewriting one:

> I taste a liquor never brewed
> In vats upon the Rhine;
> No tankard ever held a draught
> Of alcohol like mine.[46]

Aldrich strongly objects to her as "half-educated," and quotes Andrew Lang's remark that Dickinson might have been better "if she had only mastered the rudiments of grammar and gone into metrical training for about fifteen years." Aldrich's impulse to rewrite Dickinson is thus a pedagogical one: he wants to teach her a thing or two about conventions and help her to grow up, because her poems as they are "totter and toddle, not having learned to walk."[47] Dickinson's poems are not just little, they are little bodies—bodies like Undine's or Mignon's that are broken, unfinished, and disturbing.

Aldrich's negative reaction to Dickinson is related to the generic horizon of expectations that schoolroom poetry had established in American readers. The problem, for Aldrich, is not Dickinson's childishness per se but rather the physically jarring form that this childishness takes. And if most literary historians would be inclined to say that Aldrich was simply wrong about Dickinson, I think he was right to assume that she represented the loss of a certain imagined community—a community that relied on specific generic assumptions (about repetition and nostalgia) to produce responses in readers. Among the reviews that Todd pasted into her scrapbook was one from the London *Daily News* that reads, in part, "Poetry is a thing of many laws felt and understood, and sanctioned by the whole experience of humanity. Miss Dickinson in her poetry broke every one of the natural and salutary laws of verse."[48] As I have argued, the schoolroom poets made the "laws" of poetry "felt and understood" in America; that is, these conventions, inculcated in childhood, were internalized by people and understood as natural, physical rules that "everyone" remembered and could recall through poems such as "Paul Revere's Ride" and "The Barefoot Boy." Such poetry was physically comfortable: it was easy to remember and to repeat. Dickinson—despite her sporadic appearances at her father's receptions, and despite her sporadic appearances in periodicals and textbooks—broke the laws that her readers had physically internalized, and they often expressed their consternation in physical terms. As an essayist in *Scribner's* complained, "Having one's breath taken away is a very agreeable sensation, but it is not the finest sensation of which we are susceptible; and instead of being grateful for it one is very apt . . . to suffer annoyance."[49] Readers schooled in the art of rhetoric had been trained to breathe as they read, but Dickinson's dashes and line breaks (even in edited early editions) do not lend themselves to smooth repetitions by trained elocutionists.

This has social as well as literary implications. To illustrate my point, I want to return to "The Barefoot Boy," a poem that is well socialized and that was used to socialize children throughout the latter half of the nineteenth century. Whittier's poem invites repetition because of its facile rhymes and meters: "Blessings on thee, little man / Barefoot boy, with cheek of tan!" But the poem also thematizes repetition; the adult speaker imagines that the boy is exactly the same as the speaker used to be: "From my heart I give thee joy,— / I was once a barefoot boy!" And as I have discussed, this poem creates a community of readers with memories in common: memories of learning the poem, and memories of childhood as represented by the poem. This sense of community hinges in part on the poem's accessibility: like the common school system, this poem is open to all. Like all the most popular work by Longfellow, Whittier, Riley, and Field, it is easy to comprehend, so that people reading it can feel that they are all reading it in the same way, sharing an internal as well as an external experience, and building a form of subjectivity that they can hold in common. The fact that this sense of collective subjectivity is chimeric does not matter; on the contrary, its (perpetual) loss leads to nostalgia: "childhood" is a culturally constructed, closed and finished, idyllic time, a "time of June" prior to the alienation of adulthood. This is a function not just of content but of genre. As a schoolroom poem, "The Barefoot Boy" teaches people what to expect, helping them to internalize conventions as rules that are "felt and understood" so that they seem natural, and then giving them exactly what they have been taught to seek (and to long for). While this has a disciplinary component (making everyone fit in), it is also collective: the poem can accommodate all, *e pluribus unum*.

Dickinson's work registers (and hastens) the weakening of the conventions that "The Barefoot Boy" embodies, thereby also putting pressure on the collective relationships that a poem such as "The Barefoot Boy" allows readers to imagine. While her individual poems worked in social settings, her collections—as Higginson understood when he nervously allegorized her social eccentricity—make her allegiances clear. Her poems are chirographic (not oral), individualistic (not collective), and playful (not didactic). "The First Lesson," a poem from the 1890 volume, articulates Dickinson's generic difference while also imagining a different kind of schoolroom.

> Not in this world to see his face
> Sounds long, until I read the place
> Where this is said to be
> But just the primer for a life
> Unopened, rare upon the shelf,
> Clasped yet to him and me.
>
> And yet, my primer suits me so
> I would not choose a book to know
> Than that, be sweeter wise;
> Might some one else so learned be,
> And leave me just my A B C,
> Himself could have the skies.[50]

This poem, while it can certainly be read aloud to beautiful effect, is not built like a recitation piece. Its meter is uneven and one of its rhymes (life/shelf) is not "perfect," so that it leads the oral reader along a rugged road. Although twenty-first-century readers (myself included) are likely to find this ruggedness aesthetically pleasing— and might even be tempted to argue that Dickinson's poems work best when read aloud—her earliest readers (as the reviews show) did not concur. In her preface to the *Second Series*, Todd tried to soften the effect by introducing the notion of a "thought-rhyme," "appealing, indeed, to an unrecognized sense more elusive than hearing."[51] Todd's preface concedes a point that seemed obvious to Dickinson's first mass audience: these are poems for silent readers. And indeed the culture was preparing silent readers: "whole language" learning was replacing phonics in the reading classes of the 1890s, so that readers were encouraged to apprehend entire words visually instead of speaking syllables aloud. But the idea of a "thought-rhyme" also has a corollary: whatever "unrecognized sense" her poems address, this sense is not collective and intersubjective like the human voice. It is internal, isolated in the individual.

The poem also thematizes individualism. The idea that this world functions as a primer for the next is derived from the Calvinist system of correspondences perfected by preachers such as Jonathan Edwards. But the second stanza moves (as Calvinism itself eventually moved) toward a version of transcendentalism, claiming that this world is preferable to—or perhaps even the equivalent of—heaven. The purpose of education thus emerges in the second stanza: its point is not to redeem the child (who is already in the paradise of her own consciousness) but to "suit" her. In 1862, when Dickinson wrote this poem (not titling it "The First Lesson," and not punctuating it in the way that I have quoted), progressive educators were already asking what kinds of lessons might best suit children. In an 1862 article in the *Atlantic Monthly*, Elizabeth Peabody—co-founder with Bronson Alcott of the Temple School and a close friend of Higginson's—argued that children should make the world their primer:

> Anything of the nature of scientific teaching should be done by presenting *objects* for examination and investigation. Flowers, insects, shells, etc. are easily handled. The observations should be drawn out of the children, not made to them, except as corrections of their mistakes. Experiments with the prism, and in crystallization and transformation, are useful and desirable to awaken taste for the sciences of Nature. In short, the Kindergarten should give the beginnings of everything.[52]

The end result, for Peabody, is not perfect obedience but rather a revelation: the child's own individuality will be discovered and cultivated by the teacher, who recognizes different kinds of children and gives them different objects to play with. Instead of engaging in "banking" education, with periodic recitations of facts, the teacher gives children the raw materials so that observations can be "drawn out of them" in the context of solving problems. Indeed, Peabody argues, play is not necessarily the opposite of work; it can be a form of work for children.

"The First Lesson" also rethinks the beginnings of everything and, through these beginnings, the ultimate end as well: why do we learn to read? In the first stanza, it seems that the speaker's education is designed to make her move forward, according to an authoritative divine plan. But in the second stanza the alphabet turns out to be better than heaven because of its flexibility: the speaker can take it and make it her own. Peabody, like Dickinson, was a radical in the 1860s, but by the 1890s the progressive educational ideas that she promoted were beginning to catch on, as teachers like Mary Burt (author of *The Eugene Field Book*) encouraged children to follow their own inner "leadings."

There are many advantages to moving away from the old methods of repetition and rote memorization so wickedly parodied in "Sic Transit Gloria Mundi," but in "The First Lesson" the speaker acknowledges that there are costs as well. By internalizing the alphabet, the speaker makes it "*my* A B C" and gains individual control over her letters. But she also gives up the possibility of seeing another face, affirming her isolation from the community that a collective A B C, and an identity based on collaborative individualism, might offer. She constructs her syntax obliquely, offering readers the rewarding opportunity to work through her poem in ways that "suit" them, but withdrawing the possibility (proffered by the transparent "Barefoot Boy") that every reader will understand the poem in the same way. And finally, related to this issue, there is the question of her subjectivity. Is she a literal or metaphorical child? The very fact that we do not know whether this is supposed to be a child speaker, or an adult simply using the metaphor of childhood, makes it hard to picture her. Unlike the Barefoot Boy, with his red lips "redder still, / Kissed by strawberries on the hill," the childish aspects of this speaker are protean, not fixed; indeed, she changes her attitude from stanza to stanza, and ends by giving us an ambivalent picture of her own interiority. Unlike the Barefoot Boy, she is not accessible; in other words childhood for Dickinson is not necessarily easy. On the one hand she is content with her A B C, but on the other hand her contentment comes with an acute sense of what has been lost.

*   *   *

NINETEENTH-CENTURY POEMS, as I have argued throughout this study, were not just social texts but sociable texts. And the rules of engagement—accepted by poets and readers alike—were the rules of genre. A genre, as Fredric Jameson has argued, is not a fixed form but rather a provisional contract "between a writer and a specific public" that works as an agreement specifying how the text should be read and used.[53] The rules of poetry, as practiced by Longfellow, Whittier, Riley, Dodge, and Field, dictated that it be accessible by, and useful to, ordinary middle-class people; this meant that it should rhyme, that its meter should be regular, and that its language should be easy to understand, to remember, and to repeat. What the folklorist William

Newell thought he saw in the "games and songs" of American children was true of most nineteenth-century poetry: poetry as an institution was conservative in the sense that it conserved "the past" through both thematic and generic repetition.

On the thematic level American poets often personified the past as a child, such as Whittier's "Barefoot Boy," who worked as an archaic and yet youthful form of the middle-class self. But this child—this barefoot boy, this mediocre hero—was not just a personal memory that could be recovered through poetry. Rather, the child was connected to a specifically intersubjective orality: not only were children emblems of earlier, preliterate verse forms, but they were also expected to perform this orality in collective settings such as the church and the school. In other words, if the child embodied the inner self, then it embodied a "self" that was sanctioned by (and that in turn sanctioned) social institutions. Thus, when Longfellow begins "Paul Revere's Ride" with the invocation "Listen, my children, and you shall hear / Of the midnight ride of Paul Revere," he positions these children as conservators not just of a personal but also of collective—local and national—versions of the past.

On the generic level, too, repetitions of rhyme and meter were not simply mnemonic devices, mediating the poems' conservative or nostalgic content. Rather—and this was certainly true by the 1890s, as Riley understood—it seems evident that rhyme and meter had in themselves come to constitute the shape of nostalgia, that they functioned as more or less unconscious but powerful "memories" that readers had internalized and wanted to repeat. Jameson has made a similar point in reference to pop music: because it fulfills preexisting generic expectations, even a "new" top-forty hit functions as a repetition, and it is this repetitive quality that enables us to form passionate attachments that are a function, not so much of the content of the song, as of its familiarity: "the pop single, by means of repetition, insensibly becomes part of the existential fabric of our own lives, so that what we listen to is ourselves, our own previous auditions."[54] When Riley made even brand-new poems sound familiar by following generic rules, he was responding to a social contract that made American poetry not just thematically nostalgic but also nostalgic at the level of genre: the figure of a child might trigger a longing for the past, but so could the form of a poem.

Dickinson is not a nostalgic poet (although she has her nostalgic moments), but the other schoolroom poets in this study—Longfellow, Whittier, Riley, and Field—all produced work that is imbued with a strong sense of the past: with the archaic past of Hiawatha, with the republican past of the Haverhill homestead, with the rural past of the

Indiana Hoosiers, and with Little Boy Blue's lost toys. The past has its uses, as I have discussed, but its overwhelming presence is still notable if we consider that schoolroom poetry was above all instrumental, concerned with forging real and imagined connections among people. Large-scale institutions supported and disseminated poems such as *The Song of Hiawatha, Snow-Bound,* and "Little Orphant Annie," but these poems depict small-scale communities that are explicitly linked to the small world of childhood. There is a profound disconnect between the worlds that these poems depict and the institutional contexts through which they circulated—a disconnect that is pushed to its extreme with the work of Field, which located itself in the enclosed space of children's bedrooms even as it circulated through the large-scale, anonymous city of Chicago via the *Chicago Morning News.* This does not mean, however, that the schoolroom poets were out of touch with their readers' needs; on the contrary, as their extraordinary popularity shows, readers in the later nineteenth century wanted poetry to be reassuring and to represent a "tradition" to which they could always return. They wanted to "turn backward," as Elizabeth Akers Allen put it, toward poetry and childhood, and toward poetry as a form of childhood. And the childhood they expected to find was not broken, incomplete, or troubling,

When I began this book, I expected my final chapter on Dickinson to show her forging a path to the twentieth century, at which point old-fashioned schoolroom poetry would be rendered obsolete by modernism. But this narrative would have been inaccurate for two reasons: first, the demand for schoolroom poetry was so strong in the 1890s that as soon as Dickinson became a best-selling poet her work was appropriated for pedagogical purposes in textbooks and juvenile periodicals, where (like Dickinson herself, emerging once a year to host a reception) it performed quite nicely. Dickinson did not supplant schoolroom poetry; she was—at least temporarily—incorporated into its horizon of expectations. This underlines my broader theoretical point that people's (institutionally instilled) reading practices can override authorial intent in determining the meaning of a poetic text.

Second, schoolroom poetry was never really in competition with the modernist aesthetic that Dickinson anticipates in her most characteristic (challenging, playful, innovative) verses. Schoolroom poetry was part of middle-class daily life—it was a form of *popular culture*—and, as such, it competed more with comic strips or silent films than with Dickinson or Stephen Crane. In the first decades of the twentieth century, the compartmentalization, commercialization, and expansion of middle-class options for education and diversion reduced the "market share" of the schoolroom poets. Textbooks increasingly drew on a specialized niche of children's peer culture, featuring Raggedy Andy or the Sunbonnet Babies rather than Longfellow and Whittier. Many of Riley's "opera house" venues were converted into movie houses. Intimate parlor entertainments (singing around the piano, reciting poetry) were rendered obsolete by phonographs and radios, and sales of sheet music (which often featured lyrics from the schoolroom poets) flagged. New printing technologies put comics and photos into the newspaper spaces where poetry had once been used as filler. And more systematic enforcement of copyright laws (by increasingly professionalized lawyers) began to limit the casual distribution of newspaper and periodical verses. People still read the schoolroom poets, and teachers still taught them, but no longer was "everybody" exposed to the same few poems. Did this new era—the era that Walter Benjamin calls the "age of mechanical reproduction"—result in a net loss of real and imagined communities? The question is too large to be considered here. But it is certainly true that popular poetry had been supported by communities that were either disappearing or changing beyond recognition by the time of the First World War.

Indeed, if anyone forged a path for popular poetry in the twentieth century, it was not Dickinson—who, despite her initial popularity, was essentially an elite figure—but rather Mary Mapes Dodge. There is no question that Carol Muske-Dukes was right to claim, in the *New York Times,* that as the twentieth-century wore on, middle-class people became much less likely to know, and to be able to quote from, a stable archive of popular verses. Indeed, in the later twentieth century middle-class people (outside the tiny group generated by English departments) barely read poetry at all, although they continued to read novels, and novels were flourishing as a form of popular as well as elite culture—as evidenced, for example, by Oprah's Book Club. While some might point out efforts such as Robert Pinsky's "Favorite Poem Project," or cite the vibrant "spoken-word" scenes in certain cities, the fact remains that while M.F.A. writing programs flourish, most *readers* read fiction and nonfiction rather than poetry. Dana Gioia states the obvious in his essay "Can Poetry Matter?": "American poetry now belongs to a subculture. No longer part of the mainstream of artistic and intellectual life, it has become the specialized occupation of a relatively small and isolated group."[55] Of course poetry still matters to some people, myself (and Pinsky and Gioia) included. But it does not matter to most people.

However—and here is where Dodge comes in—at the end of the twentieth century it was still possible to make money writing in rhyme and meter. Shel Silverstein, Theodore Geisel, and Jack Prelutsky all managed it—and what these writers have in common, of course, is that their work is aimed at children. These authors echo and extend the innovative, playful uses of rhyme, meter, and illustration introduced by *St. Nicholas,* and their tremendous popularity takes for granted (and perpetuates) a "natural" connection between children and poetry. In the splintered, niche-driven world of middle-class popular culture, poetry has maintained a toehold in America as a children's genre, supported by the institutions of children's publishing, elementary schools, and libraries. There is nothing particularly natural about this link between children and poetry, but it is the result of assumptions and practices rooted in the literary history that I have described in this study. The infantilization of American poetry began in the nineteenth century, but it did not end there: popular verse forms became—and remain—forms of American childhood.

NOTES

Introduction: Learning by Heart (pp. xi–xlv)

1. Carol Muske-Dukes, "A Lost Eloquence," *New York Times*, 29 December 2002.

2. Ann Hanson, letter, *New York Times*, 1 January 2003. Henry H. Emurian, letter, *New York Times*, 1 January 2003.

3. Front cover flap, John Hollander, ed., *American Poetry: The Nineteenth Century*, vol. 1 (New York: Library of America, 1993).

4. See James Machor, ed., *Readers in History: Nineteenth-Century American Literature and the Contexts of Response* (Baltimore: Johns Hopkins University Press, 1993); Janice Radway, *A Feeling for Books: The Book-of-the-Month Club, Literary Taste, and Middle-Class Desire* (Chapel Hill: University of North Carolina Press, 1997); Cathy Davidson, ed., *Reading in America: Literature and Social History* (Baltimore: Johns Hopkins University Press, 1989). Joan Shelley Rubin has recently done some work on poetry specifically; see Joan Shelley Rubin, " 'They Flash Upon That Inward Eye': Poetry Recitation and American Readers" *Proceedings of the American Antiquarian Society*, vol. 106: (1996): 273–300.

5. Stephen Greenblatt has argued that "repeatable forms of pleasure and interest" generate what he calls "social energy." See Greenblatt, *Shakespearean Negotiations: The Circulation of Social Energy in Renaissance England* (Berkeley: University of California Press, 1988), 6.

6. Jeanetta Boswell has prepared a useful bibliography, *The Schoolroom Poets: A Bibliography* (Metuchen, N.J.: Scarecrow Press, 1983). The "schoolroom poets" were linked together as such by the turn of the century, in textbooks such as Sherwin Cody's *Four American Poets: A Book for Young Americans* (New York: Werner School Book Company, 1901).

7. See Joel T. Headly, *The Christian Parlor Book* (New York: 1851), 343. Reprinted in Kenneth Walter Cameron, ed. *Longfellow among His Contemporaries* (Hartford, Conn., Transcendental Books: 1978), 40. George Gilfillan, *Second Gallery of Literary Portraits*, 2nd ed. (New York, 1852), 255.

8. Hazel Felleman, ed. *The Best-Loved Poems of the American People* (1936; reprint, New York: Doubleday, 2001). Felleman compiled her selections based on queries to the *New York Times Book Review* in the 1920s and early '30s. This anthology is still a steady seller, as noted on the Wal-Mart catalogue home page. Online reader responses to the volume, at Wal-Mart and on Amazon.com, are nostalgic and effusive.

9. Olive E. Dana, "A Whittier Folk-Gathering," *Journal of Education* (December 1897): 12.

10. John G. Whittier, "The Barefoot Boy," *Little Pilgrim* 1:1 (1852): 1.

11. See Hans Robert Jauss, *Toward an Aesthetic of Reception*, trans. Timothy Bahti (Minneapolis: University of Minnesota Press, 1982). See also Jauss, "The Identity of the Poetic Text in the Changing Horizon of Understanding," in James Machor and Philip Goldstein, eds., *Reception Study: From Literary Theory to Cultural Studies* (New York: Routledge, 2001), 7–27. Jauss's use of the phrase "horizon of expectations" tends to be more literary, constituted by

other texts; I am appropriating his term and making the horizons more cultural, constituted by people's experiences of institutions and daily life as well as by their literary reading.

12. Van Wyck Brooks, *Our Literary Heritage* (New York: E. P. Dutton, 1956), 100.

13. Leslie Fiedler, "The Children's Hour; or, The Return of the Vanishing Longfellow: Some Reflections of the Future of Poetry," in Ihab Hassan, ed., *Liberations: New Essays on the Humanities in Revolution* (Middletown, Conn.: Wesleyan University Press, 1971), 177.

14. Donald Hall, introduction to *The Oxford Book of Children's Verse in America*, ed. Donald Hall (New York: Oxford University Press, 1985), xxxiv.

15. The Dickinson quote is from the poem that was printed as "Unreturned" in Emily Dickinson, *Poems by Emily Dickinson*, ed. Thomas Wentworth Higginson and Mabel Loomis Todd (Boston: Roberts Brothers, 1890), 37.

16. Agnes Repplier, "The Children's Poets," *Atlantic Monthly* (March 1892): 328.

17. Lewis O. Saum, *The Popular Mood of America, 1860–1890* (Lincoln: University of Nebraska Press, 1990), 139.

18. Kate Douglas Wiggin, *Rebecca of Sunnybrook Farm* (New York: Grosset and Dunlap, 1903), 168.

19. Lucy Larcom, "Longfellow and the Children," *St. Nicholas* (June 1882): 637.

20. For instance, in a *McGuffey's Reader* anthology, part of the Bedford Series of History and Culture designed for classroom use, selections including "The Barefoot Boy," "The Old Oaken Bucket," and "A Psalm of Life" are prefaced by a question from the editor: "Why do you think much of this literature is so sentimental in style?" See Elliott J. Gorn, ed., *The McGuffey Readers: Selections from the 1879 Edition* (New York: Bedford/St. Martins, 1988), 170.

21. Mary Louise Kete, *Sentimental Collaboration: Mourning and Middle-Class Identity in Nineteenth-Century America* (Durham: Duke University Press, 1999).

22. Ibid., 32.

23. Ibid., 251.

24. Richard Brodhead, *Cultures of Letters: Scenes of Reading and Writing in Nineteenth-Century America* (Chicago: University of Chicago Press, 1993).

25. Mary Loeffelholz, "Who Killed Lucretia Davidson? or, Poetry in the Domestic-Tutelary Complex," *Yale Journal of Criticism* 10:2 (1997): 271–293.

26. Westside High School *Hesper* (Milwaukee, 1898), 122.

27. See George Arms, *The Fields Were Green: A New View of Bryant, Whittier, Holmes, Lowell, and Longfellow, with a Selection of Their Poems* (Stanford, Calif.: Stanford University Press, 1953), 6. Arms notes the prevailing devaluation of the schoolroom poets and suggests that adults dislike them partly because they do not see a connection to modernists, and partly because these poems are too familiar, having been learned too early in childhood, "before much literary sensitivity has been developed."

28. University of Wisconsin *Badger* (Madison, 1890), 212.

29. Westside High School *Hesper* (Milwaukee, 1898), 3.

30. Alan Trachtenberg, *The Incorporation of America: Culture and Society in the Gilded Age* (New York: Hill and Wang, 1982).

31. Richard Moiser, *Making the American Mind: William McGuffey and his Readers* (New York: King's Crown Press, 1947).

32. See William McGuffey, ed., *McGuffey's Eclectic Primer* (1836; revised, Cincinnati: W. B. Smith, 1879). The *Primer* begins with the alphabet, then lists words with pictures, from Axe to Zebra, then commences with simple sentences: "Is it an ox?" "It is an ox." "It is my ox."

33. Friedrich A. Kittler, *Discourse Networks, 1800/1900,* trans. Michael Metter and Chris Cullens (Stanford, Calif.: Stanford University Press, 1990).

34. William McGuffey, ed. *McGuffey's Fifth Eclectic Reader* (1879, reprint, New York: Signet, 1962), 21.

35. Ibid., 51–54

36. Ibid., 67–68.

37. Pierre Bourdieu, *Distinction: A Social Critique of the Judgment of Taste,* trans. Richard Nice (Cambridge, Mass.: Harvard University Press, 1984).

38. Mary Antin, *The Promised Land* (New York: Houghton Mifflin, 1911), 198.

39. Ibid., 225.

40. Ibid., 267.

41. Michael Moon, "'The Gentle Boy from the Dangerous Classes': Pederasty, Domesticity, and Capitalism in Horatio Alger." *Representations* 19 (Summer 1987): 87–109.

42. Antin, 282.

43. Ibid., 338.

44. Charlotte Forten Grimké to Booker T. Washington, 2 December 1887, in Louis Harlan, ed., *Booker T. Washington Papers,* v. 2 (Champaign-Urbana: University of Illinois Press, 1972), 394.

45. Marcel Mauss, *The Gift: The Form and Reason for Exchange in Archaic Societies,* trans. W. D. Halls (New York: W. W. Norton, 1990).

46. Alphonso Newcomer, *American Literature* (Chicago: Scott Foreman, 1901).

47. "The Poetry of James Russell Lowell," *Littell's Living Age* (April 1866): 131.

48. Leon Vincent, *American Literary Masters* (New York: Houghton Mifflin, 1906), 453.

49. Joseph Conforti, *Imagining New England: Explorations of Regional Identity from the Pilgrims to the Mid-Twentieth Century* (Chapel Hill: University of North Carolina Press, 2000), 206.

50. James Whitcomb Riley, *The Complete Works of James Whitcomb Riley,* memorial edition, vol. 1 (New York: Collier and Sons, 1916), vi.

51. Riley, "The Old-Fashioned Bible," in *Riley Songs of Friendship* (New York: Grosset and Dunlap, 1915), 54. Samuel Woodworth, "The Old Oaken Bucket," in William M. McGuffey, ed., *McGuffey's Fourth Eclectic Reader* (Cincinnati: Wilson, Hinkle, 1866). The poem was retained in the 1879 edition, but Riley must have used the 1866 version in his school days.

52. "Kansas, the Prairie Queen," in Eva Ryan, ed., *Walls of Corn and Other Poems* (Hiawatha, Kans.: Harrington Printing Company, 1894), 39.

53. Robert Pinsky, *Democracy, Culture, and the Voice of Poetry* (Princeton, N.J.: Princeton University Press, 2002), 46.

54. Carolyn Steedman, *Strange Dislocations: Childhood and the Idea of Human Interiority, 1780–1930* (London: Virago Press, 1995), 19–20. See also Raymond Williams, *Marxism and Literature* (London: Oxford University Press, 1977).

55. Susan Stewart, *On Longing: Narratives of the Miniature, the Gigantic, the Souvenir, the Collection* (Baltimore: Johns Hopkins University Press, 1984), 65.

Chapter 1. Reading America: Longfellow in the Schools (pp. 1–34)

1. Anonymous writer to Henry Wadsworth Longfellow, 27 February 1882, "Birthday Letters" envelope, Henry Wadsworth Longfellow Papers, Houghton Library, Harvard University, Cambridge, Mass.

2. Eric Haralson, "Mars in Petticoats: Longfellow and Sentimental Masculinity," *Nineteenth-Century Literature* 51:3 (December 1996): 327; Matthew Gartner, "Longfellow's Place: The Poet and Poetry of Craigie House," *New England Quarterly* 73:1 (March 2000): 327–355; Virginia Jackson, "Longfellow's Tradition; or, Picture-Writing a Nation," *Modern Language Quarterly* 59:4 (December 1998): 472–473.

3. Quoted in Henry Perkinson, *The Imperfect Panacea* (New York: Random House, 1968), 80.

4. Richard Henry Stoddard, "Henry Wadsworth Longfellow," *Scribner's* (November 1878): 17.

5. John Dewey, "My Pedagogic Creed," *School Journal* 54 (January 1897): 77.

6. Henry Wadsworth Longfellow, *The Song of Hiawatha* (1855; reprint, London: Everyman, 1992), 1. Hereafter abbreviated as *Hiawatha* and noted parenthetically as *H* in the text.

7. Mary Proudfoot, *Hiawatha Industrial Reader* (New York: Rand McNally, 1915), 21.

8. John Davis, ed. Davis-Julien *Reader,* 3rd year, part 2 (Boston: D. C. Heath, 1912), 239.

9. Program for "Hiawatha, or Manabozho, an Ojibway Indian Play" (1900), Box 117, Folder 10, Dana Family Papers, Longfellow House, Cambridge, Mass.

10. *Hiawatha,* 84.

11. James Brow, "Notes on Community, Hegemony, and the Uses of the Past," *Anthropological Quarterly* 63:1 (1990): 3.

12. M. R. Atwater, *Stories from the Poets* (New York: Silver, Burdett and Co., 1898), 52.

13. See for instance Daniel Aaron's introduction to the Everyman *Song of Hiawatha,* xvii. Aaron points out that Longfellow "infused his poem with sentiments highly congenial to the thousands who rushed to buy it and utterly remote from the character and psychology of the people it was ostensibly about."

14. Cora M. Folsom to Henry Longfellow Dana, n.d., Box 118, Folder 1, Dana Family Papers.

15. "The Colored College and the Indian Schools—Hiawatha as Played by the Indians," *Cleveland Gazette* (10 May 1884).

16. Booker T. Washington, *Up From Slavery* (Garden City, N.J.: Doubleday, 1901), 98.

17. "The Colored College and the Indian Schools."

18. Henry Wadsworth Longfellow, "Paul Revere's Ride," in *Favorite Poems of Henry Wadsworth Longfellow* (New York: Doubleday, 1957), 43. Henceforth abbreviated *FP.* Further references to "Paul Revere's Ride" refer to this edition and are noted parenthetically as *FP* in the text.

19. Benedict Anderson, *Imagined Communities: Reflections on the Origin and Spread of Nationalism* (London and New York: Verso, 1983), 19.

20. John Van Schaick, *Characters in "Tales of a Wayside Inn"* (Boston: Universalist Publishing House, 1939), 29.

21. Charles Ferris Gettemy, *The True Story of Paul Revere*. (Boston: Little, Brown, 1912), xx–xxi.

22. Helen Clarke, *Longfellow's Country* (New York: Doubleday, Page and Co., 1913), 104.

23. Richard Shenkman, *I Love Paul Revere, Whether He Rode or Not* (New York: Harper Collins, 1992). Shenkman's amusing book debunks many of the myths that later-nineteenth-century schools taught as facts.

24. Abraham Isaacs, "What Shall the Public Schools Teach?" *Forum* (October 1888): 210–211.

25. Benedict Anderson, 31.

26. Benjamin T. Harris, "What Shall the Public Schools Teach?" *Forum* (January 1888): 54.

27. Margaret W. Haliburton, *Teaching Poetry in the Grades* (Boston: Houghton Mifflin, 1911), 54.

28. I am drawing, here, on the classic Victor Turner text, *The Forest of Symbols* (Ithaca, N.Y.: Cornell University Press, 1967).

29. Quoted in the *Fifty-fourth Annual Report, Common Schools of Cincinnati* (Cincinnati, Ohio: Carpenter Printers, 1881), 64.

30. Benedict Anderson, 17.

31; Ibid., 19.

32. George Lukacs, *The Historical Novel*, trans. Stanley Mitchell (1936; reprint, Lincoln: University of Nebraska Press, 2002).

33. E. B. Andrews, "Patriotism and the Public Schools," *Arena* (December 1890): 71.

34. Haliburton, 8.

35. *Boston Superintendent's Report, Document No. 6* (Boston, 1907), 42.

36. Julia A. Colby, *Reminiscences* (Springfield, Mo., 1916), 94.

37. Kete, 181.

38. From a program for the dedication of the Longfellow School, Box 24, Folder 6, Alice Mary Longfellow Papers, Longfellow House, Cambridge, Mass.

39. Sarah Pearson to HWL, 31 January 1991, "Birthday Letters" envelope, Henry Wadsworth Longfellow Papers.

40. Cecil Gandolfo to Alice Longfellow, 27 February 1899, uncatalogued materials, Alice Mary Longfellow Papers.

41. Emma May Buckingham, *A Self-Made Woman; or, Mary Idyl's Trials and Triumphs* (New York: S. R. Wells, 1873), 4.

42. Ibid., 341–42.

43. D. J. Jordan, "The Philosophy of Progress," *African Methodist Episcopal Church Review* 10 (1 July 1983): 123.

44. Jauss, "Identity of the Poetic Text," 12.

45. William Dean Howells, "The Art of Longfellow," *North American Review* (March 1907): 485.

46. "Longfellow," *The Little Chronicle* 15:8 (Sat., 23 February 1907): 1.

Chapter 2. Learning to Be White: John Greenleaf Whittier's "Snow-Bound" (pp. 35–67)

1. In 1866 James Fields, Whittier's publisher, wrote to him about *Snow-Bound*, "We can't keep the plaguey thing quiet. It goes and goes, and now, today, we are bankrupt again, not one being in the crib. I fear it will be impossible to get along without printing another batch!" Quoted in Thomas Currier,

A Bibliography of John Greenleaf Whittier (Cambridge, Mass.: Harvard University Press, 1937), 99. Currier reports that editions of *Snow-Bound* were released, after their initial printing in February 1866, in time for the Christmas gift markets of 1867, 1868, 1875, 1881, 1883, 1892, 1900, 1904, 1905, 1906, 1907, 1909, 1910, 1911, and 1913. This does not count its inclusion in numerous collected and selected Whittier volumes.

2. For a representative New Critical reading, see John Pickard, "Imagistic and Structural Unity in 'Snow-Bound,'" in Jane Kribbs, ed., Critical Essays on John Greenleaf Whittier (Boston: G. K. Hall and Co, 1980), 130–136; see also James E. Rocks, "Whittier's *Snow-Bound*: 'The Circle of Our Hearth' and the Discourse on Domesticity," Studies in the American Renaissance (1993): 339–353.

3. Geoffrey Buckwater, ed., *Buckwater's Fifth Reader* (New York: Parker P. Simmons, 1907), 294–295.

4. Steven Mailloux, "Interpretation and Rhetorical Hermeneutics," in Goldstein and Machor, 39–60. One example that Mailloux gives is the struggle over *Adventures of Huckleberry Finn* and the gradual emergence of race as an issue in that text.

5. James Russell Lowell, "Whittier's *Snow-Bound*," *North American Review* (April 1866): 631–632.

6. Alice Morse Earle, *Home Life in Colonial Days* (New York: Macmillan, 1898), 72.

7. Ibid., 74–75.

8. Ibid., 431.

9. Conforti, 206.

10. John Greenleaf Whittier to Mary Vincent Holmes, 26 January 1881, Haverhill Whittier Club Collection, Haverhill Public Library, Haverhill, Mass.

11. Oliver Capen, *Country Homes of Famous Americans* (New York: Doubleday, 1905), 174.

12. Harriet Prescott Spofford, "John Greenleaf Whittier," in George Woodbury, ed., *Authors at Home*, (New York: J. B. Gilder, 1888), 345.

13. Edmund Stedman, "Whittier," *Century Magazine* 30:1 (May 1885): 40.

14. Donald Freeman, "A History of the Whittier Club," in John Pickard, ed., *Memorabilia of John Greenleaf Whittier*, (Hartford, Conn.: Emerson Society, 1968), 61–64.

15. William Kennedy, "In Whittier's Land," *New England Magazine* (November 1892): 277.

16. James Russell Lowell, quoted in Matthew Jacobson, *Whiteness of a Different Color* (Cambridge, Mass.: Harvard University Press, 1998), 72.

17. Ruth Frankenberg, *The Social Construction of Whiteness: White Women, Race Matters* (Minneapolis: University of Minnesota Press, 1993), 1.

18. Valerie Babb, *Whiteness Visible: The Meaning of Whiteness in American Literature and Culture* (New York: New York University Press, 1998), 125.

19. Freeman, 63.

20. Jean Pickering and Suzanne Kehde, *Narratives of Nostalgia, Gender, and Nationalism* (London: MacMillan, 1997), 3.

21. John Buckham, "The Unforgotten Whittier," *New England Magazine* (September 1903). 44–51, quotation on 45.

22. George Carpenter, "John Greenleaf Whittier," in Charles Dudley Warner, ed., *Library of the World's Best Literature*, vol. 39, (New York, 1897), 5912.

23. Quoted in Louis Ruchames, "Race, Marriage, and Abolition in Massachusetts," *Journal of Negro History* 40 (1955): 273.

24. Ibid., 253.

25. A Letter," in John Greenleaf Whittier, *Poetical Works of John Greenleaf Whittier* (Boston: Houghton Mifflin, 1975), 298–300, henceforth abbreviated as *PW* and cited parenthetically in the text.

26. Albert Mordell, *Quaker Militant: John Greenleaf Whittier* (Boston: Houghton Mifflin, 1933).

27. Toni Morrison, *Playing in the Dark: Whiteness and the Literary Imagination* (New York: Vintage, 1993), 38.

28. Kate Gardner, review of "Snow-Bound," *The Ladies' Repository* (December 1867): 723.

29. Frankenberg, 17.

30. Morrison, 59.

31. Ibid., 52.

32. John Saillant, "The Black Body Erotic and the Republican Body Politic, 1790–1820," in Mary Chapman and Glen Hendler, eds., *Sentimental Men: Masculinity and the Politics of Affect in American Culture* (Berkeley: University of California Press, 1999). I am using only selected points from his discussion, which actually focuses on the homoerotics of these bodily images.

33. Sarah Wentworth Morton, "The African Chief," in Nina Baym et al., eds., *The Norton Anthology of American Literature*, vol. 1 (New York: W. W. Norton, 1997), 842–844.

34. John Greenleaf Whittier to Harriet Pitman, 20 January 1869, in Whittier, *The Letters of John Greenleaf Whittier*, vol. 3, ed. John B. Pickard (Cambridge: Harvard University Press, 1975), 191.

35. Robert Morris, *Reading, Riting, and Reconstruction* (Chicago: University of Chicago Press, 1981), 174.

36. Rocks, 349–350.

37. Rebecca I. Davis, *Gleanings from Merrimack Valley* (Haverhill, Mass.: Chase Brothers, 1887), 16.

38. Edward Pierce, untitled article, *Freedman's Journal* (May 1867): 80.

39. Lincoln Kerstein, ed., *The Hampton Album* (New York: Museum of Modern Art, 1966), 25. For a wider-ranging reading of Johnston's work, see Laura Wexler, "Black and White in Color," *Prospects* 13 (1988): 341–390.

40. Unattributed, untitled article, *Southern Workman* 8 (1899): 8.

41. *Ibid.*, 8

42. The "Hampton Idea," which produced Booker T. Washington and which many saw as too gradualist and accommodating, is critically described in James Anderson, *The Education of Blacks in the South, 1860–1935* (Chapel Hill: University of North Carolina Press, 1988).

43. Emily Harper Williams, *American Authors' Birthdays*, Hampton Leaflets (Hampton, Va.: Hampton Normal and Agricultural Institute, 1917), i.

44. Williams was one of the first African-American women to graduate from the University of Michigan; information published online by Michigan's alumni association lists her graduation date as 1896.

45. Williams, 18.

Chapter 3. A Visit from St. Nicholas: Pedagogy, Power, and Print Culture (pp. 68–98)

1. [Mary Mapes Dodge], "Children's Magazines," *Scribner's* (July 1873): 352.

2. Ibid., 353.

3. Ibid., 354.

4. *St. Nicholas Magazine for Boys and Girls* (May 1876): 470. Henceforth referred to by its shorter name, *St. Nicholas.*

5. Lawrence Levine, *Highbrow / Lowbrow: The Emergence of Cultural Hierarchy in America* (Cambridge, Mass.: Harvard University Press, 1988), 225.

6. Arthur John, *The Best Years of the Century: Richard Watson Gilder, "Scribner's Monthly," and the "Century Magazine," 1870–1909* (Champagne-Urbana: University of Illinois Press, 1981), ix.

7. Quoted in Ibid., 54. From editorials by Gilder in the *Century,* June 1896 and April 1900.

8. Both of these testimonials appeared in an advertising supplement titled "What Some Eminent Men Think of *St. Nicholas,* " bound into *St. Nicholas,* January 1875.

9. Clara Bates, "The Children's Building of the Columbian Exposition," *St. Nicholas* (July 1893): 714.

10. R. Gordon Kelly, *Mother Was a Lady: Self and Society in Selected American Children's Periodicals, 1865–1890* (Westport, Conn.: Greenwood Press, 1974), 23.

11. Bill Brown, *The Material Unconscious: American Amusement, Stephen Crane, and the Economies of Play* (Cambridge, Mass., and London: Harvard University Press, 1996).

12. William Cullen Bryant, "The Woodman and the Sandal-Tree," *St. Nicholas* (November 1873): 1.

13. Brander Matthews, "William Cullen Bryant," *St. Nicholas* (November 1894): 19.

14. See Ibid., 15–19; Henry Fenn, "The Story of Whittier's 'Snow-Bound,' " *St. Nicholas* (December 1893): 427–430; "To the Children of America," announcement in the Letter-Box, *St. Nicholas* (December 1882): 156.

15. *St. Nicholas* (December 1880): 139.

16. Ibid.

17. "The St. Nicholas Treasure-Box," *St. Nicholas* (April 1881): 483.

18. Patricia Meyer Spacks, *Boredom: The Literary History of a State of Mind* (Chicago: University of Chicago Press, 1995).

19. Dodge, "Children's Magazines," 354.

20. James Buckham, "Some Needs of the Versifiers," *Writer* (May 1888): 114–115.

21. Richard Watson Gilder, "The Poet's Day," *Century* (June 1895): 247.

22. *St. Nicholas* (October 1875): 751.

23. See Howard Chudacoff, *How Old Are You? Age Consciousness in American Culture* (Princeton, N.J.: Princeton University Press, 1989). Chudacoff does not address the role of the mass-culture industry in age grading, but his demographic work is especially useful, showing how a decrease in family size, together with a narrowing in the age gap between husbands and wives, contributed to a more age-conscious, polarized family structure by the turn of the century, with parents on one side of the gap and like-minded siblings on the other.

24. *St. Nicholas* (November 1874): 52.

25. "New Toys and Games for the Children," *St. Nicholas* (January 1874): 171.

26. Bill Brown, "American Childhood and Stephen Crane's Toys," *American Literary History* 7:3 (1995): 443–476. Brown sees this conflict recapitulated in

toys such as the steam-engine dancer, which embodies both the traditions of the rural South and the modernity of the mass-produced object. Brown also genders the emerging mass-cultural sphere as female and traditional childhood as the ruralist, male-centered province of the "boys' book."

27. Oskar Negt and Alexander Kluge, "The Public Sphere of Children," in *Public Sphere and Experience: Analysis of the Bourgeois and Proletarian Public Sphere*, trans. Peter Labanyi et al. (Minneapolis: University of Minnesota Press, 1993), 283–288. I do not mean to suggest that Negt and Kluge generally assume culture to be unified; one of their main points is that it is not. Nevertheless, like many adults confronted with childhood, they seem to make sweeping assumptions about children based on the notions that (1) children are "naturally" more free from cultural constraints than adults, and (2) capitalist society does not value children, because they are not productive workers. This latter assumption is at least debatable by anyone who studies later-nineteenth-century America, where children were almost obsessively valued.

28. *St. Nicholas* (May 1889): 90.

29. William Leach, *Land of Desire: Merchants, Power, and the Rise of a New American Culture* (New York: Pantheon, 1993), 148. See also Rachel Bowlby, *Just Looking: Consumer Culture in Dreiser, Gissing, and Zola* (New York: Methuen, 1985). Bowlby frames this phenomenon in Freudian terms: "Consumer culture transforms the narcissistic mirror into a shop window, the glass which reflects an idealized image of the woman (or man) who stands before it, in the form of a model of what she could buy or become. Through the glass, the woman sees what she wants and what she wants to be" (32).

30. This description appeared on the back of *Youth's Companion* (16 April 1827); this "family paper," it should be said, continued to be popular after the Civil War, appealing largely to a poorer and less sophisticated readership (especially in the West) that could not afford to indulge the demographic split between children's and adults' reading materials; in tone, it was more akin to, say, the *Saturday Evening Post* than to strictly juvenile periodicals.

31. In the January 1875 issue of *St. Nicholas*, part of Moore's poem was reprinted in facsimile; the accompanying commentary notes: "No matter who writes poetry for the holidays, nor how new or popular the author of such poems may be, nearly everybody reads or repeats 'Twas the Night Before Christmas' when the holidays come round; and it is printed and published in all sorts of forms and styles, so that the new poems must stand aside when it is the season for this dear old friend" (161).

32. Mary Mapes Dodge, welcome letter, *St. Nicholas* (November 1873): 5.

33. Sarah Josepha Hale, "Mary's Lamb," in Donald Hall, ed., *The Oxford Book of Children's Verse in America*, 20. The first four lines of the poem were the first electronically recorded human speech, as recited from memory by Thomas Edison in 1877.

34. One characteristic of the Letter Box is that it printed letters from a variety of locales in each issue; the "Mary's Lamb" sketch was flanked by letters from London, New York, Hartford, California, and Harper's Ferry, Virginia.

35. The exception, obviously, is "nursery rhymes" that were explicitly didactic, like "Mary's Lamb." The Puritan tradition left its stamp on early American children's literature, much more so than in Britain; certainly, America in the 1840s could not have, and did not, produce anyone akin to Edward Lear, although Lear's work was imported to the United States. It is

also notable that the nondidactic "Visit from St. Nicholas" originally appeared, not in a children's magazine, but in a newspaper; the earliest children's magazines, such as Lydia Child's *Juvenile Miscellany,* were too earnest for such fancies.

36. Laura E. Richards, "Some Funny Summer Verses," *St. Nicholas* (August 1876): 664.

37. Susan Stewart, *Nonsense: Aspects of Intertextuality in Folklore and Literature* (Baltimore: Johns Hopkins University Press, 1978), 60.

38. Richards, "Some Funny Summer Verses," 665.

39. Laura E. Richards, "The Shark," *St. Nicholas* (March 1876): 312–313.

40. Jackson Lears, *Fables of Abundance: A Cultural History of American Advertising* (New York: Basic Books, 1994).

41. Nestlé's Food ad, *St. Nicholas* (February 1902): 3. Ads were not printed in the magazine itself but were bound into the beginning and end pages.

42. "Palmer Cox" (obituary), *New York Times,* 25 July 1924.

43. "Brownie" is a term from lowland Scotland, according to the Celticist antiquarian Henry Jenner; he speculates that "Brownie, *Duine Sith,* and *Peght,* which is 'Pict,' are only in their origin ways of expressing the little dark-skinned aboriginal folk who were supposed to inhabit the barrows, cromlechs, and *allées couverts,* and whose cunning, their only effective weapon against the mere strength of the Aryan invader, earned them a reputation for magical powers." Henry Jenner, introduction to "In Cornwall," in W. Y. Evans-Wentz, *The Fairy-Faith in the Celtic Countries* (1911; reprint, New York: Citadel Press, 1990), 163.

44. Palmer Cox, "The Brownies on Bicycles," *St. Nicholas* (November 1885): 70.

45. Quoted in Anthony Esler, *Generations in History* (Williamsburg, Va.: privately printed, 1982), 45.

46. Raymond Williams notes that preromantic uses of "generation" refer to lineages, not to age-graded groups; see Williams, *Keywords: A Vocabulary of Culture and Society* (New York: Oxford University Press, 1976), 140–142.

47. "New Toys and Games for the Children," *St. Nicholas* (January 1874): 170–171.

48. *St. Nicholas* (May 1886): 554.

49. Trachtenberg, 3–4.

50. Michel de Certeau, *The Practice of Everyday Life,* trans. Steven Rendall (Berkeley: University of California Press, 1984), xxiv.

51. On the influence of Palmer Cox's Brownies on Rose O'Neill's Kewpies, see *Woman's Home Companion* (January 1914): 3–4.

52. *St. Nicholas* (September 1898): 961.

53. Daniel Harris, "Cuteness," *Salmagundi* 96 (Fall 1992): 177–186.

54. Selections from Bergen's "Pandean Pastimes" and "Nibblings and Browsings," which first appeared in the *Atlantic Monthly* in 1896 and 1893 respectively, are reprinted in Simon Bronner, ed., *Folklife Studies from the Gilded Age: Object, Rite, and Custom in Victorian America* (Ann Arbor: University of Michigan Research Press, 1987), 120–133.

55. *Literary World* (12 December 1896): 454.

56. Mary Mapes Dodge, *Rhymes and Jingles* (New York: Scribner's, 1874). This collection contained work culled from *St. Nicholas* as well as other original verses; it was released in conjunction with the bound Christmas volume of *St. Nicholas* in 1874.

57. Joan Rubin, *The Making of Middlebrow Culture* (Chapel Hill: University of North Carolina Press, 1992), 18.

58. Gelett Burgess, untitled, *St. Nicholas* (January 1899): 259.

Chapter 4. Performing Class: James Whitcomb Riley Onstage (pp. 99–125)

1. James Whitcomb Riley, *Complete Poetical Works of James Whitcomb Riley* (Indianapolis: Bobbs-Merrill, 1932), 445. Henceforth abbreviated as *CPW.*

2. *Boston Globe*, 1 March 1889.

3. Ibid.

4. Van Wyck Brooks, *America's Coming-of-Age* (Garden City, N.Y.: Doubleday, 1958), 13

5. Elizabeth J. Van Allen, *James Whitcomb Riley: A Life* (Indianapolis: Indiana University Press, 1999), 90–93.

6. Joe S. Miller, untitled rhyme accompanying cartoon illustration, *Bookman* (March 1911): 73.

7. Stuart Blumin, *The Emergence of the Middle Class: Social Experience in the American City, 1760–1900* (Cambridge: Cambridge University Press, 1989), 258.

8. Riley actually met Arnold on a train in New York State in 1882, when they were both on tour; Riley wrote to his friend Myron Reed that Arnold had no sense of humor: "A joke that tackled him would hide its head in shame, and skulk away and weep." James Whitcomb Riley, *Letters of James Whitcomb Riley*, ed. William Phelps (Indianapolis: Bobbs-Merrill, 1935), 40.

9. Quoted in Rubin, 1. Middlebrow culture, according to Rubin, was about aspiring to status; it was about bringing "high culture" to middle-class people; this is different from the "genial middle ground" of the middle nineteenth century, as carved out by writers such as Whittier, whose "genial middle ground" made readers not cultivated but comfortable, not special but ordinary.

10. The reference is to Riley's "Little Orphant Annie."

11. *Minneapolis Journal*, 11 March 1893.

12.For an assessment of Arnold's huge impact on late-nineteenth-century American culture, see John Raleigh, *Matthew Arnold and American Culture* (Berkeley: University of California Press, 1957). See also Levine, *Highbrow/Lowbrow.*

13. Riley, *CPW,* 513.

14. See Kathy Peiss, *Cheap Amusements: Working Women and Leisure in Turn-of-the-Century New York* (Philadelphia: Temple University Press, 1986). Although Peiss is concerned with working-class women in New York, her insights into the effects of urbanization and increasing leisure time are broadly applicable; moreover, as her book shows, working-class women frequently identified with and aspired to middle-class status, taking advantage of "self-culture" opportunities at, for example, the Thirty-eighth Street Working Girls' Club, and thus pressing the boundaries of "class" themselves.

15. As Levine has argued, this impulse to draw strict cultural boundaries (based on taste and cultivation, as opposed to social position per se) is largely a product of the later nineteenth century. See Levine, 14–81.

16. Pierre Bourdieu, "Social Space and Symbolic Power," *Sociological Theory* 7:1 (1989): 20. See also Bourdieu, *Distinction.*

17. Quoted from a Standard Remedy trademark, designed by Riley and reproduced in Marcus Dickey, *The Youth of James Whitcomb Riley* (Indianapolis: Bobbs-Merrill, 1919), 121.

18. See Brooks McNamara, *Step Right Up* (Garden City, N.Y.: Doubleday, 1976).

19. Dickey, 117.

20. Levine, 9.

21. Quoted in McNamara, 77.

22. Bliss Carman, "Mr. Riley's Poetry," *Atlantic Monthly* (September 1898): 426.

23. *Milwaukee Journal*, 26 October 1900.

24. Quoted in *The Bookman* (September 1904): 18; originally appeared in the Anderson *Democrat* ca. 1877. See also Charles Eastman, "The Grandfather," in William McGuffey, ed., *McGuffey's Fifth Eclectic Reader* (1879; reprint, New York: Signet, 1962), 61. Eastman's poem begins, "The farmer sat in his easy chair / Smoking his pipe of clay, / While his hale old wife, with busy care / Was cleaning the dinner away."

25. Stuart Hall, "Notes on Deconstructing 'the Popular,'" in Ralph Samuel, ed., *People's History and Socialist Theory* (London: Routledge, 1981), 233.

26. Riley, *CPW*, 745.

27. People's College Star Course of Denver, *Fourth Annual Announcement* (booklet), 1896–97. Riley Papers, Lilly Library, Indiana University, Bloomington.

28. *Memphis Commercial*, 3 April 1892.

29. Randall Knoper, *Acting Naturally: Mark Twain in the Culture of Performance* (Berkeley: University of California Press, 1993), 74.

30. Program for the "First Entertainment" at the Baptist Church, East Aurora, New York, Riley Papers.

31. *Indianapolis Herald*, 16 October 1880.

32. Will Allen, "Riley on a Tear," *Nashville Journal*, 8 February 1890.

33. Riley's prevarications included shaving five years off his age, a point that became an embarrassment when obituaries had to be written. Critics seldom held him up as a "role model," the way they did Longfellow and Whittier; the *Minneapolis Tribune*, for instance, cast him as a heathenish adolescent in a 1 February 1889, profile: "The Hoosier poet is a thorough Bohemian. He cares about as much for society as a Digger Indian cares for the fine arts. It is told of him that he was wont to call on just one young lady, and his attraction then lay in the fact that she lived on the same street as his boarding house."

34. Elsie Russell to JWR, 9 February 1916, Riley Papers.

35. Stuart Hall, 235.

36. Riley, *CPW*, 507–508.

37. *Peoria Journal*, 3 September 1882. Quoted in Carol Reed Kennedy, "The Grand Opera House of Peoria, 1882–1909," *Journal of the Illinois State Historical Society*, 78:1 (1984): 36.

38. *Peoria Daily Transcript*, 6 April 1889. Quoted in Ibid., 38.

39. H. L. Mencken, *The American Language* (New York: Knopf, 1937), 221. I do not mean to imply that chautauquas thereby gave up their pursuit of refinement; I simply mean to point out that even in cultivated circles, a taste for popular entertainment had taken hold and had to be assimilated.

40. This new middle-class access and mobility—along with its perils—is perhaps most starkly illustrated in the rise, after 1880, of the department store (with its theatricality, its multiple floors, and its bargain basement) as chronicled by William Leach in *Land of Desire*. Indeed, by the 1930s Bloch's Department Store in Indianapolis was advertising a James Whitcomb Riley

fountain room, where patrons could order a Little Orphant Annie parfait. My point is that the department store enables the consumer a certain protean mobility, moving between subject-positions within the confines of middle-class consumer culture.

41. Interview in the *Milwaukee Journal*, 26 October 1900.

42. *Rochester (N.Y.) Morning Herald*, 14 April 1888.

43. Riley, *CPW*, 462–464.

44. Interview in the *San Francisco Examiner*, 9 December 1892.

45. Bourdieu, "Social Space and Symbolic Power," 3.

46. Letter to JWR from Dan Paine, December (day unspecified) 1892, Riley Papers.

47. *Kansas City Star*, 17 November 1897.

48. Fredric Jameson, "Reification and Utopia in Mass Culture," *Social Text* 1 (Winter 1979): 141. Certainly, the "optical illusion of social harmony" that Jameson describes in this essay is operant in Riley's work.

49. Riley, *CPW*, 28.

50. Ibid., 595.

51. Emilie B. Stapp to JWR, 14 February 1914, Riley Papers.

52. JWR to Emilie B. Stapp, 20 February 1914, Riley Papers.

53. Emilie B. Stapp to JWR, n.d. [March 1914?] Riley Papers. Although this letter is not dated, it is part of the same exchange.

54. Levine makes this point in *Highbrow/Lowbrow*, 222–223.

55. Riley, *CPW*, 651. This is not Riley's only foray across the color line; see also "Ponchus Pilate" for a rewriting of "The Raggedy Man" in racial terms.

56. Clinton Scollard, "Recent Books of Poetry," *Critic* (March 1903): 234.

57. The general cultural obsession with childhood during the 1880s and '90s is well known; see, for example, James R. Kincaid, *Child-Loving: The Erotic Child and Victorian Culture* (New York: Routledge, 1992). For the flexible nature of minstrelsy, and how it expanded to deal with differences other than the black-white racial dichotomy, see Joyce Flynn, "Melting Plots: Patterns of Racial and Ethnic Amalgamation in American Drama before Eugene O'Neill," *American Quarterly* 38:3 (1986): 418–436.

58. Miles Orvell, *The Real Thing: Imitation and Authenticity in American Culture, 1880–1940* (Chapel Hill: University of North Carolina Press, 1989), 71.

59. Ibid., 370.

60. James Whitcomb Riley, *Complete Works of James Whitcomb Riley*, Vol. 10 (New York: Collier and Sons, 1916), 2575–2576.

61. Edmund Eitel, "The Real Orphant Annie," *Ladies' Home Journal* (November 1915): 54.

62. Robert Sayers, "Sing Anything: The Narrative Repertoire of a Mormon Pioneer," *Journal of the Southwest* 29:1 (1987): 70.

63. *Kansas City Star*, 17 November 1897.

64. Bierce wrote this attack in the *San Francisco Examiner*, in December of 1892, but I am quoting from a reprint of the article, published in the *Indianapolis Journal*, 20 January 1893. It is almost needless to say that the *Journal* reprinted Bierce's attack in the context of a defense of Riley—already by 1893, Riley was one of Indianapolis's most famous citizens.

65. JWR to George Smith, 21 November 1892, in Riley, *Letters of James Whitcomb Riley*, 166–167.

66. See, for instance, JWR to Rudyard Kipling, in ibid., 182–183: "For some years I've been striving to ferret out the one evident lack or defect of

our whole art guild; and I've struck it: It's business. We naturally hate that, and therefore avoid it. That's why we're all victims. So I've got to work to change that status of affairs. In consequence, I'm a revelation to myself. Am making not only oodles of money off my books, but twice over as much again by personally reading the same to packed houses."

67. *Minneapolis Tribune,* 15 January 1892.

68. Anonymous to JWR, n.d. [1914?], Riley Papers.

69. Advertising flyer, Riley Papers.

70. Jameson, "Reification and Utopia," 136.

71. Ibid., 137.

72. Keith Cunningham, ed., *The Oral Tradition of the American West* (Little Rock, Ark.: August House, 1990), 63.

73. For Levine, this sense of "collective aesthetic experience" was present in early- to mid-nineteenth-century productions of Shakespeare; under such vitally chaotic popular conditions, he argues, a "rich public culture" emerged; this is Levine's version, then, of what had been lost.

Chapter 5. "Seein' Things at Night": Eugene Field and the Infantilization of American Culture (pp. 126–155)

1. Quoted in Albert B. Paine, *Mark Twain: A Biography,* vol. 3 (New York and London: Harper Bros., 1912), 1175.

2. "Mark Twain Unveiling the Memorial Tablet in the Wall of the House Where Eugene Field was Born," *St. Louis Globe-Democrat,* 7 June 1902.

3. Michael Kammen, *Manhood in America: A Cultural History* (New York: Simon and Schuster, 1996), 183.

4. Hamlin Garland, "Eugene Field," *Review of Reviews* (September 1893): 334.

5. Edmund Stedman, Genius and Other Essays (New York: Moffat, Yard and Co., 1911), 185.

6. Eugene Debs, "Riley, Nye, and Field," *National Magazine* (1930): 616.

7. T. J. Jackson Lears, *No Place of Grace: Antimodernism and the Transformation of American Culture, 1880–1920* (Chicago: University of Chicago Press, 1981).

8. William S. Lord, untitled. From *Lines Read at the Funeral Services of Eugene Field* (Philadelphia: privately printed, 1922), Eugene Field Papers, Newberry Library, Chicago.

9. Anonymous review of *The Sabine Edition of Eugene Field, Bookman* (July 1896): 452.

10. Stedman, 189.

11. Edward Bok, *The Americanization of Edward Bok* (New York: Scribner's, 1920), 174. Bok became the editor of the *Ladies' Home Journal.*

12. Eugene Field, "To a Usurper," in *Mary Burt, ed. The Eugene Field Book: Verses, Stories, and Letters for School Reading* (1898; reprint, New York: Books for Libraries Press, 1969), 30.

13. Carl Dennis, *Eugene Field's Creative Years* (New York: Doubleday, 1924), 299.

14. Henry Ellsworth Hadon, "Eugene Field," *Chicago Sunday Times,* 10 November 1895. The poem was part of a full-page spread of newspaper poems mourning Field, and reflects the sentiments of most of them.

15. William Marion Reedy, *The Eugene Field Myth* (St Louis: privately printed, 1901), 11–12.

16. Ibid., 13.

NOTES

17. Ibid., 18.

18. Leon Mead, "Eugene Field and Bill Nye," *Bookman* (March 1899): 135.

19. Anonymous, "Point of View," *Scribner's* (January 1896): 122.

20. Quoted in Robert Conrow, *Field Days: The Life, Times, and Reputation of Eugene Field* (New York: Scribner's, 1974), 15.

21. G. Stanley Hall, "The Contents of Children's Minds," in T. L. Smith, ed., *Aspects of Child Life and Education* (Boston: Athenaeum Press, 1907), 43–45. Hall's essay first appeared in the *Princeton Review* in 1883.

22. Burt, ed. *The Eugene Field Book*, viii.

23. Ibid., ix.

24. Eugene Field, "The Sugar-Plum Tree," in Ibid., 13.

25. Isabel Moore, ed., *Eaton Fourth Reader* (Chicago: Eaton Book Company, 1906), 7.

26. Frances Chutter, ed., *Art-Literature Reader, Book Three* (Boston: Atkinson, Metzer, and Grover, n.d. [1900?]), 16.

27. Dennis, 163.

28. G. Stanley Hall, "A Study of Dolls," in Smith, ed., *Aspects of Child Life and Education*, 159.

29. Field, Sharps and Flats, *Chicago Record*, 21 March 1895.

30. Eugene Field, *Love Affairs of a Bibliomaniac* (New York: Scribner's, 1896), 9–10. Since Field died in his forties, the details here—and elsewhere in his autobiography—are recklessly misleading. Sometimes the lies are ironized and sometimes they seem (to me) pathological. But they are always theatrical, designed to advance a particular "character" to the public. It is interesting to note that Field's son, Eugene Field, Jr., became one of the twentieth century's most notorious forgers, faking (and selling) his father's signature and the signatures of other notables including Abraham Lincoln.

31. Patricia Crain, *The Story of A: The Alphabetization of America from "The New England Primer" to "The Scarlet Letter"* (Stanford, Calif.: Stanford University Press: 2000), 51.

32. Quoted in Slason Thompson, *The Life of Eugene Field* (New York: Appleton, 1927), 18.

33. Jay Leyda, *The Years and Hours of Emily Dickinson*, vol. 1 (New Haven, Conn.: Yale University Press, 1960), xlvii.

34. Mary J. Reid and Henrietta Dexter Field, "Eugene Field," *St. Nicholas* (August 1896): 836.

35. Field to Mrs. Julia Jewett, 12 July 1879, quoted in Leyda, 312.

36. Quoted in Thompson, 18.

37. Eugene Field, *Tribune Primer* (1882; reprint, New York: Grosset and Dunlap, n.d.), 26.

38. Ibid., 12.

39. Field, "The Merciful Lad," *Chicago Morning News*, 6 October 1886.

40. Eugene Field, handwritten ms. for a Sharps and Flats column, reprinted in Willis J. Buckingham, ed., *Emily Dickinson's Reception in the 1890s: A Documentary History* (Pittsburgh: University of Pittsburgh Press, 1989), 142. Buckingham expresses concern that a printed version does not exist. However, multiple editions of the *Chicago Record* were published every day and not all have survived; researchers on Field will find gaps in the Sharps and Flats run that are a function of what was and was not saved on microfilm.

41. William Wells Newell, *Games and Songs of American Childhood* (1883; reprint, New York: Dover, 1963), 200.

42. Field, "Intry-Mintry," in *With Trumpet and Drum*, 12.

43. Field, "Wynken, Blynken, and Nod," in Burt, 67.

44. See Brodhead, 13–47.

45. Field, "Child and Mother," in Burt, 5.

46. Field, "The Rock-a-By Lady from Hushaby Street," in *Love-Songs of Childhood* (New York: Scribner's, 1894), 1.

47. Field, "The Awful Bugaboo," quoted in Thompson, 77.

48. Morton Cohen, *Lewis Carroll, Photographer of Children: Four Nude Studies* (New York: Potter, 1978).

49. Nina Auerbach, *Romantic Imprisonment: Women and Other Glorified Outcasts* (New York: Columbia University Press, 1986), 168.

50. Carol Mavor, "Dream-Rushes: Lewis Carroll's Photographs of the Little Girl," in Claudia Nelson and Lynne Vallone, eds., *The Girl's Own: Cultural Histories of the Anglo-American Girl, 1830–1915* (Athens: University of Georgia Press, 1994), 170.

51. Eugene Field, *Little Willie* (Philadelphia: privately printed, 1895), n.p.

52. Lears, *No Place of Grace*, 146.

53. Conrow offers an account of *Only a Boy* and the ensuing scandal in *Field Days*, 135–137.

54. Reid and Field, 834.

55. Ibid., 834.

56. Field, "The Doll's Wooing," in *Love-Songs of Childhood*, 100.

57. Field, "Lady Button-Eyes," in *Ibid.*, 62.

58. G. Stanley Hall, "A Study of Dolls," 192.

59. Reid and Field, 834.

Chapter 6. Emily Dickinson and the Form of Childhood (pp. 156–189)

1. A reviewer in the *Boston Post* wrote, approvingly, "There is a winsome playfulness and sympathy with the trivial chills and flushes of nature, which find expression in fantastic form and almost suggest the capricious feeling of a child." *Boston Post*, 27 November 1890, 2; WJB #26. After each contemporary review cited, I will also give the number assigned to the review by Willis J. Buckingham (WJB) in his indispensable collection, *Emily Dickinson's Reception in the 1890s*.

2. See Domhnall Mitchell, "Revising the Script: Emily Dickinson's Manuscripts," *American Literature* 70:4 (December 1998): 705–737. Mitchell reviews (with some skepticism) the critical discourse surrounding Dickinson's handwritten manuscripts.

3. Willis J. Buckingham, "Poetry Readers and Reading in the 1890s: Emily Dickinson's First Reception," in Machor, ed., 164–179.

4. Both of these critics have placed Emily Dickinson (hereafter ED) in mostly early- to mid-nineteenth-century contexts, but their approaches emphasize the ways that ED did fit into cultural conventions. See Barton Levi St. Armand, *Emily Dickinson and Her Culture: The Soul's Society* (Cambridge: Cambridge University Press, 1984); Elizabeth Petrino, *Emily Dickinson and Her Contemporaries: Women's Verse in America, 1820–1885* (Hanover, N.H.: University Press of New England, 1998).

5. Quoted in Sol Cohen, ed., *Education in the United States: A Documentary History*, vol. 2 (New York: Random House, 1974), 1087.

6. I am quoting here from the poem as it appears in Mabel Loomis Todd, ed., *Letters of Emily Dickinson*, vol. 1 (Boston: Roberts Brothers, 1894), 140.

7. See Ebenezer Porter, *Rhetorical Reader* (New York: Mark A. Newman, 1835). This was one of the textbooks used at Amherst Academy when ED was a student there.

8. Mary Isabella Lovejoy, *Nature in Verse: A Poetry Reader for Children* (New York: Silver, Burdett, 1896); Ellen M. Cyr, ed., *Cyr Reader, Book Four* (Boston: Ginn and Co., 1896), 115; Sarah Louise Arnold and Charles B. Gilbert, *Stepping-Stones to Literature* (New York: Silver, Burdett and Co., 1897), 169; Abby E. Lane, ed., *Lights to Literature, Third Reader* (Chicago: Rand, McNally, 1898), 17; Katherine D. Blake and Georgia Alexander, eds., *Graded Poetry: Fourth Year* (New York: Maynard, Merrill and Co., 1906), 44–45; Geoffrey Buckwater, ed., *Buckwater's Third Reader* (New York: Parker P. Simmons,1907), 136; Clara Murray, ed., *Wide Awake, Third Reader* (Boston: Little, Brown, 1908), 76, 164–165, and Murray, ed., *Wide Awake, Fourth Reader* (Boston: Little, Brown, 1908), 323; Ellen E. Kenyon-Warner, ed., *Character-Building Reader, Third Year* (New York: Hinds, Noble and Eldredge, 1910), 112.

9. Cyr, v.

10. ED, "A Day," in Ibid., 115.

11. Kenyon-Warner, iii.

12. ED, "Out of the Morning," in Ibid., 112.

13. Anonymous writer, "Cheerfulness," in ibid., 113.

14. Lovejoy, v.

15. Ibid.

16. ED, "The Grass," in Lovejoy, 23.

17 "His Sixth Birthday," *Youth's Companion* 11 November 1897, 568.

18. ED, "Ready," *Youth's Companion*, 11 November 1897), 568.

19. *Youth's Companion* to Mabel Loomis Todd, 12 October 1891, Box 19, Todd envelope 372, Emily Dickinson Collection, Robert Frost Library, Amherst College.

20. ED, "Morning," *St. Nicholas* (May 1891): 491. The *St. Nicholas* editors amended the title from "Out of the Morning."

21. Ingrid Satelmajar, "Dickinson as Children's Fare: The Author Served Up in *St. Nicholas,*" *Book History* 5 (2002): 105.

22. Sandra Gilbert and Susan Gubar, *The Madwoman in the Attic: The Woman Writer and the Nineteenth-Century Literary Imagination* (New Haven, Conn.: Yale University Press, 1979).

23. Joanne Dobson, *Dickinson and the Strategies of Reticence* (Bloomington: Indiana University Press, 1989), 68.

24. Marietta Messmer, *A Vice for Voices: Reading Emily Dickinson's Correspondence* (Amherst: University of Massachusetts Press, 2001), 122.

25. T. W. Higginson, "Emily Dickinson's Letters," *Atlantic Monthly* (October 1891): 444–456. Higginson's article is reprinted in Willis J. Buckingham (WJB #221), 183.

26. Paolo Freire, *Pedagogy of the Oppressed*, trans. Myra Ramos (New York: Continuum, 1970), 53.

27. Freire, 61.

28. ED quoted by Higginson, 444.

29. Ibid.

30. Ibid.

31. Ibid., 445.

32. Ibid., 447.

33. Ibid., 448.

34. Ibid., 450.

35. Ibid., 453.

36. Claire Raymond, "Dickinson as the Un-named, Buried Child," *Emily Dickinson Journal* 12:1 (2003): 107. Raymond goes on to make a fascinating argument about ED's "buried child" voice, a trope that fits my argument that ED's understanding of childhood was unfinished and unnerving.

37. ED, "Unreturned," in ED, *Poems by Emily Dickinson*, 37.

38. *Overland Monthly* (May 1891): 549; WJB #150.

39. Higginson, preface to ED, *Poems by Emily Dickinson*, v.

40. Edmund Stedman, "The Nature and Elements of Poetry," *Century* (May 1892): 151.

41. Whittier, "The Seeking of the Water-fall," in *Poetical Works of John Greenleaf Whittier*, 162.

42. Zadel Barnes Buddington, "The Children's Night," *Harper's* (January 1875): 164.

43. See Paula Bennett, *My Life a Loaded Gun: Female Creativity and Feminist Poetics* (Boston: Beacon, 1986). Bennett ultimately sees Dickinson's "child" pose as a source of power, though with some significant risks as well.

44. See Jane Eberwein, *Dickinson: Strategies of Limitation* (Amherst: University of Massachusetts Press, 1985), 97.

45. Steedman, 3.

46. Thomas Aldrich, "In Re: Emily Dickinson," *Atlantic Monthly* (January 1892): 143; WJB #283.

47. Ibid.

48. This notice appears as a clipping in Mabel Loomis Todd's scrapbook in the Emily Dickinson Collection, Robert Frost Library, Amherst College.

49. "The Point of View," *Scribner's* (March 1890): 395; WJB #119.

50. ED, *Poems by Emily Dickinson*, 132.

51. Mabel Loomis Todd, preface to ED, *Poems by Emily Dickinson, Second Series, ed. Mabel Loomis Todd* (Boston: Roberts Brothers, 1891), 7.

52. Elizabeth Peabody, "Kindergarten: What Is It?" *Atlantic Monthly* (November 1862): 563.

53. Fredric Jameson, *The Political Unconscious: Narrative as a Socially Symbolic Act* (Ithaca, N.Y.: Cornell University Press, 1981), 106.

54. Jameson, "Reification and Utopia," 134.

55. Dana Gioia, "Can Poetry Matter?" in Gioia, et al., eds., *Twentieth-Century American Poetics: Poets on the Art of Poetry* (New York: McGraw-Hill, 2004), 438.

SELECT BIBLIOGRAPHY

Althusser, Louis. *Lenin and Philosophy and Other Essays.* Translated by Ben Brewster. New York: Monthly Review Press, 1971.

Anderson, Benedict. *Imagined Communities: Reflections on the Origin and Spread of Nationalism.* London and New York: Verso, 1983.

Anderson, James. *The Education of Blacks in the South, 1860–1935.* Chapel Hill: University of North Carolina Press, 1988.

Antin, Mary. *The Promised Land.* New York: Houghton Mifflin, 1911.

Arms, George. *The Fields Were Green: A New Vision of Bryant, Whittier, Holmes, Lowell, and Longfellow, with a Selection of their Poems.* Stanford, Calif.: Stanford University Press, 1953.

Arnold, Sarah Louise, and Charles B. Gilbert. *Stepping-Stones to Literature.* New York: Silver, Burdett and Co., 1897.

Auerbach, Nina. *Romantic Imprisonment: Women and Other Glorified Outcasts.* New York: Columbia University Press, 1986.

Babb, Valerie. *Whiteness Visible: The Meaning of Whiteness in American Literature and Culture.* New York: New York University Press, 1998.

Benjamin, Walter. *Illuminations.* Edited by Hannah Arendt. Translated by Harry Zohn. New York: Schocken Books, 1968.

Bennett, Paula. *My Life a Loaded Gun: Female Creativity and Feminist Poetics.* Boston: Beacon, 1986.

Bhabha, Homi K., ed. *Nation and Narration.* London: Routledge, 1990.

Bingham, Caleb, ed. *The American Preceptor.* Boston: Manning and Loring, 1813.

Blake, Katherine D., and Georgia Alexander, eds. *Graded Poetry: Fourth Year.* New York: Maynard, Merrill and Co., 1906.

Blumin, Stuart. *The Emergence of the Middle Class: Social Experience in the American City, 1760–1900.* Cambridge: Cambridge University Press, 1989.

Bok, Edward. *The Americanization of Edward Bok.* New York: Scribner's, 1920.

Bollough, William. "'It Is Better to Be a Country Boy': The Lure of the Country in Urban Education in the Gilded Age." *Historian* 35:2 (1973): 183–195.

Boswell, Jeanetta. *The Schoolroom Poets: A Bibliography.* Metuchen, N.J.: Scarecrow Press, 1983.

Bourdieu, Pierre. *Distinction: A Social Critique of the Judgment of Taste.* Translated by Richard Nice. Cambridge, Mass.: Harvard University Press, 1984.

——. "Social Space and Symbolic Power." *Sociological Theory* 7:1 (1989): 14–25.

Bowlby, Rachel. *Just Looking: Consumer Culture in Dreiser, Gissing, and Zola.* New York: Methuen, 1985.

Brodhead, Richard. *Cultures of Letters: Scenes of Reading and Writing in Nineteenth-Century America.* Chicago: University of Chicago Press, 1993.

Bronner, Simon, ed. *Folklife Studies from the Gilded Age: Object, Rite, and Custom in Victorian America.* Ann Arbor: University of Michigan Research Press, 1987.

Brooks, Van Wyck. *America's Coming-of-Age.* Garden City, N.Y.: Doubleday, 1958.

——. *Our Literary Heritage.* New York: E. P. Dutton, 1956.

Brow, James. "Notes on Community, Hegemony, and the Uses of the Past." *Anthropological Quarterly* 63:1 (1990): 1–6.

Brown, Bill. "American Childhood and Stephen Crane's Toys." *American Literary History* 7:3 (1995): 443–476.

Buckingham, Emma May. *A Self-Made Woman; or, Mary Idyl's Trials and Triumphs.* New York: S. R. Wells, 1873.

Buckingham, Willis J., ed. *Emily Dickinson's Reception in the 1890s: A Documentary History.* Pittsburgh: University of Pittsburgh Press, 1989.

Buckwater, Geoffrey, ed. *Buckwater's Fifth Reader.* New York: Parker P. Simmons, 1907.

——. *Buckwater's Third Reader.* New York: Parker P. Simmons, 1907.

Burns, Sarah. "Barefoot Boys and Other Country Children: Sentiment and Ideology in Nineteenth-Century American Art." *American Art Journal* 20:1 (1988): 24–50.

Burt, Mary E., ed. *The Eugene Field Book: Verses, Stories, and Letters for School Reading.* 1898. Reprint, New York: Books for Libraries Press, 1969.

Cameron, Kenneth Walter, ed. *Longfellow among His Contemporaries.* Hartford, Conn.: Transcendental Books, 1978.

Capen, Oliver. *Country Homes of Famous Americans.* New York: Doubleday, 1905.

Certeau, Michel de. *The Practice of Everyday Life.* Translated by Steven Rendall. Berkeley: University of California Press, 1984.

Chudacoff, Howard. *How Old Are You? Age Consciousness in American Culture.* Princeton, N.J.: Princeton University Press, 1989.

Chutter, Frances. *Art-Literature Reader, Book Three.* Boston: Atkinson, Metzer, and Grover, n.d. [1900?].

Clark, Henry Nichols Blake. "The Impact of Dutch and Flemish Genre Painting on American Genre Painting, 1800–1865." Ph.D. diss., University of Delaware, 1982.

Clarke, Helen. *Longfellow's Country.* New York: Doubleday, Page and Co., 1903.

Cody, Sherwin. *Four American Poets: A Book for Young Americans.* New York: Werner School Book Company, 1901.

Cohen, Morton. *Lewis Carroll, Photographer of Children: Four Nude Studies.* New York: Potter, 1978.

Cohen, Sol, ed. *Education in the United States: A Documentary History.* Vol. 2. New York: Random House, 1974.

Colby, Julia A. *Reminiscences.* Springfield, Mo., 1916.

Conforti, Joseph. *Imagining New England: Explorations of Regional Identity from the Pilgrims to the Mid-Twentieth Century.* Chapel Hill: University of North Carolina Press, 2000.

Conrow, Robert. *Field Days: The Life, Times, and Reputation of Eugene Field.* New York: Scribner's, 1974.

Crain, Patricia. *The Story of A: The Alphabetization of America from "The New England Primer" to "The Scarlet Letter."* Stanford, Calif.: Stanford University Press, 2000.

Cunningham, Keith, ed. *The Oral Tradition of the American West.* Little Rock, Ark.: August House, 1990.

Currier, Thomas. *A Bibliography of John Greenleaf Whittier.* Cambridge, Mass.: Harvard University Press, 1937.

Cyr, Ellen M., ed. *Cyr Reader, Book Four.* Boston: Ginn and Co., 1896.

Dana Family Papers. Longfellow House, Cambridge, Mass.

Davidson, Cathy, ed. *Reading in America: Literature and Social History.* Baltimore: Johns Hopkins University Press, 1989.

Davis, John, ed. *Julien Davis Reader.* 3rd year, part 2. Boston: D. C. Heath, 1912.

Davis, Rebecca I. *Gleanings from Merrimack Valley.* Haverhill, Mass.: Chase Brothers, 1887.

Dennis, Carl. *Eugene Field's Creative Years.* New York: Doubleday, 1924.

Derrida, Jacques. *Acts of Literature.* Edited by Derek Attridge. New York: Routledge, 1992.

Dickey, Marcus. *The Youth of James Whitcomb Riley.* Indianapolis: Bobbs-Merrill, 1919.

Dickinson, Emily. *Complete Poems of Emily Dickinson.* Edited by Thomas H. Johnson. Boston: Little, Brown, 1960.

———. *Poems by Emily Dickinson.* Edited by Thomas Wentworth Higginson and Mabel Loomis Todd. Boston: Roberts Brothers, 1890.

———. *Poems by Emily Dickinson, Second Series.* Edited by Mabel Loomis Todd. Boston: Roberts Brothers, 1891.

———. *Selected Letters.* Edited by Thomas H. Johnson. Cambridge, Mass.: Harvard University Press, 1971.

Dodge, Mary Mapes. *Rhymes and Jingles.* New York: Scribner's, 1874.

Douglas, Ann. *The Feminization of American Culture.* 1977. Reprint, New York: Anchor Press–Doubleday, 1988.

Dropkin, Ruth, ed. *The Roots of Open Education in America.* New York: Center for Open Education, 1976.

Earle, Alice Morse. *Home Life in Colonial Days.* New York: Macmillan, 1898.

Eberwein, Jane. *Dickinson: Strategies of Limitation.* Amherst: University of Massachusetts Press, 1985.

Esler, Anthony. *Generations in History.* Williamsburg, Va.: privately printed, 1982.

Evans-Wentz, W. Y. *The Fairy-Faith in Celtic Countries.* 1911. Reprint, New York: Citadel Press, 1990.

Felleman, Hazel. *The Best Loved Poems of the American People.* 1936. Reprint, New York: Doubleday, 2001.

Field, Eugene. *Love Affairs of a Bibliomaniac.* New York: Scribner's, 1896.

——. *Love-Songs of Childhood.* New York: Scribner's, 1894.

——. *Tribune Primer.* 1882. Reprint, New York: Grosset and Dunlap, n.d.

——. *With Trumpet and Drum.* New York: Scribner's, 1898.

Flynn, Joyce. "Melting Plots: Patterns of Racial and Ethnic Amalgamation in American Drama before Eugene O'Neill." *American Quarterly* 38:3 (1986): 418–436.

Foucault, Michel. *The Care of the Self.* Translated by Robert Hurley. Harmondsworth, Eng.: Allen Lane Publishers, 1988.

Frankenberg, Ruth. *The Social Construction of Whiteness: White Women, Race Matters.* Minneapolis: University of Minnesota Press, 1993.

Freire, Paolo. *Pedagogy of the Oppressed.* Translated by Myra Ramos. New York: Continuum, 1970.

Gartner, Matthew. "Longfellow's Place: The Poet and Poetry of Craigie House." *New England Quarterly* 73:1 (March 2000): 327–355.

Gettemy, Charles Ferris. *The True Story of Paul Revere.* Boston: Little, Brown, 1912.

Gilbert, Sandra, and Susan Gubar. *The Madwoman in the Attic: The Woman Writer and the Nineteenth-Century Literary Imagination.* New Haven, Conn.: Yale University Press, 1979.

Gilfillan, George. *Second Gallery of Literary Portraits.* 2nd ed. New York, 1852.

Gioia, Dana. "Can Poetry Matter?" In *Twentieth-Century American Poetics: Poets on the Art of Poetry,* edited by Dana Gioia, David Mason, and Meg Schoerke. New York: McGraw Hill, 2004.

Goldthwaite, John. *The Natural History of Make-Believe: A Guide to the Principal Works of Britain, Europe, and America.* New York: Oxford University Press, 1996.

Gorn, Elliott J., ed. *The McGuffey Readers: Selections from the 1879 Edition*. New York: Bedford / St. Martin's, 1988.

Gramsci, Antonio. *Selections from the Prison Notebooks of Antonio Gramsci*. Edited and translated by Quentin Hoar and Geoffrey Smith. New York: International Publishers, 1971.

Greenblatt, Stephen. *Shakespearean Negotiations: The Circulation of Social Energy in Renaissance England*. Berkeley: University of California Press, 1988.

Haliburton, Margaret W. *Teaching Poetry in the Grades*. Boston: Houghton Mifflin, 1911.

Hall, Donald. Introduction to *The Oxford Book of Children's Verse in America*. Edited by Donald Hall. New York: Oxford University Press, 1985.

Hall, G. Stanley. "The Contents of Children's Minds." In *Aspects of Child Life and Education*, edited by T. L. Smith. Boston: Athenaeum Press, 1907.

———. "A Study of Dolls." In *Aspects of Child Life and Education*, edited by T. L. Smith. Boston: Athenaeum Press, 1907.

Hall, Stuart. "Notes on Deconstructing 'the Popular.'" In *People's History and Socialist Theory*, edited by Ralph Samuel. London: Routledge, 1981.

Halttunen, Karen. *Confidence Men and Painted Women: A Study of Middle-Class Culture in America, 1830–1870*. New Haven, Conn.: Yale University Press, 1982.

Haralson, Eric. "Mars in Petticoats: Longfellow and Sentimental Masculinity." *Nineteenth-Century Literature* 51:3 (Dec. 1996): 327–355.

Harlan, Louis, ed. *Booker T. Washington Papers*. Vol. 2. Champagne-Urbana: University of Illinois Press, 1972.

Harris, Daniel. "Cuteness." *Salmagundi* 96 (Fall 1992): 177–186.

Hassan, Ihab, ed. *Liberations: New Essays on the Humanities in Revolution*. Middletown, Conn.: Wesleyan University Press, 1971.

Hastings, Scott E., Jr. *Miss Mary Mac All Dressed in Black: Tongue Twisters, Jump Rope Rhymes, and Other Children's Lore from New England*. Little Rock, Ark.: August House, 1990.

Haverhill Whittier Club Collection. Haverhill Public Library, Haverhill, Mass.

Hobsbawm, Eric, and Terence Ranger, eds. *The Invention of Tradition*. Cambridge: Cambridge University Press, 1983.

Hollander, John, ed. *American Poetry: The Nineteenth Century*. 2 vols. New York: Library of America, 1993.

Jackson, Virginia. "Longfellow's Tradition; or, Picture-Writing a Nation." *Modern Language Quarterly* 59:4 (December 1998): 471–496.

Jacobson, Marcia Ann. *Being a Boy Again: Autobiography and the American Boy Book*. Tuscaloosa: University of Alabama Press, 1994.

Jacobson, Matthew. *Whiteness of a Different Color.* Cambridge, Mass.: Harvard University Press, 1998.

Jameson, Fredric. *The Political Unconscious: Narrative as a Socially Symbolic Act.* Ithaca, N.Y.: Cornell University Press, 1981.

———. "Reification and Utopia in Mass Culture." *Social Text* 1 (Winter 1979): 130–148.

Jauss, Hans Robert. *Toward an Aesthetic of Reception.* Translated by Timothy Bahti. Minneapolis: University of Minnesota Press, 1982.

John, Arthur. *The Best Years of the Century: Richard Watson Gilder, "Scribner's Monthly," and the "Century Magazine," 1870–1909.* Champagne-Urbana: University of Illinois Press, 1981.

Jones, Rowena Revis. "The Preparation of a Poet: Puritan Directions in Emily Dickinson's Education." *Studies in the American Renaissance* (1982): 285–324.

Juhasz, Suzanne, ed. *Feminist Critics Read Emily Dickinson.* Bloomington: Indiana University Press, 1983.

Kammen, Michael. *Manhood in America: A Cultural History.* New York: Simon and Schuster, 1996.

Kelly, R. Gordon. *Mother Was a Lady: Self and Society in Selected American Children's Periodicals, 1865–1890.* Westport, Conn., Greenwood Press, 1974.

Kennedy, Carol Reed. "The Grand Opera House of Peoria, 1882–1909." *Journal of the Illinois State Historical Society* 78:1 (1984): 33–44.

Kenyon-Warner, Ellen E. *Character-Building Reader, Third Year.* New York: Hinds, Noble and Eldridge, 1910.

Kerstein, Lincoln, ed. *The Hampton Album.* New York: Museum of Modern Art, 1966.

Kete, Mary Louise. *Sentimental Collaboration: Mourning and Middle-Class Identity in Nineteenth Century America.* Durham: Duke University Press, 1999.

Kincaid, James R. *Child-Loving: The Erotic Child and Victorian Culture.* New York: Routledge, 1992.

Kittler, Friedrich A. *Discourse Networks 1800/1900.* Translated by Michael Metteer and Chris Cullens. Stanford, Calif.: Stanford University Press, 1990.

Knoper, Randall. *Acting Naturally: Mark Twain in the Culture of Performance.* Berkeley: University of California Press, 1993.

Kribbs, Jane, ed. *Critical Essays on John Greenleaf Whittier.* Boston: G. K. Hall and Co., 1980.

Lane, Abby E., ed. *Lights to Literature, Third Reader.* Chicago: Rand McNally, 1898.

Leach, William. *Land of Desire: Merchants, Power, and the Rise of a New American Culture.* New York: Pantheon, 1993.

Lears, Jackson. *Fables of Abundance: A Cultural History of American Advertising.* New York: Basic Books, 1994.

———. *No Place of Grace: Antimodernism and the Transformation of American Culture, 1880–1920.* Chicago: University of Chicago Press, 1981.

Levine, Lawrence. *Highbrow/Lowbrow: The Emergence of Cultural Hierarchy in America.* Cambridge, Mass.: Harvard University Press, 1988.

Leyda, Jay. *The Years and Hours of Emily Dickinson.* Vol. 1. New Haven, Conn.: Yale University Press, 1960.

Lindberg, Stanley. *The Annotated McGuffey.* New York: Van Nostrand Reinhold, 1976.

Loeffelholz, Mary. *Dickinson and the Boundaries of Feminist Theory.* Urbana: University of Illinois Press, 1991.

———. "Who Killed Lucretia Davidson? or, Poetry in the Domestic-Tutelary Complex." *Yale Journal of Criticism* 10:2 (1997): 271–293.

Longfellow, Alice Mary. Papers. Longfellow House, Cambridge, Mass.

Longfellow, Henry Wadsworth. *Complete Poetical Works.* Boston: Houghton Mifflin, 1893.

———. *Favorite Poems of Henry Wadsworth Longfellow.* New York: Doubleday, 1957.

———. Papers. Houghton Library, Harvard University, Cambridge, Mass.

———. *The Song of Hiawatha.* 1855. Reprint, London: Everyman, 1992.

Lott, Eric. *Love and Theft: Blackface Minstrelsy and the American Working Class.* New York: Oxford University Press, 1993.

Lovejoy, Mary Isabella. *Nature in Verse: A Poetry Reader for Children.* New York: Silver, Burdett, 1896.

Lukacs, George. *The Historical Novel.* Translated by Stanley Mitchell. 1936. Reprint, Lincoln: University of Nebraska Press, 2002.

Machor, James, ed. *Readers in History: Nineteenth-Century American Literature and the Contexts of Response.* Baltimore: Johns Hopkins University Press, 1993.

Machor, James, and Goldstein, Philip, eds. *Reception Study: From Literary Theory to Cultural Studies.* New York: Routledge, 2001.

Marling, Karal Ann. *George Washington Slept Here: Colonial Revivals and American Culture, 1876–1986.* Cambridge, Mass.: Harvard University Press, 1988.

Mauss, Marcel. *The Gift: The Form and Reason for Exchange in Archaic Societies.* Translated by W. D. Hall. New York: W. W. Norton, 1990.

Mavor, Carol. "Dream-Rushes: Lewis Carroll's Photographs of the Little Girl." In *The Girl's Own: Cultural Histories of the Anglo-American Girl, 1830–1915,* edited by Claudia Nelson and Lynne Vallone. Athens: University of Georgia Press, 1995.

McGuffey, William, ed. *McGuffey's Eclectic Primer.* Cincinnati: W. B. Smith, 1879.

——. *McGuffey's Fifth Eclectic Reader.* 1879. Reprint, New York: Signet Library, 1962.

——. *McGuffey's Fourth Eclectic Reader.* Cincinnati: Wilson, Hinkle, 1866.

McNamara, Brooks. *Step Right Up.* Garden City, N.Y.: Doubleday, 1976.

Mencken, H. L. *The American Language.* New York: Knopf, 1937.

Messmer, Marietta. *A Vice for Voices: Reading Emily Dickinson's Correspondence.* Amherst: University of Massachusetts Press, 2001.

Mitchell, Domhnall. "Revising the Script: Emily Dickinson's Manuscripts." *American Literature* 70:4 (December 1998): 705–737.

Moiser, Richard. *Making the American Mind: William McGuffey and His Readers.* New York: King's Crown Press, 1947.

Moon, Michael. "'The Gentle Boy from the Dangerous Classes': Pederasty, Domesticity, and Capitalism in Horatio Alger." *Representations* 19 (Summer 1987): 87–110.

Moore, Isabel, ed. *Eaton Fourth Reader.* Chicago: Eaton Book Company, 1906.

Mordell, Albert. *Quaker Militant: John Greenleaf Whittier.* Boston: Houghton Mifflin, 1933.

Morris, Robert. *Reading, Riting, and Reconstruction.* Chicago: University of Chicago Press, 1981.

Morrison, Toni. *Playing in the Dark: Whiteness and the Literary Imagination.* New York: Vintage, 1993.

Murray, Clara, ed. *Wide Awake, Fourth Reader.* Boston: Little, Brown, 1908.

——. *Wide Awake, Third Reader.* Boston: Little, Brown, 1908.

Negt, Oskar, and Alexander Kluge. *Public Sphere and Experience: Analysis of the Bourgeois and Proletarian Public Sphere.* Translated by Peter Labanyi, Jamie Owen Daniel, and Assenka Oksiloff. Minneapolis: University of Minnesota Press, 1993.

Newcomer, Alphonso. *American Literature.* Chicago: Scott Foreman, 1901.

Newell, William Wells. *Games and Songs of American Childhood.* 1883. Reprint, New York: Dover, 1963.

Ong, Walter J. *Orality and Literacy: The Technologizing of the Word.* London: Routledge, 1982.

Paine, Albert. *Mark Twain: A Biography.* Vol. 3. New York and London: Harper Bros., 1912.

Peiss, Kathy. *Cheap Amusements: Working Women and Leisure in Turn-of-the-Century New York.* Philadelphia: Temple University Press, 1986.

Perkinson, Henry. *The Imperfect Panacea.* New York: Random House, 1968.

Petrino, Elizabeth. *Emily Dickinson and Her Contemporaries: Women's Verse in America, 1820–1885.* Hanover, N.H.: University Press of New England, 1998.

Pickard, John, ed. *Memorabilia of John Greenleaf Whittier.* Hartford, Conn.: Emerson Society, 1968.

Pickering, Jean, and Suzanne Kehde. *Narratives of Nostalgia, Gender, and Nationalism.* London: Macmillan, 1997.

Pinsky, Robert. *Democracy, Culture, and the Voice of Poetry.* Princeton, N.J.: Princeton University Press, 2002.

Porter, Ebenezer. *Rhetorical Reader.* New York: Mark A. Newman, 1835.

Proudfoot, Mary. *Hiawatha Industrial Reader.* New York: Rand McNally, 1915.

Radway, Janice. *A Feeling for Books: The Book-of-the-Month Club, Literary Taste, and Middle-Class Desire.* Chapel Hill: University of North Carolina Press, 1997.

Raleigh, John. *Matthew Arnold and American Culture.* Berkeley: University of California Press, 1957.

Raymond, Claire. "Dickinson as the Un-named, Buried Child." *Emily Dickinson Journal* 12:1 (2003): 107–122.

Reedy, William Marion. *The Eugene Field Myth.* St. Louis: privately printed, 1901.

Richards, Laura E. *Melody.* Boston: Estes and Lauriat, 1896.

Riley, James Whitcomb. *Complete Poetical Works of James Whitcomb Riley.* Indianapolis: Bobbs-Merrill, 1932.

——. *Letters of James Whitcomb Riley.* Edited by William Phelps. Indianapolis: Bobbs-Merrill, 1935.

——. Papers, scrapbooks, and memorabilia. Lilly Library, Indiana University, Bloomington.

——. *Riley Songs of Friendship.* New York: Grosset and Dunlap, 1915.

Robbins, Bruce, ed. *The Phantom Public Sphere.* Minneapolis: University of Minnesota Press, 1993.

Rocks, James E. "Whittier's *Snow-Bound*: 'The Circle of Our Hearth' and the Discourse on Domesticity." *Studies in the American Renaissance* (1993): 339–353.

Roggenbuck, Mary June. "*St. Nicholas Magazine*: A Study of the Impact and Historical Influence of the Editorship of Mary Mapes Dodge." Ph.D. diss., University of Michigan, 1976.

Ryan, Eva. *Walls of Corn and Other Poems.* Hiawatha, Kans.: Harrington Printing Company, 1894.

Ruchames, Louis. "Race, Marriage, and Abolition in Massachusetts." *Journal of Negro History* 40 (1955): 250–273.

Rubin, Joan. *The Making of Middlebrow Culture.* Chapel Hill: University of North Carolina Press, 1992.

——. "'They Flash Upon That Inward Eye': Poetry Recitation and American Readers" Proceedings of the American Antiquarian Society. Vol. 106:2 (1996): 273–300.

Saillant, John. "The Black Body Erotic and the Republican Body Politic, 1790–1820." In *Sentimental Men: Masculinity and the Politics of Affect in American Culture,* edited by Mary Chapman and Glen Hendler. Berkeley: University of California Press, 1999.

Satelmajar, Ingrid. "Dickinson as Children's Fare: The Author Served Up in *St. Nicholas.*" *Book History* 5 (2002): 105–142.

Saum, Lewis O. *The Popular Mood of America, 1860–1890.* Lincoln: University of Nebraska Press, 1990.

Sayers, Robert. "Sing Anything: The Narrative Repertoire of a Mormon Pioneer." *Journal of the Southwest* 29:1 (1987): 41–79.

Shenkman, Richard. *I Love Paul Revere, Whether He Rode or Not.* New York: Harper Collins, 1992.

Spacks, Patricia Meyer. *Boredom: The Literary History of a State of Mind.* Chicago: University of Chicago Press, 1995.

St. Armand, Barton Levi. *Emily Dickinson and Her Culture: The Soul's Society.* Cambridge: Cambridge University Press, 1984.

Stedman, Edmund. *Genius and Other Essays.* New York: Moffat, Yard and Co., 1911.

Steedman, Carolyn. *Strange Dislocations: Childhood and the Idea of Human Interiority, 1780–1930.* London: Virago Press, 1995.

Stewart, Susan. *Nonsense: Aspects of Intertextuality in Folklore and Literature.* Baltimore: Johns Hopkins University Press, 1978.

——. *On Longing: Narratives of the Miniature, the Gigantic, the Souvenir, the Collection.* Baltimore: Johns Hopkins University Press, 1984.

Tanner, Tony. *The Reign of Wonder: Naivety and Reality in American Literature.* Cambridge: Cambridge University Press, 1965.

Thompson, Slason. *The Life of Eugene Field.* New York: Appleton, 1927.

Tompkins, Jane. *Sensational Designs: The Cultural Work of American Fiction, 1790–1860.* New York: Oxford University Press, 1985.

Trachtenberg, Alan. *The Incorporation of America: Culture and Society in the Gilded Age.* New York: Hill and Wang, 1982.

Turner, Victor W. *The Forest of Symbols.* Ithaca, N.Y.: Cornell University Press, 1967.

Van Allen, Elizabeth J. *James Whitcomb Riley: A Life.* Indianapolis: Indiana University Press, 1999.

Van Schaick, John. *Characters in "Tales of a Wayside Inn."* Boston: Universalist Publishing House, 1939.

Venezky, Richard. "A History of the American Reading Textbook." *Elementary School Journal* 87:3 (1987): 247–265.

Vincent, Leon. *American Literary Masters.* New York: Houghton Mifflin, 1906.

Waits, William. *The Modern Christmas in America: A Cultural History of Gift-Giving.* New York: New York University Press, 1993.

Washington, Booker T. *Up From Slavery.* Garden City, N. J.: Doubleday, 1901.

Wexler, Laura. "Black and White in Color." *Prospects* 13 (1988): 341–390.

Whittier, John Greenleaf. *The Early Poems of John Greenleaf Whittier.* Edited by N. H. Dole. New York: Thomas Cromwell, 1893.

——. *Legends of New England.* Hartford, Conn.: Hammer and Phelps, 1831.

——. *The Letters of John Greenleaf Whittier.* Vol. 3. Edited by John B. Pickard. Cambridge, Mass.: Harvard University Press, 1975.

——. *Poetical Works of John Greenleaf Whittier.* Boston: Houghton Mifflin, 1975.

Wilder, Laura Ingalls. *Little Town on the Prairie.* New York: Harper and Row, 1941.

Williams, Emily Harper. *American Authors' Birthdays.* Hampton Leaflet. Hampton, Va.: Hampton Normal and Agricultural Institute, 1917.

Williams, Raymond. *Keywords: A Vocabulary of Culture and Society.* New York: Oxford University Press, 1976.

——. *Marxism and Literature.* London: Oxford University Press, 1977.

Wishy, Bernard. *The Child and the Republic: The Dawn of Modern Child-Nurture.* Philadelphia: University of Pennsylvania Press, 1968.

INDEX

bedrooms: children's, in Field,
142–147, 149–150, 187; Field's,
151–152, 154–155
bed-wetting, 149–150
Benjamin, Walter, 188
Bennett, Paula, 179–180, 208n
Bergen, Fanny, 93, 200n
*Best-Loved Poems of the American People,
The*, xiii, 191n
Bianchi, Martha Dickinson, 157
Bible, 166; apocrypha, 179
Bierce, Ambrose, 122–123, 203n
Bingham, Caleb, 55
birthdays, poets' celebrated, xv–xvi,
24–25, 66–67; Longfellow's, 1, 12,
14, 20, 23–25, 32, 67; Lowell's,
24–25, 67; Whittier's, xxxvii–xxxviii
Bloch's Department Store, 202–203n
"Blue and the Gray, The" (Finch), xiii
Blumenthal, Sarah, 29, 32–33
Blumin, Stuart, 101
bohemianism, 108–109, 202n
Bok, Edward, 130, 204n
Bolshevism, 121
Book of Joyous Children, The (Riley), 117
Bookman, 100–101, 129
boredom, 77
Boston, Delbert, xx
Boston, Mass., xv–xvii, 23–24, 47; in
Longfellow, 15, 18; Riley in, 99
Boston Post, 206n
Boston Press Club, 99
Boston Transcript, 16
Boswell, Jeanetta, 191n
Bourdieu, Pierre, xxxiii, xli, 103, 114
Bowlby, Rachel, 199n
Bristol, F. M., 128
Brodhead, Richard, xxiii, 85, 146
"Brook, The" (Tennyson), xx
Brooks, Van Wyck, xviii, 100
Brown, Bill, 73, 82, 198–199n
Brown, James, 10
Brown University, 3
Brownie (camera), 93
Brownies, xx, 73, 89–95, 97, 157; folk
sources for, 200n
Browning societies, 102
Bryant, William Cullen, 71–72, 74–76,
84, 162–163, 166. *See also individual
works*
Buckham, John, 43
Buckingham, Emma May, 29–33

Buckingham, Willis J., 157, 205n, 206n
Buckwater, Geoffrey, 36
Buckwater Reader, 36, 161
Buddington, Zadel, 179
Buena Park, Ill., 151–152
bugaboos, 146–147
"Bugle Song, The" (Tennyson), xx
Bunyan, John, 170
Bureau of Indian Affairs, 12
Burgess, Gelett, 71, 79, 96–97
Burns, Robert, xiii; Whittier as Ameri-
can Burns, 40, 47; Riley as American
Burns, 107
Burt, Mary E., 133–134, 136, 148, 185
Burtis Grand Opera House, Davenport,
Iowa, 110

Cable, George W., 41
"Cable Hymn, The" (Whittier), 47,
57–58
Canadian Pacific Railway Company, 8
cannibalism, 54
capitalism, 124–125, 150, 199n
Captain January (Richards), 95
Carman, Bliss, 105
Carnegie Hall, 12, 133, 148
Carpenter, George, 43
Carroll, Lewis, 148–149, 159
cenotaphs, 21–22
censorship, of Field, 151, 206n
centennial, 1876, xxxix, 38
centralization, of public education,
28–29
Century, 40–41, 71, 78
Certeau, Michel de, 92
"Chambered Nautilus, The" (Holmes),
xxxviii
Character-Building Reader, 161, 163–165,
169
charisma, 28
chautauquas, 111, 202n
Chicago: Field in, 126, 129–130, 142,
148, 187; World Colombian Exposi-
tion, 72–73, 91
Chicago Morning News, 129–130, 151,
187
Chicago Record, 205n
Chicago Sunday Times, 131, 204n
Chicago Times-Herald, 132
Child, Lydia Maria, 122, 200n
"Child and Mother" (Field), 146,
148–151

INDEX